Why Buddha Touched the Earth
Zen Paganism for the 21st Century

Why Buddha Touched the Earth
Zen Paganism for the 21st Century

Tom Swiss

Megalithica Books
Stafford England

Why Buddha Touched the Earth: Zen Paganism for the 21st Century
by Tom Swiss
© 2013 First edition

All rights reserved, including the right to reproduce this book, or portions thereof, in any form.

The right of Tom Swiss to be identified as the author of this work has been asserted by him in accordance with the Copyright, Designs and Patents Act, 1988.

Cover Art: Peter Hollinghurst
Editor: Marianne Braendle
Layout: Taylor Ellwood

Set in Book Antiqua

MB0164

ISBN: 978-1-905713-90-5

A Megalithica Books Publication
An imprint of Immanion Press

http://www.immanion-press.com
info@immanion-press.com
8 Rowley Grove
Stafford ST17 9BJ
UK

"Fire Circle Rap" Copyright © William J. Thorpe. Used by permission.
"Why Are There So Many Losers in the Martial Arts?" Copyright © 1994 Dave Lowry. Excerpted by permission.
"Smokey the Bear Sutra" by Gary Snyder, "may be reproduced free forever" by grant of the author.
"A Zen Story / Enlightenment of a Seeker" by Camden Benares appears in *Principia Discordia,* "(K) ALL RIGHTS REVERSED - Reprint what you like"

Other quoted material is either in the public domain or is used under fair use provisions.

Dedicated to the memory of Piccolo and Chewbacca, the Wondermutts.

visiting the graves
the old dog
leads the way – Issa

Acknowledgments

My deep and sincere thanks go to:

Dave Landis, for detailed commentary on the first draft.

Billy Bardo (a.k.a. William J. Thorpe), for permission to include his "Fire Circle Rap." Why not check out his band's website at www.bardobrothers.com?

Isaac and Phaedra Bonewits. A casual conversation with them put me on the path to the Joseph Campbell essay *The Symbol without Meaning*, which had a large impact on the development of this book.

Ian Corrigan, for permission to quote his amazon.com review of *The Witch's Bible*, and for his and his co-organizers amazing work to keep the Starwood Festival happening every year.

John Michael Greer, who was kind enough to answer an e-mail about his article *The Red God: Woodcraft and the Origins of Wicca*, and help me track down some information about Ernest Thompson Seton.

Eric Wiegmann, Robin Gunkel, and the lovely and charming Elizabeth Rose, for showing me around Kansai.

"Kaz," the Shinto priest who took so much time to talk with me about his religion.

Dave Lowry, for permission to quote his essay "Why Are There So Many Losers in the Martial Arts?", which originally appeared in *Karate Illustrated* circa 1994.

The fine librarians at the Catonsville branch of the Baltimore County Public Library, who produced some very obscure books for me via the magic of inter-library loan, and the people at several websites that make old or rare texts available on the Internet, including the Internet Sacred Text Archive (www.sacred-texts.com), the Internet Archive (www.archive.org), and of course Google Books (books.google.com). The research behind the historical parts of this book would have difficult or impossible without them.

And finally to the poets of Zelda's Inferno, my brothers- and sisters-in-arms in the battle to put words on the page, for encouragement and friendship.

Table of Contents

Preface	8
"I Love Being Religious"	9
Zen Paganism	17
Industrial Strength Shamanism	24
The Mystic Sense	34
A Guy Who Woke Up	38
A Red Bearded Barbarian and an Illiterate Peasant	50
The Tapestry of Zen Pagan History Part I	62
It's All in Your Mind	96
The Tapestry of Zen Pagan History Part II	114
The Way of the Kami	140
Why Buddha Touched the Earth	151
How Shall We Live?	160
How to Sit Down and Shut Up	168
Zen in the Art of Magic	182
What Would Buddha Eat?	190
Sex (or the lack thereof) and the Single Gaijin	197
Law, Sausages, and Religion	204
Life and Death in the Stream	226
Zen Paganism (Reprise)	233
Appendix:	
Seton, Zen, and the Nature of Consensus Reality	238
Smokey the Bear Sutra by Gary Snyder	240
Enlightenment of a Seeker by Camden Benares	244
The Magick of Large Fire Circles	245
The "Fire Circle Rap" by William "Billy Bardo" Thorpe	247
Glossary	253
A Partial Time Line of the Pagan and Buddhist Revivals	259
The Dog Question	285
Bibliography	286
About the Author	307

Preface

> "I had nothing to offer anybody except my own confusion."
> – *Jack Kerouac*, On the Road

The word "essay" comes from a French word meaning "to attempt" or "to try." Originally, it referred to a piece where an author tried to use the process of writing to organize his or her thoughts about a topic.

This book is an essay in that original sense, an attempt to make myself come up with a coherent statement about the spiritual path I've been following since about 1990. It is most definitely not the product of some enlightened spiritual master come to bring you truth, nor is it authoritative testimony about either Zen or Paganism. While I have made every effort to keep my facts and my history straight, and have checked in with a few genuine Zen teachers along the way, I have no formal Buddhist credentials. And Pagans are a notoriously idiosyncratic lot about whom no one can make authoritative statements!

After fifteen years of messing around with the idea of "Zen Paganism," I first started trying to put my thoughts in writing during a trip to Japan in 2005. After a year and a half of historical research, it was on a longer return trip in 2007 that I first began to make significant headway on these essays, which – with a lot more research – eventually developed into this book.

In the course of our investigations, we're going to discuss a fair bit of history and go through several cultures. To help keep it straight, there's a timeline and a glossary in the back.

Except as explicitly attributed otherwise, the opinions expressed in this book are my own, and should not be blamed on anyone else.

"I Love Being Religious!"

It is a warm July evening in western New York state. About one hundred people have gathered here in the middle of an open field between the tents at a campground called the Brushwood Folklore Center, for the opening ritual of the twenty-seventh annual Starwood Festival, an event which describes itself as one of the largest "Pagan" and "Magical" gatherings in the country.

There are elders and children, men and women. Many are dressed in interesting regalia, some of the men in kilts or sarongs, a few people "skyclad" – or, as it would be called in the outside world, stark naked. The field on which we gather is also dressed and decorated, marked around its edges by symbols of the four classical elements: a tall garlanded pole to the east for air, the embers of a bonfire to the south for fire, a small man-made pond to the west for water, and a stone monolith to the north for earth.

Before the festival ends, there will be rituals in Wiccan, Druid, and Voodoo traditions (plus a late-night rock and roll ritual honoring Dionysus in the avatar of Jim Morrison), American Indian-style sweat lodges, and workshops and lectures on topics ranging from music history and renewable energy to sex magic and the proper arrangement of ceremonial altars. The heart of the festival is the fire circle, a nightly bonfire where drummers and dancers celebrate and trance until dawn, repeating what is probably one of humanity's oldest magical practices. The whole thing takes on some aspects of a "Be-in" from the 1960s, some of an old Celtic fire festival, and some of a Japanese *matsuri*.

But now, to start it all off, we invoke the spirits of the four directions, honor the ancestors and the gods and the spirits of the land, and visualize an umbrella of protective light over the whole site. Then the drummers start, and, laughing, we join hands in the spiral dance. Running and leaping and swinging each other, we make a sort of giant game of "crack the whip," which will end with us all in a cluster in the center for a final chant.

In front of me is an old festival friend, a feisty redhead who introduced herself to me at my first festival as "Lady Sue." (It was a while before I realized that she was not claiming aristocratic status, but that "Lady" is a title that some Wiccans adopt – some seriously, some in jest.) She looks back over her shoulder at me as we dance and, smiling, says "I love being religious!"

Obviously, this is a very different sense of the word "religious" than I learned as a Catholic boy in Baltimore.

So what is religion? Is it a collection of superstitions and metaphysical beliefs, doomed to be rendered irrelevant by a scientific understanding of the world? Or is it something more like applied psychology, or even poetry or art? Is it possible to build a sort of religion that's appropriate for an age of science and technology?

And why has there been such an interest over the past few decades in both Eastern spirituality and in pre-Christian Western religions, as well as in ancient practices like shamanism?

What do the answers to these questions say about how we should live our lives?

I've been pondering questions like these for most of my life, as I abandoned my childhood Catholicism, progressed to a sort of indistinct theism, and from there to agnosticism, then atheism, to end up with what I refer to as "Zen Paganism." I've had the opportunity to talk about some of these issues with Buddhist teachers, Witches, Druids, self-described "scientific pantheists," followers of Voodoo, students of Native American spirituality, leading figures of the modern Pagan revival, and even a Shintō priest. I'd like to share some of the philosophy and history I've found along the way.

So let's start with one of the big questions: what does it mean to be religious?

Our society typically measures religiosity by questions of dogma and by frequency of attendance at worship rituals. "Do you believe in God?" "How often do you go to church (or synagogue or mosque)?" The answers to these determine if you're a religious person or not.

But this sort of religion doesn't seem to be helping us much. Religious dogmas keep colliding with our expanding scientific knowledge of the world, and – perhaps in reaction to this collision – the focus of church-going often becomes dividing the world into "us" and "those corrupt and wicked servants of evil who go to that different church (or synagogue or mosque)."

As we usually experience religion, there are several different things that get mixed up and make it a mess. There is the desire for a certain experience: an experience of existence, of connection to the Universe, of the Godhead. There are ethical teachings, both the prohibitions and the prescriptions. There are myths and legends that give us role models. There are the superstitions born of fear, and the super-naturalism that arises from ignorance. There's the preservation of the knowledge needed for the community to thrive, encoded into ritual. There's the deliberate hiding of knowledge that would threaten the power of a priesthood.

With all this going on, it's no wonder that more and more people identify with labels such as "spiritual but not religious."

Are other sorts of religion possible?

I think I've been part of a different sort for almost two decades now. And for much of that time I've been trying to formulate exactly what it's about.

In 2007, in an attempt to get a broader perspective, I spent three months investigating the question in Japan – home of Zen and several other forms of Buddhism, and of the Nature-focused (and thus "Pagan," depending on our definitions) religion Shintō.*

* * *

Nanzen-ji, a large Zen Buddhist temple complex in Kyoto. There's a great big old central temple, with a painting of a dragon on its ceiling. Tourists like me can only see that from the outside, peering in between wooden bars.

Apparently there's something about sticking your hands through the bars and clapping to make an echo. An old Japanese man shows me how.

(Weeks later, on a return trip, I find, in this temple, a bunch of lay people involved in a rehearsal for some sort of ceremony – I'd almost guess a wedding, if I didn't know that Japanese

---

* I have tried to consistently use the macron and other diacritical marks on words that have not entered common English usage and for those deserving of extra respect – such as "Shintō," as the name of a religion. In the case of familiar words like "Tokyo" ("Tōkyō"), I've omitted them as distracting. The use in quoted material will follow that of the source.

In romanized Japanese, the macron indicates a "long" vowel, one that is held for a second syllable. "Shintō" is pronounced something like "Shin-toe-oh," spoken with no pause or change in inflection between the last two syllables. The short/long distinction is linguistically significant.

weddings are usually Shintō or Christian. While a family rehearses hitting their marks, two young Zen monks goof off, one apparently teasing the other about his freshly-shaved scalp.)

There are lovely gardens outside the old abbot's quarters, a great painting of Bodhidharma (the semi-legendary founder of Zen) on one wall. I sat in the temple's tea room looking out at a waterfall and garden and sipped real *o-cha*, very nice.

But to go beyond the tourist view of Japanese religion, go up the hill behind the main temple. First there's a small old sub-temple, Saisho-in; not merely a tourist attraction but an actively used Zen temple. As I stand there for a moment of meditation, a woman parks her car just outside the grounds, walks up quickly, bows to the Buddha, and hurries back out. Just stopped by to say "Hi" or "Thanks," I guess.

Behind Saisho-in, a beautiful small cemetery. I stand and watch the rain fall, see an offering of sake left on a grave. I think of a young man in the inner city pouring out a "40" for a fallen homie, consider that the Buddha was a prohibitionist, contemplate the adaptability of the dharma.

I continue on up the hill, into the woods. Small Shintō shines now on the grounds of this Buddhist temple – a tree, two rocks, girded with the braided rope that denotes objects thought to house *kami* spirits. This sort of openness and syncretism is fundamental to Japanese culture and to Eastern thought on religion in general, though it may seem odd to Westerners used to exclusivist monotheisms. (Imagine finding a small synagogue inside of a Christian chapel!)

The path keeps going up to a small waterfall, where – if I read my guidebook rightly – people will sometimes sit in the falls and meditate. A little above and to the side of that, a small cave, an altar within...a place where, perhaps, hundreds of years ago some seeker might have lived in the mountain for a while.

I touch the rock; convince myself I feel the power, the connection to the Earth.

I have the place to myself for ten on fifteen minutes. I take some photos, stand contemplating the waterfall. I hear the clapping hands of someone praying in the Shintō style, he comes up to the waterfall shine. We nod at each other; I step away a bit to free him from uncouth barbarian eyes as he prays, lights a candle and a stick of incense. As he continues up the hill, a younger man comes up and also has his little ritual at the waterfall.

A cave, a waterfall, here for thousands of years perhaps; used as a shrine for hundreds at least; still active today.

And yet...Japanese people will often tell you that they're not religious. Many don't seem to be aware of the difference between a Shintō shine and a Buddhist temple. But there are small shrines all over the place, by the sides of roads, in the middle of shopping malls. A sumo tournament can't be held without the ritual that consecrates the *dohyō*, the raised platform on which the bouts take place, and Japanese companies hire Shintō priests to bless their new buildings. The Buddhist temples don't seem short of visitors at all. Images of Bodhidharma, the founder of Zen, abound.

There's a spirituality that crops up in the oddest places. A sign on a museum display of old farming tools asks, "Please do not touch these folk arts, they are valuable gifts from our ancestors." A first-aid kit for sale in an upscale department store in Osaka bears the English message, "Nobody was made to suffer. Nobody was made to destroy," while a bag I bought in a dollar store (a "hundred yen" store, here) says "There is nothing in your life that does not have meaning." Enough Nihonjin (Japanese people) read English fluently enough to make these mottoes culturally meaningful.

There's no question that they're doing something. Is it religion? It seems to be a question of semantics.

* * *

So besides making professions of faith and visiting a church on a weekly basis, what else might qualify as religious?

When in doubt, we can turn to the essayist's cheap trick of consulting the dictionary for a word's etymology. "Religion" comes from the Latin "religere," meaning "bind again." It seems to me that a more meaningful rendering into modern English might be "to reconnect."

But to reconnect what to what? Clearly, religion is concerned with reconnecting human beings to something, but as to what that something is, opinions have varied – sometimes violently.

If we look at broad trends in the history of religion, we see two main answers to this question. When religion is used as a path of individual liberation, the goal is to reconnect us to the world in which we live – often (but not always) personified as gods, spirits, or the like.

But religion can also be used as a tool promoting social cohesion, reconnecting the individual to the community. And though there is much talk of a "relationship with God," organized religion has tended more toward enforcement of social norms than toward creating genuine experiences of the divine.

The tension between these two answers drives a lot of the history of religion. In the earliest human cultures, it seems that the target of shamanistic* practices was the connection between the individual and the world; but as society grew more complex and we became civilized, religion became a tool to resolve the tensions created by the advent of specialization of labor and hierarchical power structures.

Within civilized societies, some individuals would occasionally have a direct religious experience, but these mystics tended to be rapidly ostracized or co-opted – and if their practice avoided these fates, it almost inevitably ossified within a few generations, losing its usefulness as a means of liberation and becoming a new tradition to be enforced by priestly authority.

And so it's no coincidence that religion and politics get mixed up so often. If one sort of religion is meant to connect the individual to the community, to resolve human beings to the specific economic, political, and social roles they must fill in a complex society, then it becomes easy to reuse those exact same forms in a secular context to create a political mood, to let pledges and anthems replace prayers and hymns. Is there a significant difference between a group of Sunday school kids reciting the Lord's Prayer, and the same kids in elementary school on Monday morning reciting the Pledge of Allegiance?

(They fit together eerily well: "I pledge allegiance to our Father, who art in heaven, hallowed be thy flag of the United States of America. Thy kingdom come, thy will be done on earth as it is in the Republic for which it stands, one Nation under God

---

* The term "shaman" is of Siberian origin. Out of issues of cultural politics, some object to it being used to describe a diverse array of spiritual traditions – especially Native American traditions. But we lack a better term for the general spiritual idea being discussed here. Following Joseph Campbell's usage in his essay "The Symbol without Meaning," we will use the terms "shaman" and "shamanistic" with the understanding that they are being used in the broadest sense.

with our daily bread and liberty and justice for all and lead us not into temptation but deliver us from evil, amen.")

Human societies can be far divorced from the larger cosmos. So we are often left to choose between a quiet and harmonious relationship with our neighbors, where we don't rock the boat, observe the culturally appropriate religious rites, and keep our mouths shut; or an intimate relationship with the Universe, where we question the social norms and try to honestly investigate our own natures. This can lead to violent conflict – crucifixions, witch-trials, and the like. Even the Buddha had assassination attempts made against him.

But still, I will recommend that our relationship with the Universe take priority – it is much larger and longer-lived that your local town or nation, and less likely to screw you over for its own benefit.

Whether the goal is connection to the Universe or to the community, the tools used are those that can change human consciousness: ritual, meditation, trance through the deliberate repetition of words, actions, sounds, or ideas (prayers, gathas, creeds, dance, drumming, invocations), and biochemical change (either consuming psychoactive herbs or drugs, or promoting the release of endorphins and similar chemicals by physical ordeal). Most of these tools can be used to build either sort of connection.

In our usual notion of religion, questions of belief take a primary role. Shared beliefs are certainly one way to connect a community of people together. But this almost inevitably shades off into parroting of dogma; and so such connection is a limiting one, forcing minds into a mold – the connection shared by pieces of mass-production.

An alternative to believing together is doing together. Shared ritual, if well-designed, allows a common experience with differing interpretations. Obviously if the ritual or service involves chanting a declaration of dogma, a creed of some sort, it tends in the limit to indoctrination. But a well-designed ritual can accommodate widely varying beliefs.

In large Pagan gatherings, I have shared rituals with people who identified as several sorts of Wiccan, Druid, Buddhist, Atheist, Agnostic, Taoist, Discordian, even Jewish and Christian. (Some of us identify with more than one of these labels.) These are widely differing ideas, but we all found meaning and use in the same practice, even as we interpreted it differently. We might then break off into smaller groups, sharing ritual that was closer and more limited in scope, but at least we had all drunk once from the same well.

Another way to alter our consciousness is through the stories that we tell ourselves. The mind functions largely as a story-telling machine, assembling events into a narrative. But through any finite set of event-points, an infinite number of story-curves can be drawn. What events do we give priority, and which do we explain away as rare exceptions? Does our mythology tell stories of connection or isolation? Do we tell stories of paranoia, where everything that happens is meant to thwart us, or stories of pronoia, where everything that happens is for our benefit?

Through the practice of meditation and mindfulness, we can learn to observe and eventually control the mental process of storytelling that is consciousness.

I've come to call the blend of meditation practice and ritual that I have ended up with "Zen Paganism": a set of practices and attitudes drawn from sources both Eastern and Western, modern and ancient, all meant to transform the practitioner's relationship to themselves and to the rest of the universe. A heterodox, individualistic path of liberation.

Zen Paganism

It was some time in 1986 or '87 that my good friend, fellow karate student, and general co-conspirator Mike Gurklis and I were sitting around talking about our readings on the subject of Zen. We had begun to study a karate style that deliberately integrates elements of this philosophy, and so we were inspired to seek out more information about it and its relationship to the traditional martial arts. So we read some of the classic books, such as D.T. Suzuki's *Introduction to Zen Buddhism*, Shunryu Suzuki's *Zen Mind, Beginner's Mind*, Reps and Senzaki's *Zen Flesh, Zen Bones*, and Herrigel's *Zen in the Art of Archery*.

One thing we discovered was the idea that Zen, while arising from Buddhism, wasn't limited to it. So you could be a Zen Christian, one of us said. Or a Zen Jew.

Or a Zen Pagan.

I don't remember which of us said it. But it struck a chord with me. Months later, when I trundled off to my freshman year of college and decided to personalize my knapsack with some magic-marker graffiti, in among "Make love not war" and "Stop planetary suicide" was the inscription "Zen Pagan."

At the time, it was just something that sounded cool. I didn't have any great idea what Zen or Paganism was; I was still shaking off the lingering remnants of childhood Catholicism. But sometimes the title finds us before the piece, the work of whatever art, does.

In the summer of 1990, Mike and I were both students at the University of Maryland, College Park. Having both quickly tired of the dorms and of attempting the commute from Baltimore, we decided to share an apartment. We'd get a better deal with a third person splitting a three-bedroom place, so we put up fliers around campus seeking a roommate.

But the fellow who answered our call would turn out to be much more. Joe Galitsky became a brother.

A few months after he moved in, Joe said to me, "If you're free tonight I have some friends coming over. You ought to hang out, we do this sort of 'roll your own' religion thing – I think you'd like it."

Now by this time, though I was interested in ideas from Zen and Taoism (had I known the word then, I might have said I was moving toward Pantheism), I pretty firmly identified as an atheist. But I knew Joe well enough to rule out him being a religious wacko. And I've always had an over-sized curiosity bump.

So I checked it out. And he was right – I liked it.

There's not an exciting story of a black robed initiation rite here, just a bunch of laid-back, artistically inclined people in a suburban living room.

We started off with some improv spoken word welcoming the "spirits" of the different cardinal directions – "spirit" being left conveniently undefined, so you could regard it as of the same order as "spirit of the law" or as something more ghostly and supernatural, according to your own taste. This was referred to as "opening the Circle."

A number of occurrences blend in my memory, and now I can't recall exactly what rituals we did that first night. Perhaps somebody read a poem or story from Celtic myth or from Native American culture; maybe one of us led a guided meditation. Possibly there was a symbolic ritual, like writing on slips of paper things we wished to be free of, and then burning the papers. Maybe we did a little drumming. Then we closed the circle, saying farewell to the spirits we'd invited at the beginning. Afterward we shared a potluck meal, the only unusual thing being that a small portion of food was symbolically left outdoors for the "spirits." (I'm sure the squirrels got it.)

It was fun, and I didn't detect any cultish or evangelistic streak in anyone. So I went to the next few "Circles," as we called them.

I think it was at my third or fourth one when someone asked, "So, what got you interested in Paganism?"

Oh. Is that what this was?

The group was totally non-hierarchical; we all participated, took turns leading rituals, brought in whatever prayers and meditations and ideas we liked. So, I led Zen-style meditations, drawing on instructions from my karate sensei; shared Taoist and Zen stories from my readings; and learned bits of Wiccan and Celtic and Hindu and Native American practice and lore.

The group eventually drifted apart, as people's lives changed with new jobs and new homes. But I became connected with the larger local Pagan community, eventually becoming active in a regional group, the Free Spirit Alliance, or FSA. (And for my sins, ending up as its President.)

After many years of investigating different spiritual disciplines, that old label "Zen Paganism" seems an excellent name for the practice I've fallen into.

It was at the 2001 Free Spirit Gathering – FSA's summer solstice festival, one of the largest Pagan gatherings on the East Coast – that I first gave a public talk on some of these Zen Pagan ideas. Despite their embryonic nature, they were well received, and I've given talks on the topic several times now, at FSA events and at the larger Starwood festival.

I've found several other people using the same label. In 1979, the year before his death, John Lennon identified himself as "a pagan – a Zen pagan to be precise." (S. TURNER, 73) And Lennon seems to have done his homework regarding that designation, reading Margot Adler's history of the Pagan revival, *Drawing Down the Moon,* and also listening extensively to taped lectures by Alan Watts, a key popularizer of Zen. (S. TURNER, 190)

I was contacted by Keith Veeder, who had been using the term in his own teaching and writings for several years. I found a talk from the Zen teacher Zoketsu Norman Fischer, who mentions Zen Paganism in passing. (FISCHER, "HIGHEST MEANING") I even once saw a vanity license plate on the highway in Maryland that read ZENPAGN.

It turns out that there are significant historical links between Buddhism and Paganism: encounters with Buddhist teaching by the famous occultist Aleister Crowley and (to a lesser extent) by Gerald Gardner, the founder of modern Wicca; the role of the nineteenth century Theosophical Society in prompting both a Buddhist revival in Asia and an occult revival in Europe; all the way back to the Greco-Buddhist culture that formed in Gandhara after the death of Alexander the Great and that produced the first statues of the Buddha (FIELDS, 14-16) as well as art portraying him alongside the deities Serapis (a Hellenized version of Osiris), Isis, and Horus. (WELLS, 320)

Apparently it isn't just my own delusion that these ideas are compatible and connected. So what is the relationship?

To consider that question, some definitions are in order.

Zen is easily defined. (At this point, the reader who's already waded into Zen a bit may feel free to laugh out loud.) It is the Japanese pronunciation of the sect's Chinese name *Ch'an,* which in turn comes from the Sanskrit word *dhyana,* and simply means meditation. Zen Buddhism is a form of Buddhism focusing on meditation practice.

However, in Japan Zen snuck out of the temple to permeate fields ranging from flower-arranging to sword fighting to making and serving a good cup of tea. And in so doing, it left behind the Buddha statues and the sutras, becoming something much more vague and diffuse. Which of course (and now I hope laughing readers will forgive me) makes a lie of the claim that Zen can be easily defined. Like the cliche about jazz, if you have to ask, you're never going to know.

But over the centuries the masters in the temples and training halls have found ways to make the question unnecessary, blazing experiential paths to lead seekers to the answer rather than attempting to speak it. It is this aspect of direct experience, of a "direct transmission outside the scriptures," that has made Zen of such interest to Westerners and is most relevant to us.

And what of Paganism?

By one account, the word derives from the Latin *paganus*, meaning "rustic" or "country-dweller" and dating back to the Christianization of the Roman Empire. The temples of the Greco-Roman pantheon were torn down, and their worship could only be accomplished out in the sticks, in the fields, forests, and groves – city gods go to the country, to hide out from the intolerance of state-supported monotheism. Another theory has it that the word derives from the Latin *pagus*, the local unit of government under Roman rule. (HUTTON, 4) Whatever the etymology, the label "pagan" came to be applied to followers of the pre-Christian Roman religion.

While some strands of family traditions may have come down from this time, the Pagan revival is largely a reconstruction, not a survival – mythologized histories of various sects notwithstanding. The first hints of this revival date to the late eighteenth and early nineteenth centuries, when several tributaries including the Romantic literary movement, a revival of classical Greco-Roman and Germanic themes in art, a growing exposure to Eastern thought, and a backlash against industrialization, came together in England.

By the late 1960s, "Pagan" came to be a general term for a diversity of spiritual paths: Druidism, Wicca, Discordianism, and eclectic self-defined paths of pantheism, polytheism, or animism. Kerry Thornley (co-founder of the Discordian Society, paranoid schizophrenic, and possible pawn in CIA mind control experiments that may or may not have been related to the assassination of President Kennedy) is credited by many with giving the term its current meaning, and Oberon Zell-Ravenheart (co-founder of the Church of All Worlds, a real-life church inspired by Robert A. Heinlein's science fiction classic *Stranger in a Strange Land*) is credited with popularizing it.

It is sometimes useful to make a distinction between the "Neo-Paganism" of this revival and the "Paleo-Paganism" of cultures that were never Westernized; but we are mostly dealing with Neo-Paganism, and will use the term "Pagan" in this common sense.

What binds these diverse paths together, puts them all under the rubric of Paganism? Ask five self-identified Pagans and you're likely to get five different answers. (Quite possibly more.) But I think that the following two propositions would be accepted by at least four out of five people who label themselves Pagan:

Humanity has lost sight of its connection to the natural world. It has not lost the connection – we are of this world, part of it, and the connection cannot be broken, any more than a wave can be disconnected from the ocean. But we have neglected and ignored it, forgotten that this connection exists, and this is harming both us and the natural world.

Our ordinary experience of consciousness is not the only mode possible. Through the use of ritual and magic – the art of changing consciousness at will (STARHAWK, 6, 19) – we can explore our consciousness to positive ends, finding other ways of thinking that can be helpful. As Jeff Rosenbaum of the Association for Consciousness Exploration explains, "Everything is explored by altering it. The way you explore temperature is by seeing how different temperatures affect something. The way you explore pressure is by changing the pressure to see how that affects different things. The way you study consciousness is by changing your consciousness." (QUOTED IN KRASSNER)

So, we might tentatively define this modern version of Paganism as a pantheistic or naturalistic set of spiritual attitudes, combined with the practice of ritual magic as a means of altering consciousness.

We can pick out a few other features likely to be identified as Pagan: a focus on experience rather than dogma; a spiritual egalitarianism, holding that every person has equal access to the divine and that any "priests" or "priestesses" act as facilitators, not as special chosen representatives of deities; a belief that experiences of the divine can take many different forms, and that if one person likes to work with the Greek pantheon and another prefers the Hindu deities, that's perfectly fine; and a respect for the feminine, where Goddess imagery is as important (or more important) as the Gods.

With these definitions in mind, what is the relevance of Zen to Paganism?

As we're going to see later in our exploration, the Pagan revival and the recent interest of Western thinkers in Eastern philosophies both stem from a reaction to the upheaval wrought upon society by the Industrial Revolution, and the inadequacies of mainstream traditional religion in a scientific era. Both emerge from the need to build a spirituality capable of dealing with the radical changes in human civilization we are undergoing.

Furthermore, if we look at the historical roots of the Pagan revival, we find a strong influence by Eastern thought, Hinduism and Taoism and Buddhism. (There may be some in the Pagan community who still hold to the notion that ancient European practices have been handed down with little change, and therefore find this claim remarkable, but the history is well-established.) A look at Zen gives Pagans an opportunity to connect with some of these roots.

While the modern Pagan movement reaches back to some ancient ideas and practices, it is still a new thing, only beginning to organize itself. To prevent future bouts of dogmasclerosis – hardening of the orthodoxies – we would do well to look to Zen's model of "direct transmission outside the scriptures," of reliance on direct experience rather the revealed truth.

And for all of its emphasis on, and expertise in, bringing about transformative experiences via rituals, Paganism could do a better job in terms of integrating the experience into day to day living. It can learn from Zen how to escape the Coven, Circle, or Grove, how to penetrate everyday life.

Paganism can also use a hand with ethical teaching. The non-dogmatic compassionate teachings of Zen Buddhism could be a rich example, much more specific than the Wiccan Rede, for example, while still avoiding moralistic preaching.

Finally, if magic is understood as a means of changing consciousness, then we ought to take a serious look at the experiments and observations that Buddhists have been involved with for 2,500 years. Buddhism starts with the understanding that all of our experiences arise from mind, and that cultivating new ways of thinking are the key to spiritual progress.

And what of the relevance of Paganism to Zen? We're going to look at the nature religion hidden in Zen Buddhism, from Buddha sitting under the Bo tree and touching the Earth, to the influences of Taoism on the development of Zen, to the Beat poets going to the mountains and helping introduce Zen to the West. The world needs a strong nature religion now – the only way we'll stop destroying the Earth and ourselves, is to see the planet as sacred.

Also, as Zen seeks to spread in the West, the practices of Paganism – tied to familiar Western mythology – might offer "skillful means" to Zen teachers, ways to illustrate concepts and even on occasion to trick students into learning.

And we're going to see if Paganism can get formal Zen to let its hair down (metaphorically speaking) and party a little bit (in a non-attached fashion, of course). Zen has always had a streak of the rapscallion running through it, from stories of monks hitting the sake (flagrantly violating the precepts) to the sexually liberated "Red Thread" tradition. These Zen rascals and the joyously fornicating, Dionysus-worshiping Pagans might well be able to teach each other a few things.

Finally, while it has lessons to teach Paganism, even Zen is not immune to hardening of the orthodoxies. It was less than a century ago that the formal schools of Zen Buddhism, the supposedly contemplative way of the Compassionate One, were raising money to build bombers in support of Japanese nationalism. A little transfusion of unorthodoxy, a cocktail of Beat Zen, Pagan Zen, and Discordian Zen, may help prove protective against future bouts of Taking Oneself Too Seriously – a condition to which, alas, even Certified Zen Masters are not immune.

Industrial Strength Shamanism

From the window of a train speeding through rural Japan, you see that the hillsides are covered with forests. Some scars are visible – areas cut down to the bare ground, or even where part of a hill has been covered in cement to prevent collapse – but it looks as if Japan's strict development laws have done much to protect wilderness in such a crowded nation.

But when I decided to hike into the woods near the Tekishin Zen center in Kameoka (just outside Kyoto), I was in for a shock. I found that what appeared to be forest was straight rows of trees, an artificially replanted area with no undergrowth. When I climbed a hill, instead of soil under my feet, there was plastic netting covering the rocky hillside to prevent erosion.

In recent decades Japan has undertaken a tremendous reforestation effort. This is a praiseworthy endeavor, and the rest of the world can learn much from their example. But the deforestation that made it necessary is a stark illustration of the toll that heedless industrialization can take.

Japan had experience with environmental damage and restoration centuries ago, during the Edo period (1603 to 1868). Early in that era, deforestation of the mountainous terrain led to landslides and flooding; this taught the Japanese a quick lesson in environmentalism. So forests were protected and replanted, and a remarkably sustainable form of agriculture was developed. Hillsides were terraced to provide pure ground water, and human waste from the cities was recycled as fertilizer for rural areas. With this careful attention to ecological issues, Japan's nineteenth century farming yields per acre were ten times what they were in Europe, and the city of Tokyo could support a population of approximately one million, all without industrialization. (HARADA, 81-82)

But with the Meiji restoration of the mid 1800s came rapid industrialization in an attempt to catch up to the Western powers. During Japan's imperial expansion, World War II, and the postwar reconstruction, the environment became so devastated that by the late 1960s Japan was by some measures the most polluted country in the world. (HARADA, 88)

If this can happen in a place where the forest religions Shintō and Buddhism dominate, in a land where individual rocks and trees are seen as objects of veneration, what of Europe and America, inheritors of desert-religion Christianity that, in the most popular interpretations, directs humanity to go and subdue nature?

The Industrial Revolution first got underway in England, and so it was England that first experienced its consequences, both positive and negative. And it is no coincidence that England played a key role in the history of the modern Pagan movement.

This Revolution brought into being a whole new chapter in human existence, a change whose magnitude can be compared only to the Neolithic revolution – the dawn of civilization itself, when we settled down from nomadic hunting and gathering to live in cities, villages, and towns to be farmers. It began about two and a half centuries ago and is still continuing today; assuming we survive it, it will take centuries more for the change to play out. From our perspective in the middle of the change it's hard to see clearly, to name it accurately, but we might call it the change from agricultural to industrial humanity.

And just as the establishment of agricultural civilization created a new social structure that called for new religion, so this change will also require a new spiritual outlook.

To fully understand this change we have to start in Europe, a few centuries before the start of the Industrial Revolution, at the end of the Middle Ages. We need to start not with the Renaissance or the Enlightenment, not with the intrigues of rulers or the battles of warriors or the intellectual lives of artists and philosophers, but with the changes that had the greatest everyday impact – how peasants farmed.

In medieval Europe, the basic unit of society and of production was the manor. In this system, peasant farmers worked their own strips of farmland (in addition to working for the lord of the manor), but they also had access to common areas of pastures and woodland. These common areas were vital to the system, giving peasants grazing space for their animals and a source of firewood. (T. GREER, 189-192)

Around the fourteenth century, a cooling trend flooded farms and shortened the growing season. Helped along by the Black Death, this climate change began to alter the socioeconomic environment. (T. GREER, 245-247) English landholders began a practice of "land enclosure," in which common areas were privatized and rented out to paying tenants. (T. GREER, 446-447) As a result it became difficult or impossible for many farmers (and the village artisans who served them) to make a living.

By about 1500, serfdom had disappeared from England, and peasants were no longer legally bound to their manors. But that didn't necessarily usher in freedom and prosperity for the peasant class. The feudal lord had not so much gone away as transformed into a landlord, demanding rent from tenants; and unlike serfs, tenants could be evicted.

Along the way to the end of serfdom, major changes also happened to non-agricultural production. Craft guilds began to lose control and the "domestic system" was developed – "cottage industry," where goods were produced by semi-skilled laborers rather than by skilled artisans. For the first time, a large part of the population was primarily occupied with labor other than farming. (T. GREER, 245-251)

Medieval craft guilds had social and ceremonial functions as well as economic ones, (T. GREER, 198) and as their economic power waned these other roles took on more importance. The most significant guild in this respect was that of the masons. Stonemasons' work often involved travel from construction site to construction site, and this life on the move made the masons' guild a critical part of their lives. (STEVENSON, 13) This left the guild set up for a transformation into a social organization – Freemasonry, a fraternal organization that still thrives today.

The process of land enclosure accelerated greatly during the eighteenth century, as the intensification of agriculture increased yields (though with significant external costs) and put farmers out of work. Large numbers of people were displaced, and thus cheap labor was available for the first industrial mills. (T. GREER, 446-448)

Displaced people crowded into cities looking for work, but the cities lacked the infrastructure to handle the influx. There were no sewers, the streets were unpaved, housing was crowded and rickety. And the work lacked any satisfaction: rather than craftsmen skillfully creating finished goods, or farmers proudly producing food to feed their families and their villages, workers were machine-tenders, engaged in repetitive, mind-numbing tasks, replaceable cogs in the industrial machine.

What would the Industrial Revolution have looked like without a multitude of desperate people, victims of a political process favorable to the greed of landlords, for the industrialists to put to work? Might we have developed a more humane and less exploitative technology right from the start? We can only speculate.

By 1850, half the population of Britain had moved from farming villages to industrialized cities. (T. GREER, 454) This is remarkable because, up until this point, the **entire history of human civilization** revolved around agriculture!

We created the permanent settlements that became cities specifically to work the land, and we learned to write in order to manage the complexities that this new society entailed. This "Neolithic revolution," when we became farmers, was more than a change in how we produced food. It wrought huge changes in human culture, including religion.

In his remarkable essay "The Symbol without Meaning," famed mythologist Joseph Campbell notes that religious practices can be categorized into the Paleolithic ("old stone age," gatherer-hunter), individualistic, shamanistic, paths of the forest and wilderness; and the Neolithic ("new stone age," agricultural), group-oriented, priestly, paths of the village. This comparison is drawn in very broad terms, but it's a useful tool to contemplate the nature and purpose of religion.

In gatherer-hunter societies, there was no real specialization. There might be some division of labor by age and gender, but every member was a pretty much a full master of their culture and technology. Most significant to our consideration, religion was egalitarian: anyone could go on a "vision quest," seek to be opened to new states of consciousness. Indeed, it was often part of a young person's initiation into adulthood. Some – the shamans – might be more talented at it than others, just as some might be better hunters or better warriors, but the basic technique was available to all. (At least, to any man. There are gender issues here: some cultures have been open to women's visions and to female shamans, and some have not.)

One obtained a vision or became a shaman not by apprenticeship or appointment, but through one's own experience of relationship with the gods or ancestors or spirits of the land. While they have some mythology, because they are based on individual experience these shamanic paths don't have much in the way of fixed dogma.

But with the Neolithic agricultural revolution, life and society became much more complex. Specialization and hierarchy arose. There was too much for any one person to know: the methods for planting and harvesting and preparing the various crops, and how to breed and care for the animals, and how to make all the tools, and how to build the buildings, and the skills for fighting the neighboring town (whose inhabitants were always trying to raid your town's fields), and the organizational skills to manage all the specialists who had this knowledge and the laborers who did the grunt work. Humans began to exist as parts of a larger society, rather than as self-reliant individuals. (CAMPBELL, 142-159)

This has been the standard model of the history of civilization since about the 1920s: the invention of farming led to organized religion. However, over the past two decades or so, new archeological findings at sites like Göbekli Tepe (a colossal temple built by gatherer-hunters 11,600 years ago) have suggested that people may have first come together in large groups for religious purposes and then turned to agriculture in order to feed the crowds, or that the sequence may have been different in different areas. (MANN, 49-58) But whether one led to the other or whether they created a mutual feedback loop, the precise sequence is not really important to the point that organized religion and city-based agricultural societies grew up together.

Campbell notes that it's around the time of the agricultural revolution that complex geometric figures – mandalas – make their appearance in artwork, reflective of the geographic order of cultivated fields and of the social order of the village. (CAMPBELL, 130, 140-153)

As humanity settled into cities, religion became the domain of a designated class of priests, who generally came to their positions by the selection of the rulers or of other priests, not by their own experience. Ritual evolved from individual vision quests to elaborate group activity, consuming a large part of a society's energy. It became a way of binding the community together, of resolving the individual to his or her existence as a part of the whole rather than as a fully autonomous being. (CAMPBELL, 153-163)

Of course, over the millennia there have been some civilizations where this sort of priestly religion was less dominant. One example was Greece during its Golden Age: in keeping with their ideal of personal liberty, the religion of the ancient Greeks had no authoritative dogma and no special class of priests (T. GREER, 56) – priests were selected from the general community by election or appointment, or by purchasing the privilege, (RICE, 97) or by lottery. (FAIRBANKS, 79) Citizens could believe whatever they wished so long as they did not deny or insult the officially recognized deities. (Though there were still strong religious customs, and no important act was undertaken without due consideration to the gods.)

The official religion of classical Greece had no promise of personal immortality in an afterlife, no consolation for rough times. So alongside it there evolved the "mystery cults," most of which centered on Dionysus, god of fertility, of death and rebirth, and of course, of wine. By means such as physical ordeal, consuming intoxicants, or the use of sacred drama, members of these cults experienced altered states of consciousness and came to believe that they could join with Dionysus and share in his seasonal rebirth (T. GREER, 56-59) – the direct religious experience, in some ways more like that of Paleolithic cultures than of the civilizations of Sumer or Egypt.

This freedom from dogma, and accessibility of direct religious experience, may be why the myths from the Greek religion still fascinate us today and have had a large impact on Paganism.

But in general, civilized cultures from the first cities up to today have had religions full of dogma and ruled by priests. In some, the shamanic path of direct mystical experience was heavily suppressed; in others, some space was left available to it, but only within tightly defined social boundaries. (CAMPBELL, 159-163)

As a contemporary example, for centuries the Catholic Church has carefully confined men who had mystical inclinations to monasteries. It may be that the isolation of these institutions is not just to focus the meditations of monks, but to protect ordinary parishioners from the idea that they might directly experience God and put the priests out of work. (This is true also to some degree of convents and nuns, though gender politics are also part of the picture.)

We previously encountered the question, if "religion" means "to reconnect," just to what are we reconnecting? Here we can see two different answers. In shamanistic cultures, the goal was to reconnect the individual to the "spirit world." In priestly cultures, the goal has largely been to keep the individual bound to the community.

But the Neolithic social structure, the culture of the farming village that gave birth to priestly ways, began to break apart with the Industrial Revolution. That cracking has accelerated and spread. Sometime in 2007, it is estimated, the human race as a whole passed the point that England reached around 1850. For the first time, more human beings lived in industrialized urban areas than in farming villages. (SATTERTHWAITE, "STREETS AHEAD")

Agriculture is no longer the primary occupation and vocation of the human species. And so, agricultural religion, meant to tie a farming civilization together, is no longer enough.

Which raises the question: what else have we got?

In priestly societies, people who wanted to experience and investigate spiritual issues firsthand would often have to leave town, head out into the forest or the desert, to get away from the priests and their socially regulated religious experience. It was in keeping with this model that the Buddha left his palace to enter the forest, that Jesus went out into the desert after his baptism by John, that Thoreau went to live in the woods by Walden Pond.

It's not deep wilderness or total isolation that is necessary – Thoreau's cabin was just outside of town, and the Buddha spent time with local children during his stay under the Bo tree. While the presence of "natural" surroundings, of trees and wild animals, is helpful and pleasant, it's not strictly necessary to this part of the quest. What's needed is an environment that separates us from our social imprints. The "nature" that we are really seeking is our own unconditioned self-nature, our "wild mind" apart from the expectations and pressures of our culture.

In ancient China and Japan, for example, we find many stories of wandering Buddhist and Taoist seekers, people not so much bound for any specific destination but rather opening themselves up to new experiences. There are many stories of Taoist sages finding students in traveler's inns, people whose separation from their home village made them open to considering new ideas. (CLEARY, 63-64) It's the same drive that sends so many of us on long journeys to "find ourselves": a change in environment makes possible a change of mind.

Just as travel helps individuals break their imprints, so rapid change breaks a society's. As the Industrial Revolution radically altered the way of life in Europe and America, as the mandala began to crack, there were openings for new ideas.

Among rebellious intellectuals and artists there were three threads of thought that emerged in reaction to the social changes of the Industrial Revolution, and were clear influences on the development of Paganism.

The first was naturalism. As people moved into less

natural environments the study of nature became of more and more interest: if all this is "unnatural," just what is natural, anyway? Natural history in its modern form might be dated to 1735, when the Swedish botanist, physician, and zoologist Carl Linnaeus published the first version of his *Systema Naturae*. In this and subsequent works he provided a framework for the classification and identification of all living things which influenced every nature writer after him. (It was Linnaeus who introduced the "binomial nomenclature" whereby a species is identified by its genus and species name, e.g. *Homo sapiens* or *Canis lupus*.) Among those influenced by Linnaeus were Rousseau [STÖVER, 232-333] and Goethe [BLUNT, 215], major figures in the Romantic literary movement in France and Germany, respectively.

Gilbert White was an English follower of Linnaeus whose 1789 book *A Natural History of Selborne* was one of the seminal English language works of nature writing. Among White's appreciative readers were Darwin and Thoreau, and his legacy was more than a way of describing nature – it was a point of view in which the natural world was a haven. According to historian Donald Worster,

> The rise of the natural history essay in the latter half of the nineteenth century was an essential legacy of the Selborne Cult [i.e., White's work]. It was more than a scientific-literary genre modeled after White's pioneering achievement. **A constant theme of the nature essayist was the search for a lost pastoral heaven, for a home in an inhospitable and threatening world.** [FINCH, 19-20] [emphasis added]

In Germany, naturalism had spiritual overtones dating back to at least the Roman era. Goethe wrote in his autobiography (about an incident he dates in the early 1760s):

> [My friend] related to me circumstantially, out of Tacitus [the Roman historian], how our ancestors delighted in the feelings which nature awakens in us, in such solitudes, by her artless architecture. He had not long continued in this strain, when I exclaimed, "Oh! Why does not

this precious spot lie still deeper in the wilderness! why may we not train a hedge around it, to hallow and separate from the world both it and ourselves! **Surely no worship of the Deity is more fitting than that which needs no graven image, but which springs up in our hearts merely from intercourse with nature!**" (GOETHE, 196) [emphasis added]

The second strand of thought that emerged in response to this great upheaval of European civilization was classicism (and later, more general interest in pre-Christian society including Germanic and Celtic myth). Classical Greek and Roman elements were present in European art and literature since at least the late medieval period, but in the mid-1700s, German art historian Johann J. Winckelmann's books *Thoughts on the Imitation of Greek Art in Painting and Sculpture* (1755) and *History of Ancient Art* (1764) opened the floodgates and created what some have called the "tyranny of Greece over Germany." According to historian Frank Turner, these books "constituted one of the major turning points in the history of Western taste. Almost single-handedly Winckelmann made the Greek experience alive and vitally interesting to intellectual and creative writers throughout Germany and the rest of Europe even though he never visited Greece himself." (FRANK TURNER, 39-40)

British Romantic poets, primarily the "second wave" writers John Keats and Percy Bysshe Shelley, took that Greek experience and ran with it. They not only transformed the Greek pantheon, putting a whole new spin on the character of Pan and giving us the notion of the Goddess that has come down to contemporary Paganism, but – at least in Shelley's case – seem to have taken seriously the spiritual potential of these myths, (HUTTON, 23-46) becoming to some degree early devotees of Paganism.

The third strand of thought was Orientalism, a fascination with the East, which later developed into a broader interest in foreign "primitive" cultures including the Native American nations. Even as the exploitation of India was shifting into high gear, some European intellectuals were becoming great admirers of some aspects of Indian culture. In the 1780s, the first hints of Hindu and Buddhist thought began to spread to Europe with a translation of the Hindu epic the *Bhagavad Gītā* (WILLSON, 46) and a report in the journal of the Asiatick Society discussing Buddhism in Ceylon. (FIELDS, 44-50) Pierre Sonnerat published his *Voyage aux Indes Orientales* in which he claimed that India gave wisdom, law, and religion to every other culture, while William Macintosh connected the classical and Oriental threads when he wrote that "All history points to India as the mother of science and art. This country was anciently so renowned for knowledge and wisdom, that the philosophers of Greece did not disdain to travel thither for their improvement." (WILLSON, 25)

At their best, these three strands of thought all provided intellectuals of the time with ways of breaking the social imprint, getting outside the everyday thought-patterns of their cultures. Today they still point at a naturalistic, individual sort of spirituality, free from the constraints of modern culture and following more the way of the shaman than of the priest. They lead to a sort of "industrial strength shamanism," if you'll allow the pun, that can draw from the understanding of the physical world that was the product of the philosophical and scientific Enlightenment of seventeenth and eighteenth century Europe, but can also connect with the most primal, ancient, and mystical aspects of human existence.

The Mystic Sense

To get around Osaka, I've been doing a lot of bicycling, on a cheap secondhand bike I picked up in my local *shōtengai* (shopping arcade). The city is good cycling territory, with bike lanes on most of the sidewalks and no steep hills. Everybody has a bike here – it's not uncommon to see a housewife with two small kids and a load of groceries balanced on her shopping bicycle, or a young man peddling along with his girlfriend sitting behind him on his bike's cargo rack. (The down side is that bicycle theft is also surprisingly common – this is my second bike.)

The great thing about biking is that it's brought me right up close to the everyday beauty of the city. Tonight, heading downtown to sit in a bar and write, I had just such a moment as I was waiting at the crosswalk near the bridge by the Osaka Dome baseball stadium. A man about my age, perhaps a few years younger, an ordinary guy in khaki windbreaker holding hands on either side with his daughters, maybe six and eight years old. And the daughters were on unicycles! Unicycles, one pink, one yellow, white tires; the girls in matching outfits (unicycle team outfits? or just *kawaii* cute?): blue jeans with multicolored star patches low on the legs, pink sweatshirts, white puffy parka-type vest over top.

Me with a big smile, trying not to stare; the girls sneaking looks at the funny-looking long-haired gaijin. A moment that snaps you out of your usual state of mind, that can only be described as beautiful.

All of us have some sort of aesthetic sense, a sense of beauty: the ability to be moved and exalted by certain situations and experiences, both of the senses and of the intellect. What triggers it may be as varied as Van Gogh's "Starry Night," or Cantor's diagonalization proof that there are more real numbers than rational numbers even though both sets are infinite, or the Ramones' classic punk anthem "Blitzkrieg Bop," or an encounter with little Japanese girls on unicycles. But every human being of sound mind possesses the ability to experience beauty in some sights, sounds, words, and situations. We would hold a person without this ability to be damaged, lacking, an object of pity.

One specific, wonderfully deep type of beauty comes not

from the agreeability of our concrete sensory perceptions (such as we find in music or visual arts), nor from the relationship of abstract ideas to each other (the beauty found in mathematics and in some sorts of literature), but from the perception of a relationship between our immediate subjective experience and the broader world.

We call this sort of beauty "mystic." As D.H. Lawrence wrote (in a poem titled, simply, "Mystic"):

> They call all experience of the senses mystic,
>   when the experience is considered.
> So an apple becomes mystic when I taste in it
> the summer and the snows, the wild welter of
>   earth
> and the insistence of the sun. (LAWRENCE, 594)

The mystical experience is sometimes expressed as the sense of "the presence of the divine," sometimes as an experience of "Cosmic Consciousness," sometimes as "the perception of emptiness" or a "feeling of oneness with the universe" or "a feeling of sacredness" or as "no-mind," all depending on the social conditioning and religious training of the experiencer. Because we have a great deal of our brains devoted to recognizing other human beings and understanding their behavior, the experience often comes across with some personification – a deity, a god or goddess.

But whether we personify them or not, these are all expressions of the mystical sense, just as things as varied as the beauty of a birdsong, a Bach fugue, or a heavy metal drum solo are all perceptions of the aesthetic sense applied to music.

The mystical experience can result from experiences of sensory beauty, but it can also be triggered by experiences that would otherwise be unpleasant, or by completely mundane events. It is an experience of existence rather than of meaning, of immediate and direct connection rather than evaluation or discrimination.

Until recently, Western societies generally regarded the mystical sense as the province of a few. People who had any sort of mystical experience were sent off to the seminary, monastery, convent, or madhouse, protecting the rest of us against having our ordinary consciousness contaminated or disturbed. But in the past century or so, an increased interest in Eastern spirituality and in Western pre-Christian religious practices has begun to wear away this belief that the mystical sense was a rare possession. And the notion was badly damaged by the introduction of psychedelic drugs to the mainstream in the middle of the twentieth century. Suddenly, with the ingestion of a few hundred micrograms of LSD, housewives and investment bankers and thoroughly ordinary, boring people were "seeing the face of God."[*]

But it is important to understand that the expression of the mystical sense is heavily conditioned by culture. A Christian sees Jesus, a Hindu sees Krishna; the danger in this is that each then concludes that all the associated dogma they've been taught is therefore true, when in fact the dogma and conditioning have only provided a filter for their experience, have determined what color glasses they are wearing when they behold the Clear Light.

With practice, we can develop this sense, and even manage to perceive the mystical experience from multiple perspectives, to swap the glasses for a couple of different colors. This is one of the goals of ceremonial magic, as practiced by occultists and Pagans.

Is it worthwhile to have these experiences?

Is it worthwhile to view beautiful art, or hear beautiful music, or to fall in love, we might as well ask. The experience is its own justification.

But the danger of dogma, of mistaking these wonderful subjective experiences as revealing some truth about the objective universe (or at least "consensus reality," if one questions the notion of objectivity), is not to be taken lightly. Therefore the practice must include grounding, or good solid smacks upside the head (figurative or, if absolutely necessary, literal) if the seeker becomes too attached to the fantastic.

This is why Zen masters carry a stick, and say things like "If you say this is a stick, I will hit you thirty times, and if you say

---

[*] Two notes here. One, this is not a suggestion to go drop acid at random, without at least extensive research and self-preparation. Two, as I write this I am listening to a woman sing "House of the Rising Sun" with Nihongo (Japanese language) lyrics at "Folk Jamboree Night" at a bar called The Cellar in Osaka – in a world full of things as extraordinary as little girls on unicycles waiting at the crosswalk, and Japanese folk singers who cover old American blues tunes, are drugs really necessary?

it is not, I will hit you thirty times!" Attachment to the fantastic is rejected just as much as attachment to the mundane. The Pagan community is developing its own safeguards, primarily in the form of sacred nonsense. Rather than a stick, Discordian teachers* carry a joy buzzer, and The Church of the SubGenius will empty your wallet†, but the spirit is much the same.

Not too much can be said directly about the mystical experience. Its uniquely personal, transcendent nature means that it cannot be well-expressed in words, and attempting to do so is what tends to establish dogma. (On the other hand, we ought to consider poet Gary Snyder's observation that "It's not that 'the deepest spiritual insights cannot be expressed in words' (they can, in fact) but that '*words* cannot be expressed in words.' So our poems are full of *real presences*." (SNYDER, 114) But few of us are poets of Snyder's caliber.)

A classic Zen koan from Kyogen asks us to imagine a man hanging from a high tree branch by his teeth. He can't reach any hold for his hands or his feet. Along comes a seeker who asks, "Why did Bodhidharma [the founder of Zen] come from the West?" In Zen language, this means "Please teach me about Buddhism." If he opens his mouth to answer, he falls (some versions of the story say he falls straight to hell); if he remains silent, he fails in his duty to aid the querent (and thus, some versions say, will be killed and dammed).

What should he do?

The leading mystic who founded the system that Kyogen studied, the Shakyamuni Buddha, might have answered by holding up a flower...

---

* Did you know God is a crazy woman named Eris? Read more at www.PrincipiaDiscordia.com

† You'll pay to know what you really think! Eternal salvation or triple your money back! Only at www.subgenius.com

*A Guy Who Woke Up**

The Kamakura Daibutsu

There are Buddha statues all over the place in Japan, of course. They range from little plastic knick-knacks to giant stone or metal works of wonder. When I first saw the forty-foot high bronze *Daibutsu* (literally, "Big Buddha") at Todai-ji in Nara during the New Year's celebration, I wept.

But there is another Daibutsu in the hills outside of Tokyo, in the old feudal capital of Kamakura, that I like even more. The Kamakura Daibutsu is smaller by a hair than the one in Nara, but more striking because it sits outdoors. The hall that surrounded it was washed away in a tsunami several centuries ago, so that the giant Buddha sits there among the hills, meditating like some sort of zazen Ultraman, if you remember that old Japanese TV show. The layout of the temple hides the statue around a corner from the gate, making your first view of it quite stunning.

The Kamakura Daibutsu inspired Rudyard Kipling to write,

---

* Thich Nhat Hanh's *Old Path, White Clouds* is an excellent novelization of the life of the Buddha. The account given here draws from that and from many other sources, and should be taken more as an illustrative composite of legends than an attempt at academically accurate history, a nearly impossible task.

> But when the morning prayer is prayed,
> Think, ere ye pass to strife and trade,
> Is God in human image made
> > No nearer than Kamakura?

and Aleister Crowley to state,

> The Daibutsu, colossal amid his gardens of iris, with no canopy but the sky, does really produce a sense of his [Buddha's] universality; it does remind one of the grandeur and solidity of his teaching; of the reasonableness of his methods of attainment, the impersonal peace which is their reward; and of the boundless scope of his philosophy, independent as it is of all arbitrary assumptions, parochial points of view, sordid appeals and soul-stupefying superstitions.
> (CROWLEY, CONFESSIONS, CH. 26, 226)

The Kamakura statue is a portrayal of the Amida ("infinite light") Buddha, while the one in Nara is of the Dainichi ("great sun") Buddha – two of many ancient past, distant future, and supernaturally cosmic Buddhas that were eventually invented by various sects. But all the depictions of Buddhas are inspired by recorded descriptions of the prince Siddhartha Gautama, the person who became known as the historical Buddha. He is said to have been an extremely handsome man, which probably helped him initially in spreading his message. Whether in ancient India or in today's world, human nature is such that, all else being equal, a handsome teacher from an aristocratic family can make much more of an impact than a goofy-looking working class wise man. But if there hadn't been more to the Buddha than the right parents and a pretty face, his teachings would not have endured for 2,500 years.

The Early Years

The man who would become the historical Buddha ("awakened one," one of many titles bestowed on him by his followers) was born in northern India. Large uncertainty exists about the date; one tradition puts it around 567 B.C.E., but some scholars put his life almost a century later, while some legends have him several centuries earlier.

Siddhartha's father was a king of the Śākya clan,* and Siddhartha was his firstborn and heir. Siddhartha's mother died a few days after giving birth to him, and her sister became his stepmother.

As often happens to spiritual leaders, a number of legends have sprung up surrounding his birth. One of the more spectacular stories has it that the baby Siddhartha was not born in the usual fashion, but emerged from his mother's side, took several steps, pointed up to the sky and down to the Earth, and said "In all of Heaven and Earth, I alone am the World-Honored one!" (To which Zen master Ummon responded centuries later, "If I had been there, I would have killed the arrogant child and thrown his body to the dogs!")

Another legend is that a prophecy was made that if the young prince stayed on the worldly path, he would be a great king; but if he took to the spiritual path, he would be a redeemer of all of humankind.

We might dismiss the idea of supernatural glimpses of the future, but this mythic version highlights the tension that would later emerge between the seeker and his family: would he go off and seek enlightenment while he was still young? Or would he follow the "respectable" path, as seen by his culture: do his family duty, take the throne, produce an heir, and perhaps in his old age devote his energies and time to spiritual matters?

The mythic version also leads to the story of the Four Sights, one of the great "calls to adventure" in mythology. It goes something like this:

After the prophecy, the young Siddhartha's parents took care to keep him firmly attached to this world. He was sheltered and protected in the palace, surrounded by beauty and never exposed to anything unpleasant in the outside world.

He was taught the arts of war and of pleasure as befits a future king: wrestling and archery, dancing and music. And when he grew older, the arts of love. A marriage was arranged to a beautiful and charming princess, and a son was born.

But Siddhartha was still curious about the world that had

---

* Thus the Buddha's epithet "Śākyamuni" – the sage of the Śākya clan.

been hidden from him, and one day he was able to sneak out of the palace.

For the first time he saw sickness, old age, and death. He was horrified – was this truly the way of the world? How could anyone endure the pain of it?

Then, by the side of the road, in the middle of all this horror, he saw one man who seemed calm and serene in the midst of it, a wandering mendicant who had given up his home and possessions to live the life of a spiritual seeker.

Siddhartha returned to the palace but was haunted by what he had seen. He knew he had to learn the secret of that wandering ascetic: what did that man know that let him maintain his equanimity? A few nights later he snuck out of the palace. His charioteer accompanied him to the edge of the kingdom, where Siddhartha chopped off his own hair and headed off into the forest; his charioteer returned to the palace with Siddhartha's hair, sword, and jewels, as a farewell to his family.

Of course it probably didn't happen that way. Some sources suggest a more gradual turn to the spiritual life. One version of the tale claims that the trigger for Siddhartha to leave his comfortable life was that one night he looked around at the sleeping women of his harem and saw his concubines in the absence of their artful charms, saw how empty his diversions had been.

But whatever the details, he left his life of luxury to live as an ascetic and to study with the best teachers that he could find.

At this time, the mainstream religion of Brahmanism was riddled with corruption, including widespread abuse of religious authority and of the caste system. In opposition to it, many wisdom schools of yoga arose.

When we think of "yoga," most of us think of the system of physical culture. But the word yoga comes from the same root as "yoke" – again, we find the notion of binding, of connecting. Hinduism developed several yogas, methods of training designed to create connection or unity: the physical culture of hatha yoga, the jnâna yoga of knowledge and intellectual inquiry, the bhakti yoga of love and devotion, the karma yoga of work, and the rāja yoga of psychological experiments and mental exploration through meditation. It was on the latter that Siddhartha focused.

(It's worth noting that the other forms of yoga would all spring up again in new forms within Buddhism as it grew – the intellectual discipline of the sutra masters, the devotional forms of Shin Buddhism, the working meditations of Zen monks.)

Siddhartha sought out the best teachers in the land, but he was unable to find one who could satisfy him. With his combination of a keen mind and amazing determination, he was soon able to match every teacher he found, and plumb the totality of their methods. He learned to enter many altered states of consciousness, but he realized that this was not getting him closer to an answer to the problem of suffering.

Having tried all the mental methods available, Siddhartha turned to physical disciplines. He went for extreme asceticism – sitting perfectly still for hours, pressing his tongue to the roof of his mouth so hard that he broke into a sweat, disciplining himself to eat only a handful of beans a day, neglecting hygiene until the dirt fell off of him from its own weight.

He was as much the master of his fleshly desires as any man has been. And as asceticism was a popular spiritual path at the time, his success in this won him a small crowd of followers. But it wasn't getting him to enlightenment. In fact, according to some versions of the tale it nearly killed him – he passed out from starvation and would have died, were it not for a young girl who found him collapsed in the road, overcame her fear that this filthy and emaciated collection of bone and parchment-like skin was a demon, and fed him.

He had pursued asceticism as far as was possible, and not found what he sought. He had investigated all the schools of philosophy and yoga available, and found them wanting.

He would have to find a new way.

Under a Tree

The climate in the part of India where our story takes place was mild. Mild enough that our hero was able to take his shelter under a fig tree, among the roots, while he considered and meditated for a space of many weeks.

Having tried the extremes of asceticism and the life of luxury, he went for a "middle way," seeking neither to steel himself against pain nor to chase ephemeral pleasures. He ate enough to stay healthy, fully and mindfully enjoying the simple peasant fare that the local people gave to him. He spent time talking to and teaching some of the local children, in return for food and other support – a pattern that would persist into the monastic community he built.

He recalled a time when, as a child sitting under a rose-apple tree watching a celebration of the spring planting, he had spontaneously relaxed into a meditative state. He had not sought out any special altered state of consciousness, but had simply relaxed into his own clear mind. It seems he took that spontaneous meditation, rather than the special trance states of his teachers, as a model for contemplation during his time under the tree that came to be called the "Bo" or "Bodhi" tree.

As he sat, his mind cleared, and he began to see into his own true nature.

This is never an easy task. Legends say that he strove with demons, that he was tempted by Māra, the lord of illusion, and that the Bo tree bent down to protect him and that the Earth itself testified and bore witness to his right to seek enlightenment.

Whatever the truth of this, whether these stories represent supernatural or psychological truths, Siddhartha persevered and overcame. And a little while afterward, upon seeing the morning star, he achieved his great enlightenment. A few days later, the Buddha gave his first sermon to some of his old followers from his ascetic days, describing what he had found.

Four Noble Truths

In Douglas Adams' famous science fiction radio play, and later novel, *The Hitchhiker's Guide to the Galaxy*, an advanced civilization builds a giant computer to determine "the answer to life, the universe, and everything."

The computer announces that the problem is tricky, but can be solved in time. After thousands of years of computation, the civilization sends a delegation to receive the long-awaited answer.

The computer reports that the answer is, in fact, 42.

When the delegation expresses their incredulity and disappointment at this result, the computer claims that the answer is perfect; the problem is that the adherents never knew exactly what the *Question* was.

I imagine the Buddha's mind moving in a somewhat similar fashion. He had tried all the available schools of philosophy, pushed his body to the brink of death, and not found what he was looking for.

But just what was it that he was looking for? What was the

Question, the problem he was seeking to solve?

His realization is stated in the First Noble Truth, sometimes translated as "Life is suffering," though perhaps more accurately and less depressingly (if less concisely) rendered as "Conditioned states of existence are inherently unsatisfying." It is a statement of the problem.

The actual Pali word used is *dukkha*, which can be literally translated as "out of joint," in the same sense as a slipped axle on a cart or a dislocated shoulder.

Our lives are marked with suffering. And this is not merely a material problem, not something we can solve by feeding the hungry and housing the homeless. Of course these are wonderful things to do, but people who have every physical comfort still suffer. We see rich and famous celebrities who blow their brains out. The Buddha had lived the life of luxury himself, and still found it wanting.

To solve the problem, he would have to get to the root of it. This is expressed in the Second Noble Truth: the origin of suffering is desire and attachment.

On the most obvious level, we want material things, and make ourselves miserable when don't get them – or we do get them, and find that they are not so wonderful as we dreamed. We are often like a child at Christmas, surrounded by gifts but disappointed that we didn't get the BB gun we had fixed our heart on. Or we do get it, and then promptly shoot ourselves in the face with an unfortunate ricochet.

The romantic and sexual relationships that consume so much of our energy and attention are loaded with similar pitfalls. How often we burn with desire for the woman or man we find beautiful – then find that they don't live up to our fantasy.

We are dragged around by our desires like a man being dragged behind a horse.

But beyond the material things, beyond the sensual pleasures, we want certain things from the universe.

Number one, **we want to not die!** And we want our loved ones to not die. We want not to age, and many of us want our children to not grow up. And we want our relationships with other people to always be the same. We want stability and permanence, freedom from flux and change.

But the one inevitable constant in the world is change. Buddhism talks about this with the terms *śūnyatā*, "emptiness," and *anātman*, "no self." Everything is "empty," by which is meant lacking a separate self-existence. Everything depends on the conditions created by everything else for its existence, and those conditions are constantly changing.

For example, we consider a tree as separate from the sun, the clouds, the rain, and the soil in our minds and in our words because it's useful for practical ends. But from a deep perspective there is no such separation. When we really look closely at that tree, we see that its boundaries are so fuzzy and permeable, that its roots and leaves mingle with the soil and air so thoroughly, that to fully understand it we have to understand the entire universe. A molecule in a leaf gets created because of a bit of sunlight generated ninety-three million miles away. The tree can no more be separated from the world around it than a wave or a whirlpool can be separated from the water.

And this also applies to our own individual "selves." Buddhism teaches the idea that we are separate and independent from the world is an illusion, just as it is in the case of the tree. This idea is called anātman, and in it we see a big break with the proto-Hindu philosophy that preceded the Buddha. The individual self, the ātman, the thing that says "I am!", is a fundamental concept of Hinduism. Different schools within Hinduism take differing views on the precise nature of ātman and its relationship to ultimate reality, or Brahman; but in the Buddha's day most held with a dualistic point of view that the ātman had a totally separate identity. (SMITH, 115) And even non-dualist forms of Hinduism (which arose later and were to some degree influenced by Buddhism) hold that there is an ātman which is an identifiable and meaningful thing, even if they teach that its true nature is eventually one with ultimate reality.

The Buddha, though, pointed out that just as a house is an aggregate of wood and brick and plaster and empty spaces in a certain shape, and there is no "house self" that can be added or taken away from it, so a human being is an aggregate of physical and mental phenomena. The self, the ātman, is an illusion. Because we mistake this illusion for our true nature, we cling to it and want it to last forever, but we can't hold on to a mirage.

Well, the wanting what you can't have is certainly a depressing prospect. Can anything be done?

Yes!

This is the Third Noble Truth: the end of suffering. In the mythic version, the Buddha had the example of the mendicant who inspired his quest, as a sort of "existence proof" that a solution exists. Perhaps in reality he had only his own experience and insight to rely on, but we have his example, and the example of many who followed, to demonstrate to us that relief is possible.

If suffering arises from our thoughts of desire and attachment, then by changing our thought processes we can escape the snare. The specific path of understanding, action, and mindfulness that the Buddha recommended is laid out in the Fourth Noble Truth, the Eightfold Path.

The Eightfold Path

The eight components of the path the Buddha suggested are usually translated as "Right Understanding," "Right Thought," and so on. Actually the Sanskrit term used is *samyag*, which some scholars suggest might be better be translated as "best" than "right" – less of a right/wrong dichotomy, and more along the line of "do your best."

There are varying translations of the elements of the Eightfold Path. But it's useful to group them into three parts:

1) Best Understanding (or Comprehension or View) and Best Thought (or Intention or Aspiration or Resolve): seeing the problem, resolve to start to think in a new way.

2) Best Speech, Best Action, and Best Livelihood: in word and in deed, act in ways that don't create suffering and that cultivate positive mental habits.

3) Best Effort (or Exertion or Striving), Best Mindfulness (or Recollection), Best Meditation (or Concentration): understanding that the mind is the source of everything that we experience, undertake the task of training it, and resolve to keep trying, to return always to the path and the present moment whenever we stray, and to engage in exercises to strengthen our facilities.

The Buddha: The Rest of His Life

The Buddha laid out the Four Noble Truths and the Eightfold Path in a talk to his disciples (the ones he had lost when he left the ascetic path, and now regained), and thus started a new school of thought in the world.

But that wasn't the end of the story. He was still a young man, probably in his thirties. He spent the next several decades refining his teaching and gathering followers. Many left their homes to become *bhikkhus* and *bhikkhunis* (ordained monks and nuns) but he also taught lay people. His wife and son and stepmother eventually took the vows and joined his community of monks and nuns.

His combination of noble birth (and thus social acceptability) and transcendent insight allowed him to gain a tremendous audience. It's quite likely that others before the Buddha had just as much insight into the truth, and it's possible that previous teachers were also as articulate in their analysis and teaching. But Siddhartha had one thing more: connections.

Even if he had "abandoned the world" (understanding "the world" to be his society), the world did not abandon him. As a result, he was able to build a substantial following.

Enough of a following, in fact, to present a threat to the established power structure. Kings and princes sought his council, turning against established religious leaders and scheming courtiers. As a result, at least three attempts were made on his life. (It is interesting to speculate on what might have happened to his teaching and his followers if he, like Jesus of Nazareth, had been cut down early in his career.)

There is one episode from the later life of the Buddha that is particularly relevant to our investigations here. On this occasion, the Buddha gathered all of his followers together for a sermon. But rather than speaking to them, he mutely held up a single lotus flower.

One of his disciples, Mahākāśyapa, got the idea, and smiled.

It was on the basis of his response to this "Flower Sermon" that the Buddha designated Mahākāśyapa as his successor. So just what was it that Mahākāśyapa got in that instant?

According to orthodox Zen Buddhism, in that moment both the Buddha and Mahākāśyapa saw that flower "just as it was" – experience unfiltered by discriminating consciousness. And in that instant the Buddha's state of enlightenment was transmitted to Mahākāśyapa. This "direct transmission" is the heart of orthodox Zen; it is claimed that this state has been passed down for two and a half millennia, from Buddha through Mahākāśyapa and a series of Zen Masters to students today.

The Buddha continued teaching and preaching for decades, until he was cut down in his eighties by a digestive disorder that may – or may not – have been brought about by a meal of bad mushrooms – or bad pork. In the centuries after his death, his followers gradually split into two camps.

The Theravāda ("Way of the Elders," sometimes known by its detractors as the Hīnayāna, or "Lesser Vehicle") is conservative and monastic-oriented. Its ideal state is that of the *arhat*, a person who has purified and freed themselves from all attachments. For most of its history, the Theravāda branch attempted to keep intact all of the rules – numbering in the hundreds – of the original Buddhist community, including many trivial ones that had been established by the Buddha's responses to specific conditions and occurrences.

As the Buddha was dying, he told his followers that the trivial rules could be relaxed, but no one wanted to be responsible for determining which rules were trivial! The difficulties of maintaining this complex set of rules limited the spread of Theravāda, which until recently was primarily limited to Sri Lanka (formerly known as Ceylon) and in the warmer areas of Southeast Asia. (Consider, for example, the difficulties of a Theravādan missionary who wished to cross the mountains from India into China to spread his version of the Buddha-dharma, but whose permitted clothing was limited to a few lightweight robes.) But over the past century and a half, increased contact with the West and with Mahāyāna Buddhist cultures has had something of a liberalizing influence on Theravāda.

The more liberal Mahāyāna ("Greater Vehicle") took a more flexible approach to both rules and to doctrine, adapting to whatever environment it found itself in. It had more to offer to lay people than Theravāda, and when it encountered a new culture it soaked up the local deities, beliefs, and practices – sometimes to the point of diluting, or even losing entirely, the Buddha's teachings. It takes as its ideal the *bodhisattva*, a person of limitless compassion who vows to save all sentient beings. Mahāyāna spread widely through China, Japan, Korea, Vietnam, and Tibet.*

In India itself, Buddhism fell into decline from about the twelfth century CE until the worldwide Buddhist revival in the late nineteenth century. (Many of the Buddha's teachings were

---

* Vajrayāna, the "Diamond Vehicle" which includes Tibetan Buddhism, is seen by some scholars as being contained within Mahāyāna and by others as a separate tradition emerging out of it.

absorbed into Hinduism.) Thus the West's introduction to Buddhism came not from India, but mostly from Ceylon's Theravāda and Japan's Zen.

Zen arose from the Mahāyāna tradition, almost a thousand years after the life of the Buddha and thousands of miles away in China. Its story starts with the legend of a red-bearded barbarian named Bodhidharma.

A Red-Bearded Barbarian and An Illiterate Peasant

Daruma Figurines at Daruma-Dera

Tucked away off of a side street in Kyoto, about a mile from Nijō Castle – the spot where the last shogun announced to his followers the restoration of the Emperor and the end of the shogunate – is a small Zen temple informally known as Daruma-dera, the "Temple of Daruma." Its official name is actually Hōrin-ji, which means "Temple of the Dharma Wheel" or "Temple of the Wheel of the Law" – *dharma* means the teachings of the Buddha, and an eight-spoked wheel is a common symbol of Buddhism. (This temple shouldn't be confused with another Hōrin-ji in Kyoto, over in the Arashiyama area.)

Daruma is the Japanese name for Bodhidharma, the legendary founder of Zen. He's also regarded as the founder of many of the Asian martial and healing arts, including both karate and shiatsu. That's how I first became familiar with him.

He may be the most-portrayed *gaijin* in Japanese history. His image is everywhere – not just in portraits, but in a peculiar sort of figurine. These are weighted so that if tipped over, they right themselves, illustrating the proverb *"nana karobi, ya oki"* – "if you fall down seven times, get up eight times."

Daruma figurines come with both eyes blank, white, and there is a wonderful little ritual involved in coloring them in. When you set out to achieve some goal, you get to color in one eye. The figurine then stares at you with that one eye, encouraging you to get to work and make your goal happen so that you get to fill in the other eye. It's strong magic. (I've used one to help remind me to keep working on this book!)

It is for its collection of these figurines, ranging in size from a few inches to about three feet high, that Daruma-dera is known. Supposedly, the temple houses ten thousand of them, but in Chinese and Japanese culture 10,000 often just means "more than you'd care to count." The temple itself dates to 1718, but it was in 1933 that the tenth abbot, who used the Daruma figurines as a teaching tool, started the famous collection. ("Hoorin-ji")

The temple was not in my guidebook, but when I stumbled across a mention of it on the web I knew I had to check it out. (Fortunately it was marked on the Periplus map of Kyoto I bought for the trip.) This is a small temple, not much of an international tourist destination, so there's no English brochure or signs other that the one in front. But it's definitely worth a visit if you're familiar with Bodhidharma's legend.

Bodhidharma/Daruma is often shown wearing an enveloping cloak and cowl, presumably keeping him warm as he sat facing the wall and meditating in his cave at the famous Shaolin Temple. As I walked to Daruma-dera through the wind and rain, I composed a haiku:

> wind bends umbrella
> so my jacket's hood becomes
> like Daruma's cowl

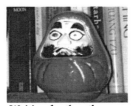
Waiting for the other eye

Not a very good haiku, perhaps, but there it is. (It was at the moment I saw the temple that the wind and rain stopped. Make of that what you will.)

When I found the temple I had the place to myself for a bit. I sat in meditation for a few minutes in the main hall with its tremendous collection of figurines, burned incense and lit a candle in prayer, then paid a few yen to go in to the inner courtyard and look at the garden. There's also a memorial hall for film stars – I'm not quite sure how that ended up here, but in

Japan it's in Buddhist temples that cemeteries and other memorials are usually found. The native religion, Shintō, considered death to be the ultimate impurity and has very little in the way of funerary ritual. It was through dealing with death that Buddhism first found its foothold in Japanese culture.

While it lacks the gravitas of the larger, more famous temples like Nanzen-ji, a visit to Daruma-dera seems a fine way to pay one's respects to the "red bearded barbarian," Bodhidharma.

According to orthodox Zen, Bodhidharma lived around 500 CE and came to China from either India or Persia. He was the successor of the Buddha through the line of direct "dharma transmission" from Buddha to Mahākāśyapa (the guy who smiled at the Buddha's "flower sermon") and down through a few dozen teachers to Bodhidharma himself, 28th in the line.

Classically he is depicted with a wild fringe of hair and a red beard – some koans (Zen teaching stories) make reference to "the barbarian's red beard." He is often shown with bulging eyes, the legend being that, frustrated with falling asleep while meditating, he cut off his own eyelids; where he threw them to the ground, the first tea plant sprouted.

Zen is replete with stories about hacking off body parts; thankfully, most of them should be taken figuratively, otherwise early Zen followers would probably have been dying from blood loss or subsequent infection at such a rate as to preclude the school's survival.

When Bodhidharma arrived in China, Buddhism was already well-established there. But this was Mahāyāna Buddhism with a thousand years of additional beliefs and teaching encrusted onto it. While it had absorbed many useful teachings it had also soaked up a bunch of superstitions and metaphysical speculation. Much of what was taught was a degraded sort of Buddhism that was less concerned with the Buddha's teachings about ending suffering in the here and now than with racking up merit ("good karma") to get a good position the next time around the cycle of reincarnation.

A traditional depiction of Bodhidharma

The story goes that the Chinese Emperor Wu was just such a Buddhist, and Bodhidharma ended up having an audience with him. The Emperor had sponsored a lot of temple-building, sutra-copying, and suchlike, and thought this had earned him a lot of good karma. He asked, "So, how much merit have I accumulated doing all this?"

Emperor Wu no doubt expected to be told that he had earned copious merit points, redeemable for a future rebirth into the Pure Land or something like that. But Bodhidharma was having none of it.

"None at all," he replied.

That's a gutsy thing to tell a man who could have you executed on a whim. But rather than running this impudent monk through, the Emperor must have figured to tap his brain on better ways to rack up the merit.

"Then, what is holy?" he asked.

And that lovable barbarian replied, "Vast emptiness. Nothing is holy."

This befuddled the Emperor more than a little bit. Perhaps suspecting that he was being toyed with, he asked, "Who are you, to give me such answers?"

Bodhidharma's answer has echoed down the ages, forming what some believe is the core of Zen: "I don't know."

"Knowing," after all, is an intellectual attachment. Perhaps you have tried to help someone learn a new skill, only to be rebuffed with protestations of "I know, I know!" And if you're honest, you can probably remember doing this yourself. (I certainly can, to my chagrin. Apologies to all the teachers I've done this to – and to the ones I'll probably do it to in the future.) "Knowing" can be excellent insulation against learning. But when we can say we "don't know," we're teachable, open to alternatives.

And if we can do this with our concept of who we are, if we can give in to "I don't know" rather than limit ourselves with attachment to socially-determined roles and labels – "I'm my father's son, so I behave thus-and-such way; I'm a poet, so I act like so; I'm an American and so I am free and brave and trustworthy and loyal and whatever" – then the freedom is boundless.

Zen calls this attitude *shoshin*, "beginner's mind." As the twentieth-century Zen master Shunryu Suzuki put it, "In the beginner's mind there are many possibilities, but in the expert's there are few." (S. SUZUKI, 21)

It's that lack of possibilities, that "sure" knowledge, that so often makes religion dangerous. You've got to be pretty damned sure of what you're doing to burn heretics at the stake in order to save their souls, or to declare that your tribal god has promised some piece of land to your people and anyone else occupying it is to be put to the sword, or to carry a bomb into a crowd of strangers and blow them and yourself into a fine red mist.

More liberal doses of "I don't know" for all religions sounds like a very, very good idea. If Zen has nothing else to offer, the treasure of "I don't know" more than justifies it as one of the world's wonders. In this sense, confusion is good for the soul.*

After his unsatisfactory interview with the Emperor, Bodhidharma went to the famed Shaolin Temple where he spent several years in seated meditation, staring at the wall of a cave – so long, according to one legend, that his arms and legs atrophied, and that's why he's represented as an armless, legless Weeble-like like figurine, symbolizing perseverance.

He supposedly found the monks at Shaolin too weak to endure the rigors of his style of meditation, and so introduced a

---

* I have tried to make a Discordian koan out of Bodhidharma's answer: "Upon hearing this great teaching of Bodhidharma, Chairman Tao exclaimed, 'I don't know?! I don't know?! Third base!'" People either look at me blankly or groan when I tell it; I "don't know" if that means it's working or not.

set of exercises, presumably with some basis in yoga, that became the basis of *wushu* (the martial art widely but inaccurately known as "kung fu"), and also of *qi gong* and Asian bodywork therapies.

Resolving the armless and legless lump with the kung fu master is left as an exercise for the reader.

Bodhidharma's method was a negation of abstract theory, focused on meditation practice and cultivating the right state of mind: stoic, not seeking any goal, practicing virtuous actions without attachment. He de-emphasized the sacred texts, saying "people nowadays who recite a few sutras or shastras [discourses of the Buddha or his prominent disciples] and think it's the Dharma are fools. Unless you see your mind, reciting so much prose is useless." (PINE, 3-7, 13)

His teaching started to chip away a lot of the junk that had adhered to Mahāyāna Buddhism over the centuries, and is considered the start of Ch'an Buddhism – or as it's known in Japan and to most of the West, Zen. (In Korea it's Seon, and in Vietnam, Thiền. These are worthwhile traditions that have developed their own distinct histories over the centuries, but for our purposes we're going to lump them all under "Zen," except when the distinction is historically important.)

Emerging out of Bodhidharma's "don't know" and his criticism of reliance on texts, Zen is sometimes perceived as anti-intellectual. But it is not that Zen asks us to stop thinking; rather, it proposes a new way of doing so. As D.T. Suzuki explained, "When this is attained, man thinks yet he does not think. He thinks like the showers coming down from the sky; he thinks like the waves rolling on the ocean; he thinks like the stars illuminating the nightly heavens; he thinks like the green foliage shooting forth in the relaxing spring breeze. Indeed, he is the showers, the ocean, the stars, the foliage." (D.T. SUZUKI, FORWARD, 7)

Bodhidharma is revered as Zen's founder and "First Patriarch." But it was another legendary master who gave Zen its distinctive flavor. This was the Sixth Patriarch, Hui Neng.

His official story goes something like this: Hui Neng was an illiterate peasant from the sticks of southern China. As a boy, he heard a man reciting the *Diamond Sutra* and was struck by its advice to "Let your mind flow free without dwelling on anything." As he was a precocious youngster, simply hearing this verse was enough to push his mind over into enlightenment. Hui Neng asked the chanting man about it, and found that he had come from the East Mountain monastery of the Fifth Patriarch,

Hung Jen.

Hui Neng headed off to Hung Jen's temple. The Fifth Patriarch recognized Hui Neng's potential and he was accepted as a disciple – but only in secret, as Hung Jen knew that the monks would not accept this country bumpkin as an equal. He was set to menial tasks, and not ordained as monk.

Some time later, Hung Jen started to look for a successor. He decided to do this with, of all things, a poetry contest, and told the monks to express their wisdom in a verse.

The senior monk, Shen Hsiu, was considered the odds-on favorite. But he was unsure of his own ability, so he wrote his poem on a wall, anonymously, and waited to see the reaction:

> The body is the Bodhi tree*
> The mind like a bright mirror standing
> Take care to wipe it all the time
> And allow no dust to cling (WATTS, WAY OF ZEN, 96)

This poem represents a fairly standard, methodical approach to cultivating wisdom. All the monks praised it, but Hung Jen told Shen Hsiu that it wasn't quite there.

Hui Neng heard the hubbub about the poem. Since he couldn't read the verse himself, one of the monks read it to him, and Hui Neng asked someone to write down a responding verse for him:

> There never was a Bodhi tree,
> Nor bright mirror standing
> Fundamentally, not one thing exists
> So where is the dust to cling? (WATTS, WAY OF ZEN, 96)

This probably seemed like nonsense to most of the monks. Publicly the Patriarch had no praise for it, but in the middle of the night, he summoned Hui Neng.

Hung Jen gave Hui Neng the dharma transmission, and the robe and the begging bowl that had been passed down from

---

* The "wisdom" tree, the tree under which the Buddha sat during the meditation leading up to his enlightenment

Bodhidharma, the symbols of the Patriarchship. Hui Neng, not even ordained but now the Sixth Patriarch, fled back south into the night to avoid the wrath of the monks. For about fifteen years he lived with hunters in the back country – though he would free animals from their snares, and would instead gather vegetables. (GODDARD, 505)

When he thought the time was right, Hui Neng went to Fa-hsing temple. Since he was still a layman, he didn't bust right out teaching, but hid his understanding until one day he overheard two monks arguing about a flag in the breeze. Was it the wind that was moving, or the flag? Hui Neng cut right through the Gordian knot, suggesting to the monks, "It is your mind that moves." With that, he was brought to the attention of the temple's master, and recognized as Hung Jen's successor. He was finally ordained as a monk and began his teaching career.

Hui Neng's teaching is marked by the idea that our true nature is already pure and enlightened. According to Liu Tsung-yuan, writing about a century after Hui Neng's death, "his teaching began with the goodness of human nature and ended with the goodness of human nature. There is no need of plowing or weeding: it was originally pure." (SHIH, 10-11)

He taught students to disregard any outside authority and put an emphasis on "sudden enlightenment": the idea that it is not enough to just follow the precepts of virtuous behavior and to study the sutras, or even to quiet the mind with meditation. A direct mystical experience is necessary, a moment of insight into one's true nature. This experience is the "satori" for which Zen is famous.

But on the other hand, satori is not sufficient by itself. We read Zen stories that end with somebody's satori and we tend to think that's the end of the process, but it's just the start. As Hui Neng's student Shen Hui (not be confused with Hui Neng's rival Shen Hsiu) explained: "All those who want to learn the Tao (Way) must achieve Sudden Enlightenment to be followed by Gradual Cultivation. It is like child-birth, which is a sudden affair, but the child will require a long process of nurture and education before he attains his full bodily and intellectual growth." (SHIH, 6-7)

The story of the Zen lineage passing through Bodhidharma and Hui Neng is a great tale – it's got a wise man who tells off one of the most powerful men in the world, an underdog who triumphs, a rag-tag bunch of spiritual rebels who prevail over hypocrisy and orthodoxy. If we buy the story about Bodhidharma being the original kung fu teacher, we can almost picture him as a Jedi Master from the *Star Wars* movies. Maybe George Lucas could turn the story of the early Zen patriarchs into a series of films.

Unfortunately, the historical evidence points to these tales being largely fabrications. The tales of Bodhidharma were not recorded until five centuries after the fact. The only contemporary account that mentions him does so only in passing, if indeed it's even the same man. (DUMOULIN, 32) Some scholars doubt he existed at all. (PINE, IX)

And Hui Neng seems to have been heavily re-invented by succeeding generations – especially by his student Shen Hui (quoted above), for the sake of arguments about the "sudden enlightenment" versus "gradual cultivation" doctrines, and possibly also due to court intrigues surrounding the Empress Wu. (KEREMIDSCHIEFF; SHIH, 4-12) (No relation to the Emperor Wu whom Bodhidharma scolded.) But their legend is so deeply rooted in Zen that it almost doesn't matter what the historical truth is. As Neil Gaiman observed, "Things need not have happened to be true." (GAIMAN, 21)

Regardless of who was responsible, Ch'an developed into a form of Buddhism with a distinctly Chinese flavor as it absorbed many ideas from Taoism.*

Taoism is the native mysticism of China, traditionally attributed to yet another mythical figure, Lao Tzu, who supposedly lived around 600 BCE. He doesn't even have a proper name, "Lao Tzu" meaning something like "Old Fellow" or "Great Old Master." Putting aside the more incredible bits – that he was conceived by a shooting star, carried in his mother's womb for over 80 years, and was born a wise old man – we still have quite a story. Supposedly Lao Tzu was an archivist who led a life of quiet virtue. In his later years, seeking to get away from the hustle and bustle he rode west into the sunset on a water buffalo. At one mountain pass a gatekeeper recognized his wisdom, and tried to get him to return to civilization. Failing in that, the gatekeeper

---

* Pronounced, and sometimes spelled, "Daoism." Conventions for rendering Chinese (and, to a lesser degree, Japanese) words in English have changed several times over the years.

persuaded Lao Tzu to stop for a while and write down some of his insights. The work he supposedly authored was the *Tao Te Ching* (loosely translated, *The Way and Its Power*), the basic text of the Taoist philosophy. (SMITH, 196-197)

The Tao of Lao Tzu is "the Way" – literally, the character "tao" means path or road or way – the way things are, in the deepest sense and the biggest picture. It is not a being to be worshiped, but something more like a current or a pattern, a way of thinking and acting, that a wise person can make use of.

Lao Tzu was one of the earliest philosophers to recognize the limitations of language in discussing states of mind. Right at the start, the *Tao Te Ching* tells us that the Tao that can be spoken of is not the true Tao – the truth of our experience comes before language.

To deal with this limitation, paradox and humor are valuable tools in the Taoist's kit. They show especially strongly in the work of Chuang Tzu, a storyteller and poet who lived around 300 BCE (HAMILL, IX) and the only Taoist who approaches Lao Tzu in stature. You may have heard about a famous dream Chuang Tzu had: he dreamed that he was a butterfly, fluttering around and doing butterfly things. He suddenly awakened to find that he was not a butterfly, but in fact Chuang Tzu. But then he wondered – was he Chuang Tzu who had dreamed that he was a butterfly? Or was he a butterfly, now dreaming that he was Chuang Tzu? (HAMILL, 18)

That's pretty radical skepticism. The Taoism of Lao Tzu and Chuang Tzu (referred to by scholars as the "Lao-Chuang philosophy") was full of "don't know" long before Bodhidharma came along.

Chuang Tzu's stories – the forerunners of Zen's koans – are fables of a sort, but like nothing that Aesop ever came up with. For example, one tells of a giant old chestnut tree with wood that is absolutely useless to craftsmen: too dense to make a boat, too subject to rot and worms to build with, too brittle to make utensils out of. But it is exactly because of its uselessness that the tree survives, while others are cut down for their wood or stripped for their fruit. (HAMILL, 30-31)

Taoism has a strong streak of naturalism in it, an ecological approach that seeks attunement with nature rather than mastery over it. As the *Tao Te Ching* states,

> Those who would take over the earth

> And shape it to their will
> Never, I notice, succeed.
> The earth is like a vessel so sacred
> That at the mere approach of the profane
> It is marred
> And when they reach out their fingers it is
> gone.(SMITH, 212-213)

And so the Taoist Sage lives a life of simplicity and balance, puts himself or herself in accordance with the natural world, and spontaneously and un-self-consciously "goes with the flow." The notion that the world consists of the interplay of *yin* and *yang*, of pairs of opposing but complementary principles that are always in motion and transformation – day and night, sun and shade, growth and decay, movement and substance – is at the heart of Taoist cosmology.

This cosmology is found not just in the Lao-Chuang philosophy, but also in the theory of *qi* (central to Chinese medicine and "Taoist yoga" such as *tai chi chuan* and *qi gong*) and in the folk religions of China. In the broadest sense, Taoism includes all of these – we could almost call Taoism a catch-all term for any native Chinese philosophy or religious practice that existed before the introduction of Buddhism and that was not Confucian or part of another easily identified historical school.

Ch'an Buddhism absorbed much from the Lao-Chuang philosophy. Scholars have recognized a close relationship between the two; Huston Smith says that "Buddhism processed through Taoism becomes Zen," (SMITH, 216) and in the view of Livia Knaul Kohn, after centuries of interaction with Buddhism, Lao-Chuang ceased to exist as an independent tradition and Ch'an may be seen as its legitimate heir. (KNAUL, 411) The *Tao Te Ching* was so influential on Chinese Buddhism that Dwight Goddard included it in his *Buddhist Bible* alongside the various sutras. (GODDARD, XXXI)

Ch'an also took from other aspects of Taoism. Taoist yoga practices influenced Ch'an's meditation style. From Chinese folk religion it picked up deities like Kuan Yin: a syncretization of a Taoist goddess with the Buddhist bodhisattva of compassion Avalokitesvara (possibly also influenced by the myths of Isis, pushed east by the empire of Alexander), she is often described as the Buddhist goddess of mercy. Taoism's simple and understated aesthetic became a part of Ch'an – while the temples of some Buddhist sects can be downright baroque, even the largest Zen temples maintain a simple design. And Ch'an absorbed Taoism's naturalist orientation.

After about seven centuries (if we accept the Bodhidharma myth) of marinating in Taoism, around 1200 Ch'an Buddhism came to Japan, where they called it Zen. It was never the most popular form of Buddhism there, but because it was favored by the samurai and the shoguns who ruled for six centuries, it came to have a disproportionate impact on Japanese culture.

While Zen/Ch'an also spread into Korea and Vietnam and established wonderfully vibrant strains there, it was from Japan that it was introduced to the West in the late 1800s, as part of a post-colonial Buddhist revival throughout the East. This revival was related in surprising ways to a revival of occultism and classicism in the West: both were connected to the Industrial Revolution, and both were parts of a historical tapestry weaving together Transcendentalists, Romantics, Buddhists, Theosophists, Magicians, the Woodcraft movement (forerunners of the Boy Scouts), Witches, Beat poets, the 1960s counter-culture, and eventually the modern Pagan movement.

The Tapestry of Zen Pagan History, Part I
or: Poets, Buddhists, and Magicians, Oh My!

> "If you know your history
> Then you would know where you coming from
> Then you wouldn't have to ask me
> Who the heck do I think I am" – "Buffalo Soldier,"
> Bob Marley

The Transcendentalists

My time in Japan has largely been a series of train trips. Thanks to the JR (Japan Railways) local and inter-city lines, the Hankyu and Hanshin privately-run railroads, and the Osaka and Kyoto subways, I have not missed having a car at all – indeed, I'm feeling disappointed that I'll have to drive when I get back home to Baltimore.

That's partly due to one of the big benefits of train travel: it is highly conducive to reading. (Well, except on a crowded rush-hour commuter train, where one barely has space to breathe.) I'm enjoying that thoroughly; I had dozens of books shipped over here because I can't imagine three months without plenty of reading material.

I've been catching up on the Transcendentalists, reading some Emerson and Whitman. It's great to read Whitman's transcription of the American carols while in a foreign land; I'm far enough away from home to silence the noise of the contemporary political "dialog," such as it is, and to really contemplate what it is to be an American.

I'm coming to see that the writers of the Transcendentalist movement – primarily Emerson, Thoreau, and Whitman – had a vision of the Unites States as a world leader. But their vision was not of political leadership, or of military power, or even of mere artistic and cultural prominence; they saw their nation as a spiritual model for the world.

It was 1837 when Emerson gave his landmark lecture "The American Scholar": (EMERSON, "AMERICAN SCHOLAR") six decades since the American colonies had declared their political independence, and a quarter-century since they had made it stick in the War of 1812. But like a teenager who has just moved out on his or her own, the

U.S. still sought to define its own identity.*

In literature and the arts it still looked to England rather than to any domestic tradition. Socially and economically it was dealing with the Industrial Revolution, and in politics it still wrestled with issues its Enlightenment-inspired founders hadn't settled – chiefly, slavery.

The question, "just what is America, anyway?" was being urgently explored, and was so divisive that within Emerson's lifetime tens of thousands would be killed trying to settle it by force.

Tumultuous times have often given impetus to spiritual or religious movements. The turmoil caused by plagues and "barbarian" attacks helped open the way for Christianity in Rome. The "Little Ice Age" and the Black Death caused such disruption in Europe that the Catholic Church split in two, each side claiming to have the genuine Pope. It was only was 25 years between Columbus's voyage and Luther's theses, and six years between the start of the English civil war and the beginning of George Fox's preaching career, the start of the Quakers.

Just so, the turmoil and conflicts of early nineteenth century America gave birth to a mass revival of "primitive" Christianity, the "Second Great Awakening". But in New England a more ecumenical and intellectual trend gave birth to the Transcendentalist literary and religious movement. They had a vision that was in some ways similar to that of the Puritan colonists, who saw the new nation as a shining "city upon a hill" that would be a guide to the world. But where the Puritans sought to build a rigid order based on received Biblical truth and a structured clergy, the Transcendentalists wanted to enable each person's individual and direct religious experience.

As Whitman wrote in the preface to the 1855 edition of *Leaves of Grass*:

> There will soon be no more priests. Their work is done. They may wait awhile ... perhaps a generation or two ... dropping off by degrees. A superior breed shall take their place ... the

---

* For a more chronological approach to the events described here, see the Timeline in the Appendix.

> gangs of kosmos and prophets en masse shall take their place. A new order shall arise and they shall be the priests of man, and every man shall be his own priest. The churches built under their umbrage shall be the churches of men and women. Through the divinity of themselves shall the kosmos and the new breed of poets be interpreters of men and women and of all events and things. They shall find their inspiration in real objects to-day, symptoms of the past and future.... They shall not deign to defend immortality or God or the perfection of things or liberty or the exquisite beauty and reality of the soul. They shall arise in America and be responded to from the remainder of the earth. (WHITMAN, "PREFACE")

Their vision was not only more individual and mystic than that of mainstream Christianity, it was also very heterodox: they were among the earliest Westerners to take a serious interest in Buddhist and Hindu thought. According to historian Arthur Versluis, the Transcendentalist movement was partly a product of such currents of Western thought as Unitarianism and Puritanism, but also of "contact with the world religions, especially Hinduism and Buddhism, which was largely seen in the light of 'universal progress'." (VERSLUIS, 3)

Emerson's famous poem "Brahma" riffs off of the Bhagavad Gītā, one of the central sacred texts of Hinduism, and Thoreau was the first to publish (in the Transcendentalist journal *The Dial* ("THE PREACHING OF BUDDHA")) an English translation of a Buddhist scripture. (FIELDS, 61) Whitman cited "the ancient Hindoo poems" as one of the influences on *Leaves of Grass*. (WHITMAN, COMPLETE POETRY, 665)

Emerson even went so far as to claim Buddhism as part of the Transcendentalist movement, in his 1842 lecture "The Transcendentalist":

> In like manner, if there is anything grand and daring in human thought or virtue, any reliance on the vast, the unknown; any presentiment; any extravagance of faith, the spiritualist adopts it as most in nature. The oriental mind has

always tended to this largeness. Buddhism is an expression of it. The Buddhist who thanks no man, who says, "do not flatter your benefactors," but who, in his conviction that every good deed can by no possibility escape its reward, will not deceive the benefactor by pretending that he has done more than he should, is a Transcendentalist.* (EMERSON, "TRANSCENDENTALIST")

Also in that lecture, we can see in the influence of Vedantist (Vedanta being the philosophy of Hinduism) and Buddhist ideas, that the world we experience is a construction of mind, and that the "self" has no existence separate from the world:

> Mind is the only reality, of which men and all other natures are better or worse reflectors. Nature, literature, history, are only subjective phenomena....
>
> I – this thought which is called I, – is the mould into which the world is poured like melted wax. The mould is invisible, but the world betrays the shape of the mould. You call it the power of circumstance, but it is the power of me. (EMERSON, "TRANSCENDENTALIST")

Both directly, and through their inspiration on the Beat poets and writers of the mid-twentieth century, the Transcendentalists had a tremendous influence on the development of Buddhism in the West.

They also helped promote to industrialized Western civilization the idea that contemplation of nature could be a spiritual activity, and their works are widely cited as examples of pantheism. Thoreau's *Walden* remains a masterpiece of nature writing, while Emerson wrote of the ordinary miracles of nature:

---

* On the other hand, perhaps confused by the concept of Nirvana, in the same year Emerson also wrote that "this remorseless Buddhism lies all around threatening with death and night." See the Timeline in the Appendix.

'Miracles have ceased.' Have they indeed? When? They had not ceased this afternoon when I walked into the wood and got into bright, miraculous sunshine, in shelter from the roaring wind. Who sees a pine-cone, or the turpentine exuding from the tree, or a leaf, the unit of vegetation, fall from its bough, as if it said, 'the year is finished,' or hears in the quiet, piny glen the chickadee chirping his cheerful note, or walks along the lofty promontory-like ridges which, like natural causeways, traverse the morass, or gazes upward at the rushing clouds, or downward at a moss or a stone and says to himself, 'Miracles have ceased'? (PERRY, 118)

And Whitman wrote of a love for the Earth with erotic overtones:

> Press close bare-bosom'd night – press close
>   magnetic nourishing night!
> Night of south winds – night of the large few
>   stars!
>
> Still nodding night – mad naked summer night.
> Smile O voluptuous cool-breath'd earth!
> Earth of the slumbering and liquid trees!
> Earth of the departed sunset – earth of the
>   mountains misty-topt!
> Earth of the vitreous pour of the full moon just
>   tinged with blue!
> Earth of shine and dark mottling the tide of the
>   river!
> Earth of the limpid gray of clouds brighter and
>   clearer for my sake!
> Far-swooping elbow'd earth – rich apple-
>   blossom'd earth!
> Smile, for your lover comes.
> Prodigal, you have given me love – therefore I to
>   you give love!
> O unspeakable passionate love. (WHITMAN, COMPLETE POETRY, 208)

While the Transcendentalists set out to create an independent

American literature, in several important ways they followed a trail blazed by the Romantic movement in Europe, especially the British Romantic poets. One of these ways was their love of the natural world, whose expression among the Transcendentalists we've just seen and which we'll see among the Romantics shortly.

Another was their attitude toward poetry. Both the British Romantics and the Transcendentalists found poetry to be far, far more than an amusing diversion: Percy Bysshe Shelley wrote that "poetry is connate with the origin of man" and called poets "the unacknowledged legislators of the world," (SHELLEY, "DEFENSE OF POETRY") while (as we saw above) Whitman predicted that "the new breed of poets" would displace the priests. Emerson went even further, rhapsodizing:

> For it is not metres, but a metre-making argument, that makes a poem, – a thought so passionate and alive, that, like the spirit of a plant or an animal, it has an architecture of its own, and adorns nature with a new thing. ... It is much to know that poetry has been written this very day, under this very roof, by your side. What! that wonderful spirit has not expired! these stony moments are still sparkling and animated! I had fancied that the oracles were all silent, and nature had spent her fires, and behold! all night, from every pore, these fine auroras have been streaming. Every one has some interest in the advent of the poet, and no one knows how much it may concern him. We know that the secret of the world is profound, but who or what shall be our interpreter, we know not. A mountain ramble, a new style of face, a new person, may put the key into our hands....
>
> All that we call sacred history attests that the birth of a poet is the principal event in chronology. Man, never so often deceived, still watches for the arrival of a brother who can hold him steady to a truth, until he has made it his own. With what joy I begin to read a poem,

> which I confide in as an inspiration! And now my chains are to be broken; I shall mount above these clouds and opaque airs in which I live, – opaque, though they seem transparent, – and from the heaven of truth I shall see and comprehend my relations. That will reconcile me to life, and renovate nature, to see trifles animated by a tendency, and to know what I am doing. Life will no more be a noise; now I shall see men and women, and know the signs by which they may be discerned from fools and satans. This day shall be better than my birthday: then I became an animal: now I am invited into the science of the real. (EMERSON, "THE POET")

This belief in the power of poetry came down to the late nineteenth and early twentieth centuries to influence occultists and the architects of modern witchcraft, and also eventually linked up with a strong tradition of poetry in Zen to help inspire the writers of the Beat Generation.

A third important way in which the Transcendentalists echoed the British Romantics was that they were not afraid to pay homage to the old gods. The Romantics, as we'll see, often invoked the classic Greco-Roman deities, and in harmony with them Emerson wrote that "every poetic mind is a pagan, and to this day prefers Olympian Jove, Apollo, and the Muses and the Fates, to all the barbarous indigestion of Calvin and the Middle Ages". (PERRY, 216) And in the space of a few paragraphs in *A Week on the Concord and Merrimack Rivers*, Thoreau pays his respects to Pan, as well as Buddha and Jesus, and throws in a reference to the necessity of the Divine Feminine for good measure:

> I am not sure but I should betake myself in extremities to the liberal divinities of Greece, rather than to my country's God. Jehovah, though with us he has acquired new attributes, is more absolute and unapproachable, but hardly more divine, than Jove. He is not so much of a gentleman, not so gracious and catholic, he does not exert so intimate and genial an influence on nature, as many a god of the Greeks. I should fear the infinite power and

> inflexible justice of the almighty mortal hardly as yet apotheosised, so wholly masculine, with no sister Juno, no Apollo, no Venus, nor Minerva, to intercede for me.... The Grecian are youthful and erring and fallen gods, with the vices of men, but in many important respects essentially of the divine race. In my Pantheon, Pan still reigns in his pristine glory, with his ruddy face, his flowing beard, and his shaggy body, his pipe and his crook, his nymph Echo, and his chosen daughter Iambe; for the great god Pan is not dead, as was rumoured. No god ever dies. Perhaps of all the gods of New England and of ancient Greece, I am most constant at his shrine.
>
> I trust that some may be as near and dear to Buddha, or Christ, or Swedenborg, who are without the pale of their churches. It is necessary not to be Christian to appreciate the beauty and significance of the life of Christ. I know that some will have hard thoughts of me when they hear their Christ named beside my Buddha, yet I am sure that I am willing they should love their Christ more than my Buddha, for the love is the main thing, and I like him too.
> (THOREAU, A WEEK... 55-58)

In their syncretism – Whitman, for example, said that he "had perfect faith in all sects, and was not inclined to reject a single one" (KAPLAN, 231) – in their insistence on individual experience over revealed truth, and in their love of nature as a spiritual force, we can see much that contributed to the modern Pagan movement.

It might even be argued that, depending on definitions, the Transcendentalists were the first American Pagans. Tim Zell, who was one of the first to use the word Pagan in its modern sense, included them in an explanation of the term in the newsletter *Green Egg* in 1968. (ADLER, 293)

And perhaps they were the first American Buddhists as well. That argument is strongest in the case of Thoreau; he published the *Lotus Sutra*, name-dropped the Buddha as we saw above, and owned a copy of R. Spence Hardy's *A Manual of*

Buddhism, a book which he respected enough to bequeath to his friend A. Bronson Alcott. (BICKNELL, 31) His peers seem to have thought it apt to call him Buddhist: his classmate John Weiss said of Thoreau that he "went about like a priest of Buddha who expects to arrive soon at the summit of a life of contemplation."

In the words of Buddhist writer and historian Rick Fields, "[Thoreau] forecast an American Buddhism by the nature of his contemplation, in the same way that a certain quality of transparent predawn forecasts a clear morning.... He was certainly not the only one of his generation to live a contemplative life, but he was, it seems, one of the few to live it in a Buddhist way." (FIELDS, 62)

But whether we draw the lines of these movements to include them or not, the Transcendentalists certainly laid down a groove that influenced the later development of Paganism and Buddhism on American shores. They prepared the ground that would receive the seeds of modern witchcraft and occultism from Britain, and the seeds of Buddhism – especially of Zen – from Asia, and sprout forth many strange and interesting flowers in the twentieth century.

They were just one thread in the tapestry of the Buddhist and Pagan revivals of the nineteenth and twentieth centuries: a strange weave of poets, Theosophists, Buddhists, magicians, witches – and jesters.

Poets

One of the other books I've brought with me is Ronald Hutton's *The Triumph of the Moon*. It's an excellent history of the revival of Pagan witchcraft in England. Besides covering the roles of the usual suspects – such as occultist Aleister Crowley, anthropologist Margaret Murray, and the founder of modern Wicca, Gerald Gardner – Hutton makes the point that the literary environment of the eighteenth and nineteenth centuries played a significant role, especially the work of the British Romantic poets.

The Romantic poets had a great admiration for the Greeks myths. Even before them, European artists in the late Middle Ages and Renaissance were attempting resolve their Christianity with the classical Pagan roots of their civilizations. This is evident in the *Divine Comedy*, where Dante's guide through Hell is the great Roman poet Virgil; also in Chaucer's *Canterbury Tales*, where the "Knight's Tale" is a story of Theseus of Athens that involves the Greco-Roman pantheon as active characters. Works like this had made it acceptable to at least mention the old gods.

Then the "Enlightenment" of the seventeenth and eighteenth centuries did much to weaken the hold of organized Christianity on the western mind. It emphasized "Reason" – or at least, a version of "Reason" – over religious dogmas, and saw the triumph of patriarchal monotheism over more natural religions as a regrettable thing. (HUTTON, 21)

The end of the Enlightenment, and the beginning of the Romantic era, is generally regarded to be around the late eighteenth or earth nineteenth centuries. In the bloody upheaval of the French and American Revolutions and the Napoleonic Wars, and with the Industrial Revolution wrecking havoc on established social structures, it became clear to many that "Reason," at least in the form proposed, was not enough. So the Romantics looked to the emotional and to the natural, and some of them followed the thread of their intellectual heritage back to a point before both the Enlightenment and Christianity, to the ancient Greco-Roman pantheon.

Friedrich von Schiller's 1788 poem "The Gods of Greece" is a clear and influential literary expression of this idealization of the Greek religion: (HUTTON, 21-22)

> Celestials left their skies
> To mingle with thy race, Deucalion ;
> And Pyrrha's daughters saw, in shepherd guise,
> Amid Thessalian vales, Latona's son.
> Beautiful links with Gods and Heroes then,
> The Loves uniting, interwove for us ;
> Heroes and Gods were worshipers with Men
> In Cyprian Amathus!
>
> Your gentle service gay,
> Nor self-denial, nor sharp penance knew;
> Well might each heart be happy in that day —
> For, were the happy not akin to you ?
> The Beautiful alone the Holy there !
> No pleasure shamed the Gods of that young race;
> So that the chaste Camaenae favoring were,
> And the subduing Grace ! (SCHILLER, 297-298)

The Romantic poets, such as William Wordsworth, also looked to nature to inform their spirituality, in "Lines Composed a Few Miles Above Tintern Abbey":

> ...well pleased to recognise
> In nature and the language of the sense,
> The anchor of my purest thoughts, the nurse,
> The guide, the guardian of my heart, and soul
> Of all my moral being. (T. GREER, 424)

and Lord Byron's "The Prayer of Nature," which says simply and directly

> Father! no prophet's laws I seek, —
> Thy laws in Nature's works appear (BYRON, 617)

Wordsworth and Byron also dipped their toes into the admiration of Pagan deities seen in von Schiller's work, but it was the second wave, primarily John Keats and Percy Bysshe Shelley, who dove right in. By the 1820s, Keats and Shelley were invoking the Goddess through images from Greek mythology.

The Romantics did much to give us the idea of a single composite Goddess. (HUTTON, 33-35) Where ancient pantheons had a multiplicity of diverse goddesses, the Romantic poets seem to have found it a useful literary device to combine them into one image of the Divine Feminine; also, it's possible that a single Goddess was seen as a better counter to Christian monotheism.

However, they looked at goddess mythology in a post-Enlightenment context. Thus Shelley could write a treatise titled *The Necessity of Atheism*, explicitly targeted against the idea of a creator god who stands outside of the universe, (SHELLEY, WORKS, 300) and be excited about the possibilities offered by science and technology:

> What a mighty instrument would electricity be in the hands of him who knew how to wield it? What will not an extraordinary combination of troughs of colossal magnitude, a well arranged system of hundreds of metallic plates, effect? The balloon has not yet received the perfection of which it is surely capable; the art of navigating the air is in its first and most helpless

infancy. It promises prodigious facilities for locomotion, and will enable us to traverse vast tracts with ease and rapidity, and to explore unknown countries without difficulty. Why are we still so ignorant of the interior of Africa ? – why do we not despatch intrepid aeronauts to cross it in every direction, and to survey the whole peninsula in a few weeks? (QUOTED AT DEFORD, 550-551)

But he could also invoke in his poetry the "Sacred goddess, Mother Earth / Thou from whose immortal bosom / Gods and men and beasts have birth", (SHELLEY, "SONG OF PROSERPINE") and could perform devotions to an ancient Greek deity, as he described in a letter to his friend Thomas Jefferson Hogg:

I am glad that you do not neglect the rites of the true religion. Your letter awoke my sleeping devotions, and the same evening I ascended alone the high mountain behind my house, and suspended a garland, and raised a small turf altar to the mountain-walking Pan. (QUOTED AT HUTTON, 25)

It was thanks to Romantics like Shelly that Pan became a Great God rather than a bit player. The sun god Apollo had long been seen as the patron of poets, in the original Greco-Roman tradition and in its Renaissance revival. But his restraint and moderation didn't fit well with Romantic ideals, with their rebellion against the coldness and hyper-rationality of the Enlightenment. Pan, with his wild nature, was much more in their line.

Keats's 1818 epic poem "Endymion" contains a 70 line invocation of Pan which calls him "forester divine" and "satyr king," (KEATS, "ENDYMION BOOK I") while Shelley's "Hymn of Pan," posthumously published in 1824, portrays Apollo listening with envy to Pan's "sweet pipings." (SHELLEY, "HYMN OF PAN")

"Endymion" also features a notable example of the strain of Orientalism found in Romanticism: it has the Greek goddess Diana assume the form of a woman of India, and tell a pantheon-mixing tale in which "Great Brahma from his mystic heaven groans, / And all his priesthood moans; / Before young Bacchus' eye-wink turning pale." This may be a reference to ancient myths in which Bacchus/Dionysus either visits, or actually originates from, India; and these myths themselves are another fascinating connection between the Greek pantheon upon which so much of modern Paganism rests, and the Hindu/Buddhist world of India.

By the 1890s, Pan the satyr had trumped Apollo the sun god. William Hazlitt gladly declared that English poetry "has more of Pan than of Apollo," (HAZLITT, 569) and by the end of the century Maurice Hewlett had him say, "I am Pan and the Earth is mine." (QUOTED AT HUTTON, 45) In Kenneth Grahame's 1908 *The Wind in The Willows* Pan appears as an awe-inspiring demigod who protects the animal children of the forest. (GRAHAME, 144)

The Romantics and those who followed them made Pan an incarnation of the natural world. Not bad for a little rural god who was considered comic at best, grotesque at worst, by the ancient Greeks.

Of course there was a backlash by more traditional and Christian writers. As an early example, Elizabeth Barrett Browning's 1844 poem "The Dead Pan" was meant as a rebuttal of Schiller. (HUTTON, 25) Decades later, G.K. Chesterton felt the need to make a dismissive mention of Pan in his 1908 Christian allegory *The Man Who Was Thursday*. (CHESTERTON, 190, 192) (Chesterton also felt a need to address Buddhism, with one character proclaiming "I am a Buddhist, I suppose; and Buddhism is not a creed, it is a doubt." (CHESTERTON, 189) A description which Chesterton may have meant as an aspersion, but one I think fully in alignment with Bodhidharma's "I don't know.")

It is not a coincidence that the image of Satan took on the satyr-like goat-horned and goat-legged appearance we know today during the nineteenth century. Prior to this, the devil was portrayed with the horns of a bull and the wings of a bat or dragon, or had dog- or snake-like attributes. (HUTTON, 46) This re-imaging of Satan was almost certainly a reaction – conscious or unconscious – against the resurgence of Pan.

Shelley and Keats influenced generations of poets. Among them was Algernon Charles Swinburne, whose work was later admired and quoted by Aleister Crowley and Gerald Gardner, (HUTTON, 26) two key players in the history of Paganism.

Swinburne consciously imitated Shelly, (HUTTON, 25) and he was also a big fan of Walt Whitman (KAPLAN, 240, 325-326) in the years that he wrote his most significant work. His 1866 collection *Poems and Ballads* caused a sensation; but perhaps the best example of how the Pagan image of the Goddess had been developed in the poetry of the nineteenth century is Swinburne's 1870 poem "Hertha," which he described as "another mystic atheistic democratic anthropologic poem" (SWINBURNE, "LETTERS," 45) and "the poem I think which if I were to die tonight I should choose to be represented and judged by…[i]t has the most in it of my deliberate thought and personal feeling or faith." (SWINBURNE, "LETTERS," 85) It also illustrates some of the same Bhagavad Gītā-inspired thought as Emerson's "Brahma":

> I am that which began;
>   Out of me the years roll;
> Out of me God and man;
>   I am equal and whole;
> God changes, and man, and the form of them
>   bodily; I am the soul.
>
> Before ever land was,
>   Before ever the sea,
> Or soft hair of the grass,
>   Or fair limbs of the tree,
> Or the flesh-coloured fruit of my branches, I
>   was, and thy soul was in me.
>
> First life on my sources
>   First drifted and swam;
> Out of me are the forces
>   That save it or damn;
> Out of me man and woman, and wild-beast and
>   bird: before God was, I am.
>
> Beside or above me
>   Naught is there to go;
> Love or unlove me,
>   Unknow me or know,
> I am that which unloves me and loves; I am
>   stricken, and I am the blow.
>
> I the mark that is missed
>   And the arrows that miss,
> I the mouth that is kissed
>   And the breath in the kiss,
> The search, and the sought, and the seeker, the

> soul and the body that is.
> I am that thing which blesses
>   My spirit elate;
> That which caresses
>   With hands uncreate
> My limbs unbegotten that measure the length of
>   the measure of fate.
>
> But what thing dost thou now,
>   Looking Godward, to cry
> "I am I, thou art thou,
>   I am low, thou art high" ?
> I am thou, whom thou seekest to find him; find
>   thou but thyself, thou art I.
>
> For truth only is living,
>   Truth only is whole,
> And the love of his giving
>   Man's polestar and pole;
> Man, pulse of my centre, and fruit of my body,
>   and seed of my soul
>
> One birth of my bosom;
>   One beam of mine eye;
> One topmost blossom
>   That scales the sky;
> Man, equal and one with me, man that is made
>   of me, man that is I. (SWINBURNE, "HERTHA")

About two decades later, another admirer of Shelley enters the story. David Hewavitarne, more widely known by his Buddhist "Dharma name" Anagarika Dharmapala, was a Sinhalese man who played a key role in the Buddhist revival, first in Ceylon and then world-wide. But it took an outside force to help set him on his way. It wasn't just his native Buddhism that inspired him, nor was the work of the Romantics enough. It took the Theosophists to help connect him to Buddhists outside of Ceylon, and to bring him to the attention of the world.

Theosophists

H.P. Blavatsky

The story of the Theosophical Society begins with Helena Petrova Blavatsky. "Madame Blavatsky," as she was often known, was born in Russia but traveled extensively in Europe, America, and the Far East.

While in Paris in 1858, she discovered Spiritualism – an American trend that had begun a decade before. It was based around "mediums" who could supposedly communicate with the deceased in the "spirit world," and who demonstrated this with evidence such as coded rapping noises, the sounds of bells and voices, movement of furniture, claims of clairvoyance, and even the apparent materialization of solid objects. (FIELDS, 83-84)

(You may have a relic of Spiritualism in your house – it is from Spiritualism that the planchette, the "pointer" used on an Ouija board, originated.)

Blavatsky supposedly "discovered" that she had mediumistic abilities, and eventually brought them to the United States. Now, before proceeding any further with this part of the tale, we ought to reveal that Blavatsky's abilities – like those of Fox sisters who started the Spiritualist movement – were eventually revealed as a fraud.

There may have been some honest Spiritualist mediums, people of extraordinary intuition who attributed their own insights to external influences. But as for the more exotic apparitions, while it took magicians like Houdini to uncover the most clever tricks, no one was able to produce their exotic phenomena under controlled conditions.

Blavatsky may have had good intentions. She may have been trying to bring about positive social and political changes. She may have been using a version of what the Buddhists refer to as "expedient means" to get her spiritual ideas across. She may have even managed to convince herself that she genuinely had powers. But for the record, your author stands squarely on the side that declares Spiritualist phenomena a bunch of trickery.

In 1874, Blavatsky was attracted by spiritualistic goings-on to the Eddy farm in New York. There she met and befriended Henry Steel Olcott, a journalist and lawyer of sterling reputation. Blavatsky and Olcott became the center of a social circle focused on the investigation of spiritualist phenomena and of the "laws which lie in back" of them – in Blavatsky's word, Occultism. They soon founded the Theosophical Society to pursue these investigations.

The Society's stated purposes included helping members to "acquire an intimate knowledge of natural law, especially its occult manifestations," "to oppose the materialism of science and every form of dogmatic theology, especially the Christian, which the Chiefs of the Society regard as particularly pernicious," "to make known among Western nations the long-suppressed facts about Oriental religious philosophies," and "to aid in the institution of a Brotherhood of Humanity, wherein all good and pure men, of every race, shall recognize each other as the equal effects…of one Uncreate [sic] Universal, Infinite, and Everlasting Cause." (BLAVATSKY, 377)

Blavatsky claimed that in her travels she had encountered a group of teachers, variously referred to as "Masters," "Adepts," "Mahatmas," or "Chiefs," who represented the peak of spiritual evolution and who were the source of the teachings she presented. Conveniently, these teachers were located in far-off places like Tibet and were incarnated in bodies that were too sensitive to come out into the everyday world, but they would sometimes appear in "etheric" form (LUTYENS, 10-11) or send letters.

The idea of a hidden order of adepts is found in the 1790s work of the Christian mystic Karl von Eckartshausen, *The Cloud Upon the Sanctuary,* (VON ECKARTSHAUSEN, 14, 25) a book that had a great impact on later occult societies. Blavatsky's Mahatmas may have been inspired by von Eckartshausen, or she may have adopted the idea of "Unknown Superiors" found in the Rosicrucian Freemasonry of her great-grandfather. (K. JOHNSON, 20)

Most skeptics have assumed that Blavatsky's Secret Chiefs

were entirely fictional. But more recently, historian K. Paul Johnson has suggested that Blavatsky was initially in league with Masonic and Rosicrucian societies who wanted to undermine dogmatic Christianity and revive occultism, and that she later allied herself with anti-colonial activists in India. With a bit of adaptation and disguise, Johnson concludes, the leaders of these groups became the Masters who guided her and Olcott. (K. JOHNSON, 7-8)

If this is the case, how should we regard Blavatsky's fraud? Her mediumistic tricks were a way to promote her Theosophy, but was her Theosophy merely a way to get people to follow her political causes? Or was there a genuine spirituality, and the mediumistic phenomena an expedient means to draw attention to the teachings she thought true? The question of Blavatsky's motives will probably never be resolved.

In 1877 Blavatsky, claiming direction from her Masters, published *Isis Unveiled*, which proposed that the world's religions were decayed fragments of the wisdom of an ancient civilization of Atlantis. It was an idea she seems to have borrowed (without credit) from an 1837 work by Godfrey Higgins, *Anacalypsis: An Attempt to Draw Aside the Veil of the Saitic Isis*. Blavatsky, however, placed more emphasis on Eastern philosophy, and identified the Atlanteans with her Mahatmas. (HUTTON, 19)

Isis Unveiled was a great success, selling out its first run of 1,000 copies within ten days. But the Society itself started to dissipate soon after: Blavatsky refused to produce mediumistic phenomena, claiming that the underlying philosophy was more important, and Spiritualists drifted away from her movement.

Olcott and Blavatsky decided to follow up contacts in India and Ceylon, where anti-colonial and nationalist movements were causing renewed interest in Vedanta and Buddhism. At the end of 1878 they departed for India. (FIELDS, 92-94)

Buddhists

Blavatsky and Olcott spent most of 1879 establishing the Theosophical Society in India. The Society's headquarters have remained there from 1882 (LUTYENS, 10) until the present day, and it has had a great influence on several traditions. Theosophist A.P. Sinnett's 1883 book *Esoteric Buddhism* did much to introduce some Buddhist concepts to a wide audience in the West (HUTTON, 19-20; FIELDS, 97). Anna Kingsford, president of the Society's London Lodge in the early 1880s, was an associate of, and perhaps a mentor to, two of the founders of Hermetic Order of the Golden Dawn, (PERT 127-132, 148; HUTTON 74) an important group in the history of ceremonial magic. It was Theosophy that introduced the spiritual teacher J. Krishnamurti to the world, and many Theosophical concepts – such as its ideas about Atlantis – have come down to the contemporary "New Age" movement.

But it's Blavatsky and Olcott's actions in Ceylon (present day Sri Lanka) that are of the most interest to our story.

Ceylon had been a stronghold of Theravāda Buddhism since the Indian emperor Ashoka sent missionaries there in the third century. But by the late nineteenth century, its people had been repressed by European colonialism for almost 500 years.

Things weren't as bad under the British as they were when Portuguese missionaries, the first Europeans in Ceylon, slaughtered Buddhist natives, burned the sutras, and wrecked the temples. Still, under British rule only Christian marriages were officially recognized, Bible study was mandatory in the schools, and Christian missionaries waged a continual campaign to try to discredit Buddhism.

The ground was ripe for a cultural and religious revival, and the Sinhalese people of Ceylon were overjoyed to see Westerners treating Buddhism with respect. (FIELDS, 21-22, 96-97)

Blavatsky and Olcott arrived there on May 17, 1880. A few days later, on May 25, they performed the ceremony of *pansil*, vowing to uphold the five precepts for Buddhist lay practitioners. In so doing they apparently became the first Americans to formally enter the Buddhist fold. (Blavatsky had become a naturalized American citizen the year before.) (FIELDS, 97-98)

To be sure, their Buddhism was somewhat idiosyncratic. The Theosophists claimed that their Masters practiced a sort of "pre-Vedic" Buddhism, supposedly identical to the "Wisdom Religion of the Aryan Upanishads" (FIELDS, 97) – in other words, they papered over some significant differences between their own interpretation of Buddhist philosophy, the Sinhalese practice of Buddhism, and Vedanta (the Hindu philosophy of the Upanishads). But neither side cared to argue fine points, and they readily accepted each other as allies.

Blavatsky had been briefly exposed to Tibetan Buddhism as a child (K. JOHNSON, 19) and had identified herself as a Buddhist as early as 1875 (FIELDS, 97-98); however, in an 1887 letter to her sister she revealed that deep in her heart, she always remained a Russian

Orthodox Christian. (HUTTON, 18; VERA JOHNSON)

But Olcott seems to have taken firmly and wholly to Buddhism. Along with Sumangala Nayaka Maha Thera, a Sinhalese high priest and scholar, he helped develop a "Buddhist Catechism" to educate the Sinhalese about their native religion. This work was eventually translated and published in Japan and India. (FIELDS, 101-106)

Ceylon wasn't the only place where Buddhism was challenged; Western imperialism had an impact on cultures throughout Asia. After the U.S. sent Commodore Perry and his "Black Ships" to forcibly end Japan's isolation in the mid-1850s, leading to the restoration of power to the Meiji Emperor in 1868, the Japanese government made a perverted form of Shintō the state religion and tried to repress Buddhism with the slogan "Haibutsu Kishaku" – "Expel the Buddha; Destroy the Teachings." (FIELDS, 80)

Though the government soon returned to religious neutrality, the policy must have remained a concern to Japanese Buddhists, already struggling to deal with rapid Westernization. So in 1888, Olcott's efforts in reviving Sinhalese Buddhism earned him an invitation to Japan. (FIELDS, 107) It is remarkable that just three decades after America pried Japan open to the world and threw their nation into turmoil, Japanese Buddhists asked an American to help strengthen their religion.

Olcott was accompanied on his trip by a young Sinhalese man, the admirer of Shelly we mentioned a little while back. Anagarika Dharmapala, born David Hewavitarne, joined Olcott and Blavatsky's circle in Ceylon shortly after their arrival. Blavatsky became a sort of mentor to him, and Dharmapala became a great promoter of the Colombo Buddhist Theosophical Society. In an interesting twist on evangelism, Dharmapala at one point wanted to find the reincarnations of Shelley and Keats so that he could introduce them to the Buddhist teachings they'd never had a chance to hear. (FIELDS, 98-105)

On this journey, Olcott carried a letter from Sumangala to the Japanese Buddhists – probably the first official communication between the Mahāyāna and Theravāda branches of Buddhism in several centuries. On his three month visit he gave 75 lectures, attended by 187,000 people. He then returned to Ceylon, bringing three Japanese priests who intended to study Theravāda and Pali, the language of the oldest Theravādan texts. (FIELDS, 107-108) The scattered schools of Buddhism were starting to revive and to unite into a world religion, with Theosophy as a catalyst; this may have given the Theosophists significant influence on how Buddhists came to see themselves and their religion.

But Olcott and Sumangala were not the only ones working to strengthen ties between Japanese and Sinhalese Buddhists. In 1887 the Japanese monk Soyen Shaku, from the Rinzai school of Zen, came to Ceylon to study how Theravāda monks lived and practiced. He spent three years in Ceylon before returning to Japan; shortly thereafter, in 1891, he became the master of the Engaku-ji temple. (FIELDS, 109) We'll encounter Shaku again in a little while.

It was also in 1891 that the Buddhist revival gained an important focal point. In that year Dharmapala made a pilgrimage to India to visit Bodh-Gaya, the site of the Buddha's enlightenment. His visit was prompted by an article by Edwin Arnold – the author of *The Light of Asia*, the first popular account of the life of the Buddha to be published in the West – decrying the decay of the site, and suggesting that it should be returned to Buddhist ownership.

Dharmapala ended up dedicating his life to that goal, and he helped start a movement that united the Buddhist world. (FIELDS, 115-118) The goal would not be achieved until 1949, sixteen years after his death, when a newly independent India turned the site over to Buddhists. (FIELDS, 135)

But in the meantime, his work on Bodh-Gaya and his connection with Olcott and Blavatsky – along with his own healthy portion of natural charm – got Dharmapala noticed. He was invited to the 1893 World Parliament of Religions as the representative of the Buddhists of Ceylon.

The Parliament was part of the Columbian Exhibition, the World's Fair held in Chicago to celebrate the 400th anniversary of Columbus's voyage. Its chairman, John Henry Barrows, saw the opening of the East as a new opportunity to spread Christianity, and he may have invited the Asian delegates with the goal of introducing them to Western faith. But the Parliament did more to introduce Asian religions to the West than to introduce Christianity to the heathen Orient.

In many ways, the Parliament was the formal introduction of Buddhism to the West. Representatives included Buddhists from the Theravāda, Zen, Jōdo Shinshū, Nichiren, Tendai, and Esoteric (Shingon) schools; also represented were Hindus, Parsis,

Sikhs, Jains, and a Confucian. They came from Japan, India, China, Siam, and Ceylon.

The Zen Buddhist representative was Soyen Shaku, the Japanese master who had visited Ceylon just a few years before. His lectures were presented by Barrows, reading from an English translation provided by Shaku's student Daisetz Teitaro Suzuki – a man who became better known by his initials, D.T. Suzuki.

During Shaku's appearance at the Parliament, he made connections that led to a return visit to the U.S. twelve years later, in 1905. On that visit he spent nine months traveling and teaching, cementing his place in history as the first Zen master to teach in the United States. (FIELDS, 168-174)

And D.T. Suzuki's translation of Shaku's address ended up getting him invited to the U.S. for a few years to work for Paul Carus at Carus's publishing company, Open Court Press. This began Suzuki's career as a key popularizer of Buddhism to the West. (FIELDS, 138-139) He returned to Japan for several decades, but after World War II Suzuki settled in New York, where his work inspired the Zen boom of the late 1950s. (FIELDS, 195-196)

But all that came later. The immediate result of the Parliament was to induce enough fascination with Buddhism – especially the Buddhism of the charismatic Sinhalese representative Dharmapala – that within a few years some Westerners were heading to Ceylon to learn more.

One of these Westerners was Allan Bennett, a Briton who became the second man from his country to become an ordained Theravādan bhikkhu. (BATCHELOR, 41) A dedicated evangelist for the dharma, he is also known to history by his Buddhist name, Ananda Metteyya.

Another Briton who went to Ceylon to learn about Buddhism was Bennett's old roommate, the famed occultist and magician described by one writer as "the wickedest man in the world": Aleister Crowley. (REGARDIE, 40-42, 112)

Magicians

Trying to puzzle out the history of the ritual magic movement of the nineteenth century is tricky. The trail is complicated both by the casual attitude towards literal truth held by some of the principal players, and by the nature of the secret societies that contributed, directly or indirectly, to the magical tradition.

We'll start with a few words about one of those societies –

Freemasonry, which was always a background presence.

As the guilds of the Middle Ages lost economic power, their fraternal and ceremonial functions became more important. This was particularly true of the mason's guild: since a stonemason's work involved a life on the move, traveling from construction site to construction site, they had always relied heavily on the social support of their guild. (STEVENSON, 13) This made the guild an organization ripe for transformation into a fraternal organization.

By about 1600, modern Masonic lodges had been established in Scotland. These admitted members who were not stoneworkers, and used highly ritualized and esoteric initiation rituals based on a mythical history of the guild. (HUTTON, 53) Their egalitarian, confidential, and non-denominational nature – Masons must acknowledge a "divine architect," but beyond that they may be Deists,* Christians, Jews, Muslims, whatever – made Masonic societies an important resource for intellectuals. It also made them a target for the hostility of the clergy and a favorite subject for conspiracy theories.

From the early 1600s also comes the first mention of the "Rosicrucians," a supposed hidden society of adepts possessing secret knowledge and dedicated to religion and healing. (HUTTON, 69-70) Many groups, including several Masonic societies, would later claim connections with the Rosicrucians. One of these was the "Societas Rosicruciana in Anglia," or SRIA, founded in 1865 by several high-ranking British Freemasons.

The SRIA claimed to be linked with the Rosicrucians via the initiation of one its founders into a German Rosicrucian organization, the "Order of the Gold and Rosy Cross," while he was traveling in the Austrian Empire (HUTTON, 73) – conveniently far away and difficult to verify. Its stated purpose was to "search out the Great Secrets of Nature," by studying Western mystical philosophies such as cabala (Jewish mysticism) and the Hermetic tradition of alchemy (which is more about self-transformation

---

* Deists believe in a creator god who started the world going, but does not interfere in it. They reject miracle stories and holy texts. Deism was a popular belief among the U.S.'s "Founding Fathers," including Jefferson, Franklin, and Madison, as well as Tom Paine, author of both the key pro-Independence essay *Common Sense* and the Deist tract *The Age of Reason*.

than about transmuting lead into gold). (HUTTON, 72-73) Among the SRIA's members were William Wynn Westcott and his protegee, Samuel Liddel – who later used the name, and became better known as, MacGregor Mathers. (REGARDIE, 73, 75; HUTTON 74)

About twenty years later, Westcott and Mathers became part of another group with a similar mission, the Hermetic Society in Britain. (HUTTON, 74) This was founded by a British mystic named Anna Kingsford, who had been president of the London Lodge of the Theosophical Society. (PERT, 108) But Kingsford encountered political friction within that group. She was a devout Christian (HUTTON, 74) whose interests lay more in the Western traditions than in the Eastern philosophies then being emphasized by Blavatsky and Olcott. (But she was definitely not hostile to Buddhism – she worked to have a play based on *The Light of Asia* produced in London. (PERT, 143))

Anna Kingsford

So in 1884, she and her friend Edward Maitland founded this new group, to further study the mystical side of Christianity, as well as cabala and the "Greek mysteries and the Hermetic

Gnosis." (PERT, 127-132) Westcott and Mathers were closely involved with this society, and presented lectures during its final series of meetings. (PERT, 148)

The Hermetic Society was short-lived; Kingsford fell gravely ill at the end of 1886, (PERT, 156) bringing to an end its activities. In 1887, Westcott and Mathers, along with two other men (William R. Woodman and Alphonsus F.A. Woodward), started to organize a new group: the Hermetic Order of the Golden Dawn. (REGARDIE, 70-71; HUTTON, 74-75) The Golden Dawn was formally chartered on March 1, 1888, just a week after the death of Anna Kingsford. (HUTTON, 76)

Westcott taught initiates that the Golden Dawn was a close cousin to Theosophy, rooted in the "same stock of Magi," and that women had a major role in occultism, with emphasis on the works of Blavatsky and Kingsford. (HUTTON, 76)

Upon Blavatsky's death in 1892, Mathers claimed to have been contacted by her "Secret Chiefs" and authorized by them to create an inner order to the Golden Dawn, which he called the Rosy Cross, (HUTTON, 76) another Rosicrucian allusion.

And here is where things get interesting.

All the groups mentioned so far – the SRIA, the Hermetic Society, and the original Golden Dawn – were strictly philosophical societies, dedicated to spiritual development through the study of mystical teachings. But initiates into the Rosy Cross were permitted to perform actual ritual magic. (HUTTON, 76)

What is this ritual magic? According to Ronald Hutton, historian extraordinaire of the witchcraft revival, prior to the nineteenth century learned ritual magic

> promised to give the operator control of...forces, which...placed superhuman powers at the disposal of the magician: demons, angels, or the hidden names of God. Those powers were still, however, expected to be used for practical ends...the classic grimoire is designed for somebody who is impoverished, embittered, and (above all) very lonely.

As Hutton puts it, "Traditional scholarly magic was at basis an elaborate way of ringing for room service." (HUTTON, 82)

What Mathers and Westcott – building on work by the

French occultist Eliphas Levi – did, was to combine the Hermetic goal of spiritual development with this ritual high magic. The spirits or deities were invoked not for practical ends, not for wealth or worldly power, but instead to allow the magician to become spiritually empowered – to experience a change in consciousness, a release of spiritual energy and a feeling of unity with the divine forces involved. (HUTTON, 82-83)

For the Golden Dawn, those divine forces were rather Christian in appearance. For example, initiation to the inner order involved the candidate being tied to a cross and having the stigmata (wounds of the Crucifixion) traced on them; (REGARDIE, 180) while the "Lesser Ritual of the Pentagram," designed by Mathers and taught to novices as a daily practice, involved a recitation of part of the Lord's Prayer in Hebrew and the invocation of angels.

However, Mathers came out of the Theosophical tradition that held that the same basic truths lie behind all religions: (HUTTON, 79) in his words, "whatever the errors, corruption, or mistakes in any particular form of religion, all are based on and descended from the acknowledgment of Supreme Divine Powers." (MATHERS, SACRED MAGIC, 8)

Also, the Golden Dawn arose in the context of the revival of the classic Pagan deities brought about by the Romantics. Thus, in among the Christian imagery both the Great God Pan and the Goddess also made their appearance: Pan as the "Goat of Mendes," and the Goddess under the syncretized identity "Isis-Urania," after whom the Golden Dawn's first temple was named. (HUTTON, 79-80)

And Mathers' Golden Dawn work made another important contribution to the theory of magic. While they were by no means materialists, the Golden Dawn did understand that the spirits invoked in ritual magic could be understood as psychological rather than supernatural in nature. As Mathers and Crowley wrote in a preface to their version of *The Lesser Key of Solomon*:

> ...What is the cause of my illusion of seeing a spirit in the triangle of Art?
>
> Every smatterer, every expert in psychology, will answer: "That cause lies in your brain."
>
> The spirits of the Goetia are portions of the human brain.

If, then, I say, with Solomon:

"The Spirit Cimieries teaches logic," what I mean is:

"Those portions of my brain which subserve the logical faculty may be stimulated and developed by following out the processes called 'The Invocation of Cimieries.'"

...There is no effect which is truly and necessarily miraculous.

Our Ceremonial Magic fines down, then, to a series of minute, though of course empirical, physiological experiments, and whoso, will carry them through intelligently need not fear the result. (MATHERS AND CROWLEY, 8-12)*

This idea is much like Buddhist teachings, especially in Zen, that tell us that there are no powers outside of ourselves to search for – and yet recommend meditations and rituals devoted to a whole host of Bodhisattvas and deities. As the Zen teacher Nyogen Senzaki explained regarding a ritual of reciting sutras before a painting of the Bodhisattva Manjusri, "A true Mahayanist [Mahāyāna Buddhist] never worships anything but his own true inner self. The recitation is an expression of our prajna, perfect understanding, and nothing else." (FIELDS, 182)

For these ceremonial magicians, the portions of the brain they wanted to stimulate included those that would produce psychic powers like clairvoyance and telepathy. But we need not – and given the state of the evidence, should not – believe in such phenomena, in order to find the methods of magic useful.

So this was the system into which Allan Bennett and his roommate Aleister Crowley were initiated in the 1890s: magical practice used as a tool for spiritual development, and compatible

---

* The writing style suggests to me that the preface in question may be primarily the work of Crowley.

with religious beliefs of many sorts.

Bennett (who some sources say was Mather's foster son (BRUNTON)) explored many spiritual paths before coming to the Golden Dawn: Hindu literature and the practice of yoga, as well as Spiritualism, Theosophy, the Western mystical traditions, and psychology. He discovered Buddhism in 1890 when he read Edwin Arnold's *The Light of Asia*. (HARRIS, 7)

He joined the Theosophical Society in 1893, (CROW) and was initiated into the Golden Dawn in 1894. Here he gained a reputation as "the one Magician who could really do big-time stuff," in Crowley's words. (QUOTED AT HARRIS, 7)

In 1900, driven both by an interest in Eastern mysticism and by a need to seek warmer climes to treat his severe asthma, Bennett went to Ceylon. Crowley paid his way – with money he obtained from an old love interest under questionable pretenses (REGARDIE, 200; CROWLEY, CONFESSIONS CH 21, 181) – hoping that Bennett would help spread Western occultism in the East. But things turned out the other way around, and Bennett took strongly to Buddhism. In late 1901, finding the Buddhism of Ceylon lacking, he traveled on to Burma to take ordination as a bhikkhu, and a few years later returned to England as a Buddhist missionary. (HARRIS, 8-11)

(Regarding the state of Buddhism in Ceylon, remember that it had only recently begun to recover from the wounds of centuries of colonialism – Sinhalese bhikkhus had even abandoned meditation. Dharmapala had also found Ceylon's Buddhism wanting and had finally received guidance from a Burmese teacher. (FIELDS, 100, 114) Of course Burmese Buddhism did not escape unscathed from colonial rule either.)

But before he left for Burma, Bennett was joined in Ceylon for a few months by his friend and student, Aleister Crowley. (REGARDIE, 229-232)

Aleister Crowley

Crowley is one of the most perplexing figures in the history of ritual magic and of the introduction of Eastern philosophy to the West. His influence on occultism is unmatched, and he was a dedicated investigator of matters spiritual who wrote some wonderfully clear texts on magic, yoga, and on philosophy. Yet he was also a self-pitying classist sexist ^(REGARDIE, 420-442) asshole of the first rank, whose collection of mental health issues could have kept a small team of expert therapists busy.

But Crowley always delighted in yanking people's chains, and some of what he claimed to think and do must be understood not as a report of truth but as a jest or provocation. For example, when he once claimed to have performed human sacrifice about 150 times in a single year, he was making a coded reference to sexual intercourse. ^(REGARDIE, 372) Sorting the truth from the chain-yanking is often a matter of guesswork.

Crowley's father died while he was very young, and he was raised by his mother and his uncle in the fanatical Christianity of the Plymouth Brethren. He had no affection for his mother, ^(CROWLEY, CONFESSIONS CH. 6, 69) whom he regarded as a "brainless bigot of the most narrow, logical and inhuman type." ^(CROWLEY, CONFESSIONS CH. 1, 36) His uncle he hated with a white-hot passion: in Crowley's assessment, "No more cruel fanatic, no meaner villain, ever walked this earth." ^(CROWLEY, CONFESSIONS CH. 4, 55) He learned their faith forward and backward – and loathed it. When his exasperated mother called him "a beast," he took it to heart and throughout his life delightedly identified himself with the Beast of the Book of Revelation, the Anti-Christ. ^(REGARDIE, 45-51) He chose as his last magical motto "To Mega Therion," "Great Wild Beast." When the numbers corresponding to the Greek letters of this phrase are added up, they total 666. ^(REGARDIE, 345)

His "autohagiography," *The Confessions of Aleister Crowley,* gives a demonstration of how disturbed a child he became:

> There is one amazing incident; at the age of fourteen as near as I can remember. I must premise that I have always been exceptionally tenderhearted, except to tyrants, for whom I think no tortures bad enough. In particular, I am uniformly kind to animals; no question of cruelty or sadism arises in the incident which I am about to narrate.

> I had been told "A cat has nine lives." I deduced that it must be practically impossible to kill a cat. As usual, I became full of ambition to perform the feat. (Observe that I took my information unquestioningly au pied de la lettre.) Perhaps through some analogy with the story of Hercules and the hydra, I got it into my head that the nine lives of the cat must be taken more or less simultaneously. I therefore caught a cat, and having administered a large dose of arsenic I chloroformed it, hanged it above the gas jet, stabbed it, cut its throat, smashed its skull and, when it had been pretty thoroughly burnt, drowned it and threw it out of the window that the fall might remove the ninth life. In fact, the operation was successful; I had killed the cat. I remember that all the time I was genuinely sorry for the animal; I simply forced myself to carry out the experiment in the interest of pure science.* (CROWLEY, CONFESSIONS CH. 6, 73-74)

Note the way in which he disassociates himself from his cruelty in relating this incident – it is an important symptom he exhibited repeatedly.

Crowley was initiated into the Golden Dawn in 1898. Shortly thereafter, he invited Bennett (who was then in dire financial straits) to share a flat with him. They lived together for about eighteen months, and Bennett became Crowley's mentor in occultism – and probably also in Hinduism and Buddhism – as Crowley moved quickly up the initiated ranks of the Order. (REGARDIE, 40)

Bennett's mentorship was immensely important to Crowley. In his *Confessions*, he wrote, "I did not fully realize the colossal stature of that sacred spirit; but I was instantly aware that this man could teach me more in a month than anyone else in five years." (CROWLEY, CONFESSIONS, CH 21, 181) *Confessions* is dedicated in

---

* We might take this whole story for another Crowley jape; given the context, and the fact that Crowley later performed animal sacrifice on at least one occasion, I don't believe it to be. But, as stated previously, the history is tricky.

part to Bennett, with the notation, "who did what he could." (CROWLEY, CONFESSIONS, CH. 1) More, his admiration for Bennett is proved by the negative: he was one of the very few people against whom Crowley never spewed his vitriol. (REGARDIE, 201)

After Bennett went to Ceylon, Crowley visited him there for several months and joined his studies of Yoga, Vedanta, and Buddhism. (REGARDIE, 229) For a while Crowley enthusiastically embraced Buddhism – in a 1902 article "Berashith" he stated "I confidently and deliberately take my refuge in the Triple Gem," (CROWLEY, "BERASHITH") and he repeated this allegiance in his 1903 "Science and Buddhism." (QUOTED AT REGARDIE, 263-265) (Taking refuge in the "Triple Gem" of the Buddha, the Dharma, and the Sangha is the formal ritual means of declaring one's self a Buddhist.)

But by 1904 Crowley had begun to move away from Buddhism. (REGARDIE, 281) Some of his arguments are reminiscent of Zen's deliberate blasphemies, intended to bring the student away from reliance on external salvation. Given his later unfavorable comparison of the Buddhism he encountered to the Taoism of Lao Tzu, (CROWLEY, CONFESSIONS, CH. 27, 234) I sometimes wonder what would have happened had Crowley met Zen (with its Taoist ancestry) rather than Theravāda – a wounded Theravāda, at that. If while visiting Kamakura, passing through Japan on his way to Ceylon, he had followed up on an impulse to settle for a while in one of the monasteries there, (CROWLEY, CONFESSIONS, CH. 26, 227) we might have a quite different tale.

But beyond his objections to what he saw as hollow practice among Buddhists he encountered, his move away from Buddhism followed shortly after the writing of *The Book of the Law*, an event central to Crowley's life and the origin of his system, Thelema.

In April 1904, Crowley had a mystical experience in which he "channeled" a "being" named Aiwass, and wrote down a text called *The Book of the Law* (or *Liber AL vel Legis*). *The Book* is written from a perspective of vicious and hostile strength: for example, "Compassion is the vice of kings: stamp down the wretched & the weak: this is the law of the strong: this is our law and the joy of the world." (QUOTED AT REGARDIE, 483)

At first Crowley rejected the "message" he received: "The fact of the matter was that I resented *The Book of the Law* with my whole soul. For one thing, it knocked my Buddhism completely on the head." (CROWLEY, CONFESSIONS, CH. 50, 403) But it maintained a hold on him.

From his training in the Golden Dawn system, Crowley had learned that the spirits that appear in magical rituals are aspects of the magician's own mind. But he was never able to understand Aiwass in this way. For many years he claimed that Aiwass was one of the "Secret Chiefs" that Blavatsky and Mathers claimed to be agents of; later, he identified Aiwass as his "Holy Guardian Angel," a reference to the magical practices of Abramelin the Mage. (REGARDIE, 463)

This inability to understand Aiwass as a fragment of his own personality, this disassociation from cruel attitudes, is the same symptom that we saw when he related the story of killing the cat as a teenager. It lies at the root of Crowley's tragic failure. Illuminated visions and mystical experiences are of no use if they are not built on that firm foundation proscribed by the Delphic Oracle millennia ago: Know Thyself.

At first Crowley didn't attach too much importance to the Aiwass experience. In different circumstances, maybe it could have been the start of a "healing crisis" that brought about an integration of Crowley's damaged personality. But that was not to be.

In 1905 Crowley – a skilled mountaineer – took part in a disastrous attempt at scaling Kanchenjunga that resulted in five deaths. (CROWLEY, CONFESSIONS CH. 52, 436, 441; REGARDIE, 287) In early 1906, while traveling across China he began intense long-term magical work, his "Augoeidies" ritual, which placed a great strain on his mental energies. Upon returning to England in June he learned that while he had been at this, his daughter had died of typhoid. He blamed his wife; (REGARDIE, 320-325) she subsequently slipped deeper into alcoholism, and they divorced in 1909. (CROWLEY, CONFESSIONS, CH 66, 615)

The stress during these years had to have been enormous.

We saw Crowley above claiming refuge in the Triple Gem: the Buddha, the enlightened or divine nature within all beings; the Dharma, the wisdom teachings; and the Sangha, the supportive community of seekers. He was indeed learned in many teachings, and pursued the divine with great zeal. But Crowley had no Sangha to turn to for support. The Golden Dawn organization had fragmented before Crowley was initiated into the inner order. Bennett had gone to Asia, and they saw each other only a few times after that. He was estranged from Mathers. He did keep some contact with his original sponsor in the Golden Dawn, George Cecil Jones, and they did some work together.

(REGARDIE, 326) But it was clearly not enough.

To put it bluntly: Crowley lost his grip on consensus reality. Always a fractured personality, he seized on *The Book of the Law* and came to believe that he had been specially anointed by the rulers of the world, the Secret Chiefs: that he "was the chosen prophet of the Masters, the instrument fit to interpret their idea and work their will." (CROWLEY, CONFESSIONS, CH 65, 610) In his words he was "the Prophet chosen to proclaim the Law which will determine the destinies of this planet for an epoch," he was "in a class which contains only seven other names in the whole of human history." (CROWLEY, CONFESSIONS, CH 66, 615)

You don't need to be a psychiatrist to looks at those assertions and declare that Crowley had gone off the rails.*

That doesn't mean his work is valueless – crazy wisdom is great. But we have to be careful to distinguish crazy wisdom from just plain crazy: and with Crowley, the closer something is to the specifics of Thelema and Aiwass, the more likely it is to be plain crazy rather than wise crazy.

An example of the wise crazy is that even as he lost himself in Thelema, Crowley could see a Pagan nature religion coming. In a 1914 letter to George Jones, he wrote:

> ...the time is just ripe for a natural religion. People like rites and ceremonies, and they are tired of hypothetical gods. Insist on the real benefits of the sun, the Mother-Force, the Father-Force, and so on; and show them that by celebrating these benefits worthily the worshipers unite themselves more fully with the current of life. Let the religion be Joy, but with a worthy and dignified sorrow in death itself; and treat death as an ordeal, an initiation....In short be the founder of a new and greater Pagan cult.
> (QUOTED AT HUTTON, 178-179)

Crowley knew that he would not be the one to bring this Paganism about. He was here suggesting that Jones take it up.

---

* Unless, of course, the whole thing was Crowley's biggest jape – an unlikely but not impossible explanation.

But instead the person who would play the key role was a much younger man, who was then in Malaya working on a rubber plantation and befriending the natives and the primitive tribes of the jungle: Gerald Gardner.

We'll pick up with Gardner's story in a bit. But first let's take a break from the history, and look more deeply into the psychological nature of the ritual magic that Crowley practiced, and of the trap that he fell into.

It's All In Your Mind

> "All statements are true in some sense, false in some sense, meaningless in some sense, true and false in some sense, true and meaningless in some sense, false and meaningless in some sense, and true and false and meaningless in some sense. A public service clarification by the Sri Syadasti School of Spiritual Wisdom, Wilmette".

> "The teachings of the Sri Syadasti School of Spiritual Wisdom are true in some sense, false in some sense, meaningless in some sense, true and false in some sense, true and meaningless in some sense, false and meaningless in some sense, and true and false and meaningless in some sense. Patamunzo Lingananda School of Higher Spiritual Wisdom, Skokie." – Principia Discordia

Sam and Dave's is a popular nightclub in the heart of Osaka. It caters to the gaijin crowd but attracts lots of Nihonjin. Walk in on a Saturday night and you'll see plenty of people engaged in the drinking and dancing mating rituals that are common to contemporary industrial cultures.

The drinks are a bit pricey, as they always are at such places, but they have a good selection of beers. And they serve food too – place your order at the bar and they give you a number to put on your table, then send a server out to you when your food's ready.

It's a fine place, lots of fun. It's not the sort of place you'd expect to see an illustration of the magical underpinnings of the Universe. But one fine evening at Sam and Dave's, after a couple of drinks, I was holding forth to my friend David Hess about the Law of Fives.

The Law of Fives is one of most fundamental teachings of Discordianism, a "spoof" religion (or perhaps a very true religion wrapped in a protective coating of jokes) that was created in the 1950s and was inspired by certain elements of Zen and occultism. As stated in the *Principia Discordia*:

The Law of Fives states simply that: ALL THINGS HAPPEN IN FIVES, OR ARE DIVISIBLE BY OR ARE MULTIPLES OF FIVE, OR ARE SOMEHOW DIRECTLY OR INDIRECTLY APPROPRIATE TO 5.

The Law of Fives is never wrong.

In the Erisian Archives is an old memo from Omar to Mal-2: "I find the Law of Fives to be more and more manifest the harder I look."(MALACLYPSE, 23)

That last bit is very important: the harder you look, the more you will see the Law of Fives in action. Sometimes you have to look really hard, but if you do, you will find a connection between any situation and the number five.

(Why not pause for a moment and try it? I look around the cafe where I'm sitting with my laptop writing this, and I notice that there a five tables in the room. There are five people in the room. One hands another a five dollar bill.)

I was trying to explain this to David, and I said, "Now, for example, if we looked out at this room right now, I'll bet we could see the number five somehow." I turned around; the people at the table directly behind me, only a few yards away, had placed a food order and been given a number to set on their table.

Sure enough, right there in black and white, several inches high, was the number 5.

* * *

When you step on to the path of magic, "coincidences" like this are typical, bizarre synchronicities that seem to drip with meaning and portent. Robert Anton Wilson gives an excellent account of his experience of this phenomenon in his book *Cosmic Trigger*, and it was an important factor in the life of Aleister Crowley, who took the seemingly mundane incident of stumbling across his misplaced manuscript of *The Book of the Law* as a communication from the "Secret Chiefs." (CROWLEY, CONFESSIONS, CH. 65, 595)

From the skeptical point of view, such oddly meaningful coincidences have a simple explanation: when we set out on the path of magic or mysticism, we are exercising our brains' pattern recognition abilities. We're good at seeing patterns, even if they aren't there. We can look at two dots and a line and see a face, or can see in the dark patches on the surface of the moon a human face (the "man in the moon"), or a rabbit (the Japanese interpretation), or Arabic letters.

Usually this is harmless, even amusing, but much trouble can result if we take such patterns to be real. For example, in the 1960s concerned parents came to believe that the indistinct vocals to The Kingsmen's rock and roll classic "Louie Louie" contained various obscenities. The song was banned from the airwaves in Indiana, and the FBI and the FCC opened investigations. The possibility of federal obscenity charges hung over the band for two and a half years before the FBI concluded that the lyrics were unintelligible. (SADLER, 250-251)

Even trained observers can fall into such traps. In 1877, the Italian astronomer Giovanni Schiaparelli reported seeing a series of fine lines on the surface of Mars. The Italian word he used was *canali*, which merely means "channels" or "grooves" – but was translated into English as "canals," which has a clear implication of something constructed.

The idea of canals on Mars was vigorously taken up by the American astronomer Percival Lowell. Because of atmospheric turbulence, it was impossible to photograph such fine features; the observer had to sit and wait for extended periods for just an instant of clear air – too short for a photographic exposure with the primitive equipment of the time – when the canals would become visible. Many astronomers were unable to see any such features, but Lowell and Schiaparelli were not alone in reporting them.

Based on these supposed constructions, Lowell argued that there must be an advanced civilization, with a global government, on Mars. He even identified its capital, where several canals came together. His concept of Martian civilization influenced the science fiction of H.G. Wells and Edgar Rice Burroughs.

It took decades before it was understood that these "canals" were never there, that they were a sort of optical illusion. (SAGAN, 104-107)

I was delighted to discover that there are words for these misfirings of the brain's pattern recognition system: *apophenia* is the general term for seeing connections in random data (finding meaning in coincidences, for example), while *pareidolia* is the more specific word for misclassifying sense perceptions (such as the Martian "canals").

With our pattern recognition systems already primed for action, it's not surprising that a process of training the intuition can result in apophenia and pareidolia. Any time we increase the sensitivity of a detector to a signal, we make it more vulnerable to noise as well. So we must be very careful in how we interpret the patterns we perceive – especially in the realm of religion and spirituality. As Carl Sagan noted, regarding Lowell and the "canals" on Mars,

> If scientists can be fooled on the question of the simple interpretation of straightforward data of the sort that they are routinely obtaining from other kinds of astronomical objects, when the stakes are high, when the emotional predispositions are working, what must be the situation where the evidence is much weaker, where the will to believe is much greater, where the skeptical scientific tradition has barely made a toehold – namely, in the area of religion? (SAGAN, 108)

So, perhaps we ought not be too hard on people like Wilson and Crowley when they fall into apophenia.

To take another apophenia example from my own experience: as I've worked on this book and learned about the role that the Theosophical Society – a group about which I previously knew next to nothing – played in the history of both Buddhism and Paganism, I've begun to see references to them everywhere. A recent example was a science fiction novel by Joe Haldeman, *The Accidental Time Machine*, in which a time traveler ends up in a future where religion dominates and MIT has become the "Massachusetts Institute of Theosophy" (with no connection to the Theosophical Society other than the name). Another was the program of an exhibit by Baltimore "symbolic artist" Dr. Robert R. Hieronimus, which lists Blavatsky's *The Secret Doctrine* in its suggested reading list and mentions how U Thant, former Secretary General of the United Nations, introduced Hieronimus to his spiritual teacher U Maung U Ji – "a Buddhist scholar, statesman, diplomat, and disciple of the Master

Koot Hoomi." (HIERONIMUS, 1) Koot Hoomi was the foremost of Blavatsky's Mahatmas.

Should I take these incidents as some sort of signal? A message from the Secret Chiefs? That could be a tempting explanation, to believe that I was a chosen agent of the Masters! (Just like Crowley.) But another recent "coincidental" encounter shows what's really going on. Reading Aldous Huxley's novel *Island*, I was struck by mentions of Koot Hoomi and Theosophy - but this was in a book I had already read at least twice. I had seen these mentions before, but they had not been meaningful to me and passed without special notice. But now, with Theosophy on my mind, I cannot help but read the exact same text differently.

Sometimes things go a little further than just coincidences. We see minor incidents of what appear to be "poltergeist manifestations" or the work of "mischievous fairies," small objects seeming to move or disappear when no one is looking. It's one thing when these occur in ritual environments where imagination might run wild, but when they start to invade everyday mundane life, significant questions are raised.

To take a small example of this from my own experience, let us consider the Case of the Confounding Keys:

One Wednesday evening in September a few years ago, I went to the ball court at the neighborhood middle school to get some exercise playing solo wallball - throwing, bouncing, and chasing a rubber ball around the court. I remember that while running around, I took my key-ring (a good sized one with about a dozen keys on it) out of my pocket so it wouldn't bounce around or fall out, and put it on the ground.

Later that evening, back home and searching unsuccessfully for those keys, I began to think that I had left them at the court. I went back over for a look - no keys. (I should mention that my vision is 20/20 in both eyes, and that I had a flashlight to illuminate my search.)

I posted a note about the lost keys, with my phone number, by the court's only entrance.

The next morning I visited the school office to check if anyone had found the keys and turned them in. No luck, and no phone calls responding to my note. That night, and two more times the next day, I checked back around the court. No keys. (Fortunately, I had spares for the most important ones.) I put a few more signs up around the school area, this time with mention of a cash reward.

Saturday afternoon, around 4 pm, I went back over to the school. *Sitting on the court, right by the wall, plain as day, were my keys.**

What are we to make of that? Was I temporarily delusional, suffering from the mental equivalent of the "48 hour flu"? Afflicted with some strange short-term, and highly specific, malfunction of my visual cortex? If so, how was it that over several days no one else found them and turned them in, even with the promise of a reward? Was someone playing a trick? Who? How and why? Did my keys fall into some sort of inter-dimensional rift? Were they hidden by mischievous faeries?

I don't have an answer. If I label the experience an illusion or a hallucination, then I'm forced to question the reliability of any observation I make – and if I can't trust my own eyes, why would I trust anyone else's? So all observations and reports become suspect. If it was a bizarre prank, then I have to wonder in what other ways I'm being fooled by others, and again have to question anything I witness or am told. As for paranormal explanations, if space warps or the fey folk were responsible, why is there no reliable evidence for their existence? Misplaced keys are not sufficient for proof of the supernatural.

Faced with these sorts of odd experiences, the best we can do is accurately report what we observe – or at least what we recall observing, keeping in mind that recall is subject to distortions of its own – and for the rest, honestly say we don't know.

(But one useful observation does emerge: the strange but common urge that makes us look again and again in the place where a lost item "should" be, even when we logically know that it can't be there because we already checked, can pay off!)

Sometimes the magical experience goes a lot further than small items moving around. Some people report full-blown visions and other such extraordinary experiences.

Let's take as an example a report from self-described "chaos magician" Grant Morrison. In his day job, Morrison is one of the most popular and successful comic book writers around – perhaps not the profession most associated with sober reflection

---

* Note that it was the fifth time that I looked, that the keys were found – in accordance with the Law of Fives.

and disciplined observation, but certainly anyone whom DC Comics and Warner Brothers trust with their cash cows Superman and Batman, can't be dismissed as mentally incompetent.

Morrison describes his visionary experience like this:

> The short version is that I was sitting up on the roof garden of the BajaRat Hotel and this thing happened and – it's hard to describe, we're going into areas that are unusual, so all I remember is getting back downstairs and laying on the bed and – some unusual things happened, and then it seemed like there were entities in the room it was like those silver morphing blobs you see in rave videos. It was like computer generated things and they claimed to be cross-sections of fifth-dimensional entities as expressed through four-dimensional spacetime and they claimed that I was one of them and that I had to come back and see what the old homestead was like. And that was when I felt like I was peeled off the surface of spacetime and they took me out of my body and then to what seemed to be the fifth dimension because I could see the entirety of space and time as a dynamic object in which Shakespeare was over here, and I was over here and the dinosaurs were here and we were all in the same object, and time was a thing.
>
> So, I appeared to be in a fifth dimensional fluid, an information space that I could say was maybe kinda bluish, extending out infinitely. These things swam through it and interacted with it and they told me that what the universe was, was a larval form of what they are, which is fifth-dimensional entities. And the only way to grow a fifth-dimensional entity is to plant it in time, henceforth our universe. (METZGER)

(Morrison admits that at the time of this experience he was no stranger to psychedelic drugs, but says that this event was of an entirely different order than a drug experience.)

For believers in the paranormal, all these coincidences and visions and unexplained events are evidence of some sort of supernatural entities or powers. To the skeptical, they are explained by apophenia, or by failures of memory, or as illusions or delusions or hallucinations, malfunctions of the sensory nervous system.

From a Zen Pagan perspective, neither of these explanations is satisfactory. The true believer's approach makes claims about the objective universe that don't hold up to controlled experiment and observation, but the skeptic's neurological reductionism neglects the fact that most events in the universe occur outside of laboratory controls, and ignores the person to whom the experience is happening. The subjective dimension is flattened out.

When we practice ritual, or engage in deep meditation, or seek otherwise to alter our consciousness, we expect to see and experience strange and unusual things. To encounter "spirits" or to have some other sort of transpersonal experience after staying up all night dancing or drumming around a bonfire, or fasting for days, or sitting unmoving in mediation for hours at a time, or ingesting strange herbs, or working yourself into a ritual frenzy, is not odd. To the practitioner, these experiences are the goal of the work.

Dismissing the experience as "mere delusion" is like calling a performance of Bach fugue a "mere disturbance of air." It is technically correct, and even captures important information – understanding that disturbance of air allows for the proper acoustic design of concert halls, after all. But it introduces an irrelevant element of judgment ("mere") and misses the aesthetic dimension that makes the whole thing worthwhile.

In the same way, calling a shaman's vision a "hallucination" may be accurate, even useful in certain contexts. (If someone was going to risk their life or well-being on information that came to them in a vision, for example, it would be good to point out that such information is not a reliable guide to objective, "consensus" reality.) But it misses the mystical element, the deep emotional content, of the experience.

Let's return to Morrison's experience. In discussions of his encounter he clearly states that he believes that it was a psychological experience that did not involve physical contact with extraterrestrial or extradimensional beings. But it was a deeply moving experience, one that has had a tremendous impact on his life and his art:

> If the same experience had occurred in Biblical times I would no doubt have described burning bushes and celestial voices. If it had happened in the Dark Ages I would have used the language of angelic hosts and infernal spirit hierarchies. If I was Aleister Crowley I'd have called it Aiwass and founded a religion. If I'd been brought up with a lot of fear in the last few decades perhaps I could have explained it as Satanic Abuse or Temporal Lobe Epilepsy. I'm a comic writer, so my attempts to frame the experience in language sound read like surrealist science fiction.
>
> Following the apparent 'encounter' which was real enough emotionally and experientially that it rewired my entire head and changed my life forever, I began to experience all manner of weird synchronicities and I plunged deeper into some very odd and dangerous magical spaces for a few years.... [F]rightening as it was at the time, I have to say that the ordeal was a breakthrough which changed my entire life - made me happier, freer, more creative, sexier and younger by the minute. I don't do magic now, it does me. I feel like I'm living in one of my own stories. (ELLIS)

Angels or epilepsy? Gods appearing in burning bushes, or five-dimensional intelligences incarnating as silver blobs?*

The answer towards which you are biased, the model you adopt for your investigations, determines the observations that you choose to make and the interpretation of the data. Therefore, for any reasonably interesting question with sparse data, the

---

* Not six dimensional. Not eight. Five, of course, in accordance with the Law.

harder you investigate, the more you tend to see your model.

For example, in the early twentieth century some physicists held firmly to the notion that light was composed of a stream of particles. They devised experiments to detect these "photons" – and sure enough, they found them.

Other physicists were sure that light was a wave phenomenon. They devised experiments to watch these waves interact – and sure enough, that's just what they saw.

We're oversimplifying a bit here to make a point, but the conundrum was perplexing enough that Albert Einstein stated in 1924 that "there are therefore now two theories of light, both indispensable...without any logical connection." (QUOTED AT GRIBBEN, 85)

The "truth," as it turned out, was the tautology that light is light. It does what light does, and sometimes the equations for particles are useful, and sometimes the wave equations are a fair description. "Particle" and "wave" are models, mental constructions which don't bind the behavior of light in the least. But when you latch on to a model, you are caught in an observational bias that will often tend to confirm it.

So if you accept the notion that lost keys are stolen by the fey folk, you will see evidence for their existence everywhere you look – that glimpsed motion out of the corner of your eye, the strange feeling of a presence even when no one is there, the small items that seem to have moved or disappeared.

If you adopt the model that all this is the result of illusion and mental failing, you'll see how much you keep forgetting, how you overlook items right in front of you. You'll notice how unreliable your vision is, that out of the corner of your eye you sometimes see things that aren't there. Tremendous discrepancies in the memories and reports of different witnesses to the same events will become apparent. You will shake your head at the unreliability of human observation, and worry about how common outright delusion seems to be.

An old Taoist story from Lieh-Tzu shows how observations tend to conform to our biases:

> A man, having lost his axe, suspected his neighbour's son of having taken it. Certain peculiarities in his gait, his countenance and his speech, marked him out as the thief. In his actions, his movements, and in fact his whole demeanour, it was plainly written that he and

no other had stolen the axe. By and by, however, while digging in a dell, the owner came across the missing implement. The next day, when he saw his neighbour's son again, he found no trace of guilt in his movements, his actions, or his general demeanour. (GILES, 111)

The same idea is expressed in Eleanor Porter's classic children's novel *Pollyanna*: "When you look for the bad, expecting it, you will get it. When you *know* you will find the good — you will get that." (PORTER, 227)

But this process doesn't apply only to how we judge other people. It comes into all of our perceptions. The Cabalist sees how perfectly his tools, the Sephiroth and the Tree of Life, model the world, and knows that he must be following the path of ultimate truth. And the Taoist sees the actions of Yin and Yang at play everywhere, and knows that they are the basis of the cosmos. And astrologers see the influences of the planets at play in everyone's lives, and know that they have the key to reality.*

Rather than ask which is "true," it is perhaps better to ask which model is useful and applicable in any given situation. Modern physicists and engineers know that sometimes they must use the particle model of light, and sometimes the wave.

Bringing spirits into your calculations for a rocket launch is not particularly useful. But during a creative endeavor, the muses, the spirits of creativity – in one guise or another, whether understood as metaphysical or psychological entities – must be appeased.

To a trial lawyer, the unreliability of eyewitness observation and of hearsay evidence is fundamental, while an astronomer or physicist relies on the assumption that precise observations can be made and accurately communicated.

A gambler who believes that his wishes can influence the roll of the dice will quickly end up broke; but go to a football stadium and insist to the rabid fans there that all their wishing doesn't change the action on their field, and not only will you be

---

* Apart from the Sun and Moon, astrology (and alchemy) feature *five* classical planets, the ones visible to the naked eye: Mercury, Venus, Mars, Jupiter, and Saturn. Even astrology is subservient to the Law of Fives.

surprised by the reality of the "home field advantage," but if you assert your belief too strongly, you're liable to get punched in the nose.

(With that said, some models are useful more often than others, and there are some whose only use is to understand those unfortunate enough to be trapped in them: racism, bigotry, delusions of grandeur, religious extremism, and so on.)

The industrial-strength shaman must be able to move from model to model, from reality tunnel to reality tunnel, as needed to be effective in any given situation. He or she must understand that even the notion that there are multiple models, is itself a model, to be adopted or to be dropped as needed.

Robert Shea and Robert Anton Wilson illustrate the point brilliantly in their Discordianism-inspired psychedelic science-fiction classic *The Illuminatus! Trilogy*. After leading the reader and the characters on for hundreds of pages of twisted conspiracy theories involving the Law of Fives, as well as fictional versions of the Discordian Society, the Bavarian Illuminati, and John Dillinger, we're given a look at the truth behind it all:

> [Hagbard] reached into his pocket and took out a photo of a female infant with six fingers on each hand. "Got this from a doctor friend at Johns Hopkins."
>
> Joe looked at it and said, "So?"
>
> "If we all looked like her, there'd be a Law of Sixes."
>
> Joe stared at him. "You mean, after all the evidence I collected, the Law of Fives is an Illuminati put-on? You've been letting me delude myself?"
>
> "Not at all." Hagbard was most earnest. "The Law of Fives is perfectly true.... But you have to understand it more deeply now, Joe. Correctly formulated, the Law is: All phenomena are directly or indirectly related to the number five, and this relationship can always be demonstrated, *given enough ingenuity on the part*

> *of the demonstrator."* The evil grin flashed. "That's the very model of what a true scientific law must always be: a statement about how the human mind relates to the cosmos. We can never make a statement about the cosmos itself—*but only about how our senses (or our instruments) detect it, and about how our codes and languages symbolize it.* That's the key to the Einstein-Heisenberg revolution in physics, and to the Buddha's revolution in psychology much earlier."
>
> "But," Joe protested, "everything fits the Law. The harder I looked, the more things there were that fit."
>
> "Exactly," said Hagbard. "Think about that."
> (SHEA AND WILSON, 741)

With this understanding, watching the Law of Fives – or any other magical system of understanding – manifest itself, lets us see how the mind connects the dots of our observations to create the stories we tell ourselves, the stories we call "reality." And when this mental story-telling process is understood, we can begin to change the stories. That is the application of magic.

And this sort of magic can work even for those who are skeptics in their conscious minds. In his account of his life as a slave in pre-Civil War Maryland, Frederick Douglass mentions how African root magic played a role in a turning point in his life, when he fought back against the white man, Covey, to whom he had been hired out by his "owner":

> I found Sandy an old adviser. He told me, with great solemnity, I must go back to Covey; but that before I went, I must go with him into another part of the woods, where there was a certain root, which, if I would take some of it with me, carrying it always on my right side, would render it impossible for Mr. Covey, or any other white man, to whip me. He said he had carried it for years; and since he had done so, he had never received a blow, and never

expected to while he carried it. I at first rejected the idea, that the simple carrying of a root in my pocket would have any such effect as he had said, and was not disposed to take it; but Sandy impressed the necessity with much earnestness, telling me it could do no harm, if it did no good. To please him, I at length took the root, and, according to his direction, carried it upon my right side…All went well till Monday morning. On this morning, the virtue of the ROOT was fully tested. Long before daylight, I was called to go and rub, curry, and feed, the horses. I obeyed, and was glad to obey. But whilst thus engaged, whilst in the act of throwing down some blades from the loft, Mr. Covey entered the stable with a long rope; and just as I was half out of the loft, he caught hold of my legs, and was about tying me. As soon as I found what he was up to, I gave a sudden spring, and as I did so, he holding to my legs, I was brought sprawling on the stable floor. Mr. Covey seemed now to think he had me, and could do what he pleased; but at this moment – from whence came the spirit I don't know – I resolved to fight; and, suiting my action to the resolution, I seized Covey hard by the throat; and as I did so, I rose. He held on to me, and I to him. My resistance was so entirely unexpected that Covey seemed taken all aback.

This battle with Mr. Covey was the turning-point in my career as a slave. It rekindled the few expiring embers of freedom, and revived within me a sense of my own manhood. It recalled the departed self-confidence, and inspired me again with a determination to be free…. My long-crushed spirit rose, cowardice departed, bold defiance took its place; and I now resolved that, however long I might remain a slave in form, the day had passed forever when I could be a slave in fact. I did not hesitate to let it be known of me, that the white man who

> expected to succeed in whipping, must also succeed in killing me.
>
> From this time I was never again what might be called fairly whipped, though I remained a slave four years afterwards. I had several fights, but was never whipped. (DOUGLASS, CHAPTER X)

Given the significance of Douglass to the abolitionist movement, this fight with Covey might fairly be called a turning point in American history.

Later in his narrative, Douglass speaks of the man who gave him the root, and disclaims any belief in its effectiveness:

> We used frequently to talk about the fight with Covey, and as often as we did so, he would claim my success as the result of the roots which he gave me. This superstition is very common among the more ignorant slaves. (DOUGLASS, CHAPTER X)

But if he was thoroughly convinced that the power of the root was just meaningless superstition, why did he mention it at all?

It seems Douglass was of two minds on the subject, his conscious mind rational and skeptical, but his unconscious credulous and superstitious. His rational mind may have been willing to fight back, but it wasn't until his credulous side could be told a magical story of empowerment that change could happen.

Of course Douglass is not alone in this state of schizophrenia. We are all of split mind, to some degree.

So if magic seems at times irrational, we must remember that we are not and can never be purely rational beings. Our neocortex, wherein resides our capacity for rationality and language, floats on top of about a half billion years of vertebrate evolution. To disregard the more "primitive" parts of the mind that make up the bulk of our selves and pretend that the forebrain and the verbal consciousness is all that matters is, ultimately, an irrational act.

As Aldous Huxley put it in his final novel, *Island* (through the character of the Old Raja of Pala), "We cannot reason ourselves out of our basic irrationality. All we can do is to learn the art of being irrational in a reasonable way." (HUXLEY, 211)

What might this reasonable irrationality look like? In

Huxley's story, the Palanese religion is mostly Buddhist, with a bit of Shivaism mixed in, and all leavened with secular humanism. In the following excerpt, one Palanese character describes his society's attitude toward religion, which we can pretty much take as Huxley's ideal. This passage occurs just after the interlocutors have watched a young girl make an offering of flowers to a statue of the Amitābha Buddha:

> "We accept [religion]....as we accept that spider web up there on the cornice. Given the nature of spiders, webs are inevitable. And given the nature of human beings, so are religions. Spiders can't help making fly-traps, and men can't help making symbols....Sometimes the symbols correspond fairly closely to some of the aspects of the external reality behind our experience; then you have science and common sense. Sometimes, on the contrary, the symbols have almost no connection with external reality; then you have paranoia and delirium. Most often there's a mixture, part realistic and part fantastic; that's religion. Good religion or bad religion – it depends on the blending of the cocktail....
>
> "....With one part of her mind, [that child] thinks she's talking to a person – an enormous, divine person who can be cajoled with orchids into giving her what she wants. But she's already old enough to have been told about the profounder symbols behind Amitabha's statue and about the experiences that give birth to those profounder symbols. Consequently with another part of her mind she knows perfectly well that Amitabha isn't a person. She even knows, because it's been explained to her, that if prayers are sometimes answered it's because, in this very odd psychophysical world of ours, ideas have a tendency, if you concentrate your mind on them, to get themselves realized. She knows too that this temple isn't what she still likes to think it is – the house of Buddha. She

> knows it's just a diagram of her own unconscious mind – a dark little cubbyhole with lizards crawling upside down on the ceiling and cockroaches in all the crevices. But at the heart of the verminous darkness sits Enlightenment. And that's another thing the child is doing – she's unconsciously learning a lesson about herself, she's being told that if she'd only stop giving herself suggestions to the contrary, she might discover that her own busy little mind is also Mind with a large M." (HUXLEY, 219-221)

Just as a Buddhist temple can be a diagram of the unconscious mind, so can the Law of Fives, the Tree of Life, the signs of the Zodiac, or any other magical system. And since the unconscious mind is most of the mind, and since our entire experience of life takes place in the mind, they can be powerful tools indeed.

But problems arise when we take one of these diagrams to be the only one available, when we insist that the diagram that helps us track our unconscious must be the right one for our neighbors, or when we take it to be a map of "objective" reality. Indeed, since "objective" reality is largely a matter of what we agree with our neighbors about (thus the alternate term "consensus" reality), these are perhaps aspects of the same error.

A beautiful illustration comes from the Discordian writer Camden Benares:

> Today I heard about a new thing called whatamores. I now believe in whatamores. If you can believe in whatamores and if we can form a mutually acceptable definition, we will discover large amounts of circumstantial evidence proving the existence of whatamores. When we believe enough, there will be whatamores. Do we really want any? (BENARES, ZEN WITHOUT ZEN MASTERS, 89)

The history of Zen provides a lovely example of application of the "whatamores" principle in the story of the origin of Nanzen-ji, one of the most historically important Buddhist temples in Japan.*

In 1264, Emperor Kameyama built a retirement villa in a beautiful spot on the outskirts of Kyoto. But he soon encountered a major problem with his new digs: they seemed to be haunted. Kameyama asked several priests to exorcise the ghosts, but all failed until he invited Fumon, a priest of the relatively new Zen sect of Buddhism, to take a crack at it.

Rather than chanting or using some ritual to dispel the haunting, Fumon and his disciples sat in silent meditation. The ghosts disappeared. (MARTIN, 176)

Kameyama was so impressed that he became Fumon's student and donated the villa to become a Zen temple. The favor of an Emperor – even a retired one – greatly increased the prestige and power of Zen, and had a significant impact on Japanese history.

Fumon knew how to get rid of the whatamores: stop believing in them.

It is the key to meditation, shamanism, and magic in all their forms: change your mind, change the world.

---

* The same temple mentioned at the start of this book.

The Tapestry of Zen Pagan History, Part II
or: Witches, Woodcraft, and the Counter-Culture

Gerald Gardner

"Hardly a pure science, history is closer to animal husbandry that [sic] it is to mathematics in that it involves selective breeding. The principal difference between the husbandryman and the historian is that the former breeds sheep or cows or such and the latter breeds (assumed) facts. The husbandryman uses his skills to enrich the future, the historian uses his to enrich the past. Both are usually up to their ankles in bullshit." – Another Roadside Attraction, *Tom Robbins*

Witches

Gerald Gardner, generally regarded as the founder of modern Wicca, first met Aleister Crowley in May 1947, just a few months before Crowley's death. (HUTTON, 217) But their paths had come within hailing distance when both were in Kandy, Ceylon, at around the same time in 1901. (BRACELIN, 25; CROWLEY CONFESSIONS CH. 27, 236)

It's interesting to compare Crowley the occultist, the foremost popularizer of intellectual and learned "high" magic, with Gardner the witch, popularizer of "low" magic. While

Crowley grew up in a family that afforded him no intellectual or emotional support, Gardner's father was kind and gentle, and his mother was an intellectual of wide literary interests. (BRACELIN, 13)* Where Crowley believed that any sort of manual labor was degrading work that should be left to lower classes, (REGARDIE, 420) Gardner worked on tea and rubber plantations in Ceylon, Borneo, and Malaya. (BRACELIN, 25, 27, 35) Where Crowley went through women as disposable means of satiating his physical needs, and never respected them in the least, (REGARDIE, 442) Gardner was happily married for over 30 years. (BRACELIN, 125, 191; HUTTON, 205)

But it is an odd coincidence how their paths crossed in Ceylon – and how it was asthma that drew them both there. Like Crowley's mentor Alan Bennett, Gardner looked to find relief from his asthma in a warmer climate. (BRACELIN, 14, 21-22)

(Crowley also suffered from asthma; his heroin addiction resulted from a prescription for bronchial spasms. And Crowley's secretary Israel Regardie, who became a noted writer on the occult in his own right, also suffered from asthma. Regardie notes a theory – from an unnamed English author and occultist – that asthma is an occupational hazard to magicians and mystics. (REGARDIE, 114-115) It is interesting to consider. Or maybe it just says something about air pollution in England at the time!)

From 1900 (BRACELIN, 22) until 1936 (HUTTON, 205) Gardner made his home in the colonies in Ceylon, Borneo, and Malaya. (BRACELIN, 110) In Ceylon he encountered Buddhism and was interested by (what he interpreted to be) its idea of reincarnation, (BRACELIN, 25) but that seems to have been the extent of its impact on him. On one of his occasional visits to England he became interested in Spiritualism, and while he found some mediums to be frauds, believed that others had genuine abilities to contact the spirits of the dead. (BRACELIN, 117-124)

In the years he lived in the East, Gardner spent much time learning about the local cultures. He witnessed the religious and magical rites of the Dyak and Sakai tribes, (BRACELIN, 40-68) and studied the mythology and folk magic of the Malays, especially that centering around their traditional blade, the *kris*. (BRACELIN, 69-94) (His

---

* I take all opinions expressed in Bracelin's biography of Gardner to be those of Gardner himself, as it was his "authorized" biography, written by his secretary Idries Shah. See Hutton, 205

fascination with the kris may explain the predominance of the athame – ritual dagger – in Wiccan ritual. (HUTTON, 230)) He became interested in anthropology and archeology, and his work was published in the *Royal Asiatic Society's Journal*.

The magic that he saw the Dyak and Sakai tribes perform was quite different from the high ritual magic of Mathers and Crowley. This was not work done in isolation by intellectuals, referencing ancient tomes and grimoires. What he saw with the Dyaks was more like Spiritualism, with a medium acting as a voice for spirits; while the Sakai danced and sang themselves into a frenzy, and treated disease with spells to cast out demons. It was paleolithic, shamanistic, community activity. In the Muslim culture of the Malays he saw sympathetic folk magic and divination practices not too different in character from those found in European cultures, though perhaps more widespread.

Two other influences from his time in the East came through clearly in his later development of Wicca. First, during his time in Ceylon he became a Freemason. (BRACELIN, 32, LAMOND 9) Second, after suffering a minor medical mishap in a Singapore hospital, he turned to the most ancient and natural healing treatment: sunbathing. The relief he obtained from sunshine and fresh air turned him into a naturalist, in the "nudist" sense. (BRACELIN, 59)

Gardner retired to England in 1936, and in 1938 – looking for a safe location for his collection of archaeological artifacts and exotic weapons if the looming war came to pass – he moved to the New Forest district of Hampshire. During lulls in his work as an air raid warden, he followed his interest in the unusual by visiting a group in Christchurch that styled itself a "Rosicrucian Theatre."

Despite some Masonic and Theosophical ties, it was a generally silly group – its leader claimed to be immortal, and to have in his possession the Holy Grail! But there was a small clique that he got on well with: a group of newcomers, Co-Masons who had followed Mabel Besant-Scott when she moved to the New Forest area. (BRACELIN, 145-150; HUTTON, 205, 213; ADLER, 61) (Besant-Scott was the daughter of Annie Besant, former president of the Theosophical Society and founder of Co-Masonry, a Masonic tradition that accepted women. (HUTTON, 213))

According to Gardner's later claims, this inner group was in fact a witch coven, practitioners of a pre-Christian European religion that had survived down the ages, and he was initiated into it in 1939.

Ten years later, he published a novel, *High Magic's Aid*, which contained disguised descriptions of (according to his later claims) the rituals and beliefs of this group. He portrayed their witchcraft as equal in status to the "high magic" of ritualists such as the Golden Dawn, but less elitist and more closely linked to the forces of nature. (HUTTON, 206, 224)

The descriptions had to be fictionalized because under the 1736 Witchcraft Act and the 1824 Vagrancy Act, it was a crime to claim to practice witchcraft in Britain. (HUTTON, 107) After the repeal of these laws in 1951, Gardner published another book, *Witchcraft Today*. This was a (purported) non-fiction work in which he posed as an independent anthropologist reporting on the discovery of a surviving pre-Christian religious system. (HUTTON, 206)

Between his (claimed) initiation and the publication of *High Magic's Aid*, Gardner also joined a Druid revival group called the Circle of the Universal Bond (a.k.a. the Ancient Druid Order), and by 1946 became a member of its governing council. (HUTTON, 224) And he met with Aleister Crowley, who initiated him into the Ordo Templi Orientis. (HUTTON, 206)

The O.T.O. was originally a German offshoot of Freemasonry founded in 1904. Based on the mythology of the Knights Templar, it also was influenced by the "high magic" of Eliphas Levi, and by Indian yoga and tantra. Crowley was a natural for the organization, and they approached him in 1912; he became the head of its English branch. By the time of his meeting with Gardner, Crowley was running the whole show, and had converted the O.T.O. into a Thelema organization.

After World War II the O.T.O. was moribund, and Crowley seems to have planned that Gardner would work to revive it in England. (HUTTON, 222)

So, leading up to 1949 Gardner (apparently) had experience, connections, and sympathies in the worlds of both "high" magic – the O.T.O. – and "low" magic – the witch coven, and the tribal shamans he had seen in the Far East.

When he visited the U.S. in 1947 (HUTTON, 222), he was also able to make some contact with Voodoo practitioners. (BRACELIN, 159) And sometime around here, by the 1950s at least, Gardner was also familiar with a British group called the Order of Woodcraft Chivalry (HUTTON, 216) – a sort of Paganish offshoot of Scouting, connected more with Ernest Seton's Woodcraft Indians than with Baden-Powell's militarist, jingoist youth movement. (We'll return to the Woodcraft movement in a bit.)

After Crowley died in 1947, some in the O.T.O. viewed Gardner as his successor in the organization. But Gardner seems to have abandoned plans to revive the O.T.O., and decided instead to throw his lot in with the witches. (HUTTON, 222-223; BRACELIN, 155-158)

Assuming, that is, that there was a group in New Forest doing some sort of ritual work, and that they were, in fact, witches.

We have to use all these qualifiers in relating Gardner's encounter with the New Forest Coven for two reasons. First, historical analysis casts much doubt on the claim that this group was a survival of ancient Paganism.

Gardner's description of the witch rituals matches up well with the discredited anthropological theories of Margaret Murray. (HUTTON, 225) Murray published two books, *The Witch Cult in Western Europe* (1921) and *The God of the Witches* (1933), about her theory of an "Old Religion." This theory is notable for two ideas.

The first is that the victims of the witch trials of the fifteenth through eighteenth centuries had been practitioners of a Pagan religion. This religion supposedly had its origins not just in pre-Christian times but all the way back in the Paleolithic era, and it was said to have been spread across all of Western Europe and organized into small covens.

The second notable idea is that this religion was a fertility cult based around a horned god representing Nature's generative powers. (HUTTON, 195-196) In her theory, Pan was just one aspect of the Horned God – as were Ammon, Osiris, the Minotaur, Dionysus, a Gallic antlered deity whom the Romans may have referred to as Cernunnos, and a host of others. (MURRAY, 23-24) While the image of the Gallic Cernunnos, rather than the Greek Pan, became a primary face of the Horned God for Murray and the British proto-Pagans who followed her theory, there was no mythology or legend of Cernunnos in written or oral form (even the name is based on a single archeological site (HUTTON, 196)); the mythology of Murray's Horned God seems very much influenced by that of the version of Pan created by the Romantics and their literary descendants.

Murray's theory might have been accepted by laymen in the 1930s – especially by Gardner, who knew Murray through the Folk-Lore Society (HUTTON, 224) – but was not well regarded at the time by experts, and has been thoroughly overturned by later research. (HUTTON, 132, 195-201; ADLER, 47-49) This points at an attempted reconstruction, by either Gardner or by the New Forest group before he encountered them, of witchcraft based on theories that were current in the 1920s and 1930s, rather than to a survival of an actual ancient religion.

Furthermore, the rituals that Gardner used in the late 1940s and early 1950s show many elements borrowed from other sources: the works of Crowley and Mathers, the poetry of Kipling, and the rituals of Masonry, the O.T.O., and Thelema. Gardner's explanation was that the New Forest coven's ceremonies were "fragmentary" by the time he encountered the group, and he used this other work to fill in the gaps. (HUTTON, 227-238)

But that brings us to our second reason for richly qualifying any statements about the origins of Wicca: Gardner had what his student Frederic Lamond calls a "devious creative attitude to factual truth." (LAMOND, 10) He was known to make bogus claims of university degrees, including a Ph.D. (HUTTON, 207, 218-219) In *Witchcraft Today*, he falsely claimed to be a disinterested observer, rather than admitting to be a member of the culture he was describing. (HUTTON, 206-207) He claimed that the New Forest coven was led by a woman named Dorothy Clutterbuck, but historical evidence shows her to have been a pious Christian with no links to any sort of witchcraft – it seems he used Clutterbuck's name either as a prank, or as a blind to conceal the identity of the real leader (if the New Forest coven actually existed). (HUTTON, 207-214)

So with all these caveats, what can we clearly say about Gardner and Wicca?

He didn't pull it out of some deep dusty closet where it had rested since the Stone Age. Nor did he make it up out of whole cloth.

Instead he wove together threads that had been floating around since the early nineteenth century. From the Romantic poets and the work of Murray came the notions of the Horned God and of the Goddess. From the Theosophists came connections between Western and Eastern traditions.

From Whitman up through D.H. Lawrence and (in an incomplete way) Crowley, came the re-sanctification of sexuality. His Wicca even had a bit of kink – Gardner thought drugs overly risky as a means of altering consciousness (though his *Book of Shadows* does say that even cannabis might be used if the "strictest precautions" are taken (GARDNER, 37)), and as an asthmatic could not dance himself into ecstasy, and so made use of bondage and scourging to achieve trance states. (LAMOND, 10; HUTTON, 235) That's not quite as dramatic as it might sound: binding was used to control blood flow and produce dizziness, while the scourging was light and rhythmical – more like an extreme version of the tapotement a massage therapist might use rather than a flogging with a cat-o'-nine-tails.

From the occultists came ritual elements of initiation and invocation, and the idea of magic as a tool for spiritual development. From naturalism, came the practice of working "skyclad." From the Dyak and Sakai tribes, came the raw methods of trance and the emphasis on natural forces. And from Gardner's wide-ranging experience and exposure to Buddhism and Islam came an inherent respect for diversity in religious practice.

With these elements, Gardner developed something special. It wasn't the first modern attempt at a Pagan religion, but it was the first to "break the surface," to spread widely and to gain some degree of mass appeal. It combined methods from low magic and high magic, and applied them to small groups instead of solitary practitioners.

And it emphasized the role of the priestess and brought the Goddess, the divine feminine, to a new prominence. (ADLER, 82)

Woodcraft: Indians and Chivalry

We've seen how the Romantics and the Transcendentalists looked to the cultures of pre-Christian Europe and of the East for cures to the ills of their societies. In a similar manner, in the U.S. at the turn of the twentieth century, Ernest Thompson Seton looked to the culture of the Native Americans.

Seton was a Canadian naturalist, artist, explorer, and writer who became an early advocate for nature conservation. Born in England in 1860, while he was still a boy his family moved to upper Ontario to become homesteaders in the virgin forest near the town of Lindsay. The family failed at farming and soon moved to Toronto, but the young Seton longed for the woods he'd left behind, and would often seek refuge from bullies – at school and, in the person of his ultra-Calvinist father, at home – in the bits of wilderness that remained in the area.

As a teen he suffered from a lung ailment, and to get him out in the fresh air his mother arranged to have him spend part of his summer vacation each year at the old Ontario homestead, where the new owners welcomed him warmly. (The theme of a mystic with respiratory problems who is forced to relocate for his health, repeats.) During these visits he spent time with neighborhood boys, camping out in the woods in homemade tepees and playing at being Indians. (ANDERSON, 1-15) During this time he made the acquaintance of an old woman he called the Lindsay Witch – a suggestive appellation! – from whom he learned much woodlore. (SETON, TRAIL, 111)

Seton displayed a talent for art, and in 1879 he went to London to study at the Royal Academy. He attended classes only for a brief time, and returned to Canada in 1881, but during his stay he was greatly inspired by visits to the library of the British museum, where he read the work of pioneering naturalists like Audubon and Thoreau. (ANDERSON 18-20, SETON, TRAIL, 139)

Also during his time in London, Seton began to have mystical experiences. He lived a self-denying, sexually repressed, ascetic life – partly from poverty, partly from a disposition towards it – and began to hear a "voice" which urged him to go to Western Canada and then to New York.* (SETON, TRAIL, 146-147)

After returning to Canada, Seton spent the 1880s moving between homesteading attempts and nature watching in Manitoba, art and natural science work in New York, and his family's home in Toronto. In the course of his Manitoba explorations, Seton became acquainted with members of the Cree and Sioux tribes. (ANDERSON, 22-38)

He became a popular nature writer and lecturer, but it was Seton's work popularizing Native American culture and spirituality that has had the most lasting effect. He studied several Native languages and was an early member of the Sequoya League, a group dedicated to improving conditions for tribes on the West Coast. By 1902 he was personally acquainted with several tribal chiefs, was acknowledged by the U.S. Bureau of Indian Affairs as an authority on Native American culture, (ANDERSON, 127-137) and was honored by his Native friends by being one of the first whites to be made a "pipe carrier." (J. GREER, 53)

Like many in the Progressive Era, Seton saw the cure for society's ills in proper youth education and development.

---

* Several authors have claimed that Seton studied Zen Buddhism during this time, but this does not seem to be correct. See the Appendix.

Combining that with his admiration for the Native Americans, he set up the "Woodcraft Indians," a youth movement dedicated in part to the preservation and promotion of "the culture of the Redman." (HUTTON, 162-163; SETON, TRAIL 374-376)

Seton's scheme for youth education was based around what he saw as natural human instincts:

> Hero-worship, gang instinct, love of glory, hunter instinct, caveman instinct, play, fear of dark, initiation instinct, etc., etc.
>
> Each of these is deeply rooted in human history and full of possibilities as ready-made power when rightly guided.
>
> With these basic thoughts I set about my scheme of education in outdoor life. First, guided by my own preferences, I selected a hero as a model. Not Robin Hood, not Rollo the Sea King, not King Arthur, but the ideal Indian of Fenimore Cooper, perfectly embodied in Tecumseh, the great Shawnee – physically perfect, wise, brave, picturesque, unselfish, dignified.
>
> Then I framed a code of exploits, beginning with things physical, rising through mental and spiritual, to find climax in the idea of service to one's people.
>
> For each exploit there was a badge, and all were earned by standards, not by competition. Competition means downing the other fellow; standards means raising yourself.
>
> Eventually I convinced Edward Bok of *The Ladies Home Journal* there here was something the nation needed. I called the members Woodcraft Indians, except when under definite commission, when they became Scouts. My first public announcement of the organization was in the *Journal* issue of May, 1902. (SETON, TRAIL, 376)

The Woodcraft movement became a fast success, with approximately 200,000 members in the U.S. by 1910. (J. GREER, 50)

In 1906, Seton was lecturing in England and met Robert Baden-Powell. Baden-Powell took Seton's Woodcraft idea and applied it to his goal of molding young men into fit subjects and soldiers for the British Empire, and the Boy Scouts were born. Seton became the leader of the Scouts in the U.S., but moved away from Baden-Powell's jingoism in the years leading up to World War I. He split with the Scouts in 1915. (HUTTON, 162-163)

Seton wanted to bring Native spirituality to adults as well as to youth. By 1912 he had started the Red Lodge, a group for men:

> This is the purpose of the Red Lodge :-
>
> That we who enter it may, for the helping of our spirits and our bodies, preserve such of the Redman's ways, his sayings, and his picture writings, and his thoughts about the world, and the God of blue air and power, and such secrets of the Medicine Lodge as have proven wise, and will help us to know our own natures, and to profit while we live the life that knows neither roof nor doorway.
>
> And further, to realize, as did the Redman, that this body is the sacred temple of the spirit, that the body must be held in subjection for the spirit's clearer insight; that all things in our lives may be made beautiful, and that there is no crime more shameful than being afraid.
>
> For this is a Lodge of Masters and of Powers for the helping of mankind, and the Gateway to power is mastery of one's self. (SETON, RED LODGE, 3)

By 1917, the men's "Red Lodge" had evolved the co-educational "Sun Lodge." (SETON, BIRCHBARK ROLL, XV)

Seton's spiritual side was not limited to Native American teachings. He was also familiar with Theosophy – his first wife, Grace Gallatin Seton, was a practicing Theosophist. (ANYA SETON)

A most interesting and more subtle connection with Theosophy, one which ties Woodcraft into other threads of our story, is a story related in a preface to the 1937 edition of his book *The Gospel of the Redman*. His second wife, Julia M. Seton, claims that in 1905 Seton met a mysterious woman – described as "a Mahatma from India, although born in Iowa" who had "spent many year studying under the Great Masters" – who told him that he was an Indian Chief "reincarnated to give the message of the Redman to the White race, so much in need of it." (SETON, GOSPEL, XVI) This would seem to be a reference to the Theosophical "Mahatmas" whose authority was also claimed by Blavatsky, Mathers, and Crowley.

Seton's 1915 secession from Scouting prompted several leaders in the British Scouting movement to also leave and follow him down the path of Woodcraft. In 1916 Ernest Westlake founded the Order of Woodcraft Chivalry, with Seton as its honorary Grand Chieftain; in 1920 John Hargrave left the Scouts to start the Kindred of the Kibbo Kift, a group whose members would eventually include H.G. Wells, Havelock Ellis, and Maurice Hewlett.

The Kibbo Kift, and its later splinter group the Woodcraft Folk, took spiritual inspiration from Native American ways (or at least, a Seton-derived concept of Native American spirituality), but also took elements from African, Polynesian, and Inuit cultures and from Freemasonry. (HUTTON, 163-164) The Order and the Kindred were close allies – Hargrave was also on the Order of Woodcraft Chivalry's leadership council and apparently wrote some of its rituals. (J. GREER, 54)

The Order of Woodcraft Chivalry included Seton's Sun Lodge as its innermost circle (in the worlds of Audrey Westlake, Ernest's son, "in a sense, the church of the movement"); and the Kibbo Kift also formed a "Lodge of Initiation" based on the Sun Lodge. But the groups looked to ancient British traditions as much as, or even more than, Native American ones. According to Hargrave:

> The Kindred has sent roots into a cultural soil which shows most clearly the strata of Anglo-Saxon, Viking, Celt, and Neolithic builders of barrow, dolmen, and the old straight track. In these traditions it finds something necessary, something clean and bright and true: something sensed by Rudyard Kipling in his *Puck of Pook's Hill*. (QUOTED IN J. GREER, 54-55)

The reference to Kipling's *Puck of Pook's Hill* – a collection of faerie stories meant to instill nationalism into British youth – is suggestive. Part of it (an excerpt from "A Tree Song," the famous "Oak and Ash and Thorn" poem) ended up in Gerald Gardner's Book of Shadows, the original Wiccan liturgy. (HUTTON, 153; GARDNER, 22) And this is by no means the only connection between Woodcraft and Wicca.

Both the Order and the Kibbo Kift met in the New Forest area, the same area as Gardner's supposed coven. Both groups practiced nudism (or "naturism"), used rituals based on bits of old British folklore, and took "Kin names" or "Woodcraft names," (J. GREER, 54-56) a practice similar to the Wiccan use of "Craft" names. Gardner was friendly with members of the Order of Woodcraft Chivalry, and was seen at their meetings in the 1950s. (HUTTON, 216) He may have been an active member at some point in the late 1930s – around the same time that he claimed to encounter his coven. (J. GREER, 56)

This has led to speculation that Gardner's "coven" was in fact the Order of Woodcraft Chivalry. Certainly there are suggestive elements here.

However, neither the Order nor the Kibbo Kift identified itself as Pagan. For the Order, Westlake proposed to "link this movement up with organized Christianity by providing the natural basis of Christianity," while Hargrave denied that the Kibbo Kift attempted to define or prescribe any religion, leaving it up to individuals to decide what the rituals meant. (HUTTON, 164, 166) There are also difficulties in matching up the chronology, as the Order seems to have become moribund during the time when Gardner supposedly encountered the coven (HUTTON, 216).

But on the other hand, Westlake also called the Order "a Dionysos [sic, British spelling] movement," identified Dionysus with the Green Man ("Jack-in-the-Green") known in British folklore, declared that the "Trinity of Woodcraft" consisted of Pan, Artemis, and Dionysus, and also suggested the worship of Aphrodite. (HUTTON, 165) This would certainly make for an odd form of Christianity.

And after Westlake's death in 1922, up through 1931, Harry Byngham – who changed his name to Dion in honor of Dionysus – led a decidedly more Pagan faction within the Order. (HUTTON, 166-169)

As for the Kibbo Kift, one member, Vera Chapman, reported that they did "quite a little bit of mysticism, ritualism, what John Hargrave particularly called 'magik', spelt with a 'k'." (QUOTED AT J. GREER, 55)

Several smaller, less formal Woodcraft groups also existed around this time, and some had distinctly Pagan elements – one of these groups, for example, practiced meditation and vegetarianism, and initiated boys as "Warriors of Pan" who swore to "take care of the sacred land and the flora, fauna and people upon it." (HUTTON, 163-164)

The Dionysus and Aphrodite factors in Woodcraft Chivalry were definitely a break with Seton's philosophy. Seton was an advocate of Prohibition (ANDERSON, 201) and of chastity (SETON, GOSPEL, 40), who believed that alcohol atrophied the pineal gland and thereby destroyed man's capability for clairvoyance (SETON, GOSPEL, 18) and that lust "makes wreck of the body" and was an evil on par with fear, anger, and falsehood. (SETON, RED LODGE, 7)

But all that considered, it seems safe to say that, directly or indirectly, Woodcraft was among Gardner's influences in the early days of Wicca; and that it's at least possible that the "New Forest coven" was actually a Woodcraft group, perhaps an offshoot of the Order of Woodcraft Chivalry or the Kindred of the Kibbo Kift.

Whether the British version of Seton's Woodcraft movement became the heart of Wicca, or were merely an influence, Seton's work had an impact on its development. And his popularization of Native spirituality helped make the American Indian a role model for the mid-twentieth century United States counter-culture that would contribute so much to the wider Pagan movement.

Pagans and the Counter-Culture

Gerald Gardner was living in the East during most of World War I and its aftermath. He spent a few months as a hospital orderly in Liverpool, but a recurrence of malaria forced him back to Malaya, so he missed directly experiencing the most wrenching period of change in Europe in centuries. By 1918, war, disease, and famine had killed almost nine and a half million soldiers (KAGAN, 920) and thirty million civilians. (T. GREER, 495)

Political, social, and artistic systems all over the continent were thrown into flux. The Dada and Surrealist movements in art, the Communist revolution in Russia, the emergence of psychology as a major social force – all of these were consequences of the post-World War I shakeup. (T. GREER, 553)

An example of the spiritual and literary impact of the war can be found in Herman Hesse's 1919 novel *Demian*. This coming-of-age story, set in the years leading up to the war, has its hero Emil Sinclair fall in with a group that pursues a spiritual practice centered around Abraxas, "a godhead whose symbolic task is the uniting of godly and devilish elements." (HESSE, 78)

In the novel, Sinclair's mentor Demian describes the state of Western civilization leading up to the war:

> ...You are only afraid if you are not in harmony with yourself. People are afraid because they have never owned up to themselves. A whole society composed of men afraid of the unknown within them! They all sense that the rules they live by are no longer valid, that they live according to archaic laws – neither their religion nor their morality is in any way suited to the needs of the present...[War] will reveal the bankruptcy of present-day ideals, there will be a sweeping away of Stone Age gods. (HESSE 115)

Hesse's work was lauded by people like Aldous Huxley and Timothy Leary, and became popular with the American and British counter-culture of the 1950s and 60s. It provided an important literary and cultural link to an earlier German counter-culture, which included the *Lebensreform* and *Naturmenschen* ("life-reform" and "natural men") movements that presaged the hippies. (KENNEDY, 52-61)

Germany, France, and the other mainland nations where the battles of World War I were fought were hit harder than Britain, but Britain still suffered enormous loss of life and of wealth. After 1921 it slipped into chronic economic depression, lasting until the Second World War. (T. GREER, 515) It's not much wonder that some Britons in the 1920s and 30s were looking for an alternative to their mainstream culture and religion. Legends of their ancestors, myths (however inaccurate) of an ancient witch-religion, provided a pleasant alternative for some.

World War I was less destructive to the U.S. Entering the war late, and experiencing it as something "over there," it suffered only a fraction of the casualties that the U.K. did. And, partly due to a strong market in exports to war-ravaged Europe,

America enjoyed an economic boom during most of the 1920s.

But by the Great Depression of the 1930s the idea that something had gone awry with Western civilization had gained some traction in the U.S., and new spiritual ideas began to circulate in the culture. For example, this passage from John Steinbeck's classic period novel *The Grapes of Wrath* shows an idea of the soul and self radically different from conventional Christianity and more in line with Eastern philosophy:

> Tom laughed uneasily. "Well, maybe like Casy says, a fella ain't got a soul of his own, but on'y a piece of a big one – an' then – "
>
> "Then what, Tom?"
>
> "Then it don' matter. Then I'll be all aroun' in the dark. I'll be ever'where – wherever you look. Wherever they's a fight so hungry people can eat, I'll be there. Wherever they's a cop beatin' up a guy, I'll be there. If Casy knowed, why, I'll be in the way guys yell when they're mad an' – I'll be in the way kids laugh when they're hungry an' they know supper's ready. An' when our folks eat the stuff they raise an' live in the houses they build – why, I'll be there...." (STEINBECK, 572)

The Depression saw the publication of the first edition of Seton's *The Gospel of the Redman* in 1935, and also of another important work on Native American religion: John Neihardt's *Black Elk Speaks*, the life story of a Sioux holy man. Neihardt's book is more well-known today, but Seton's decades of defending Native American culture as a writer, lecturer, and educator did much to open the way for it.

The 1930s also saw the first stirrings of the "back to the land" movement, such as Ralph Borsodi's "School of Living," started in 1934. ("RALPH BORSODI") If industrial society was so fragile and brittle that bankers and stockbrokers could destroy it, some reasoned, perhaps we ought to reconsider whether or not it truly represented progress. The back-to-the-landers found their prophet in Thoreau, especially in *Walden*.

Another counter-cultural movement during the

Depression, small but historically significant, was an attempt at a strict classical Pagan revival. In 1938, Gleb Botkin established the Church of Aphrodite in West Hempstead, Long Island. But though it may have been the first consciously Pagan modern church, this monotheistic, dogmatic group never really took off. (ADLER, 233)

Zen Buddhism, on the other hand, successfully began to put down American roots during the 1930s. In 1931 two teachers from the lineage of Soyen Shaku (the Japanese master who had represented Zen to the Parliament of Religions) formed groups to teach Americans. D.T. Suzuki's former roommate Nyogen Senzaki started the Mentorgarten Meditation Hall in Los Angeles, while in New York Sokei-an Sasaki formed the Buddhist Society of America. (FIELDS, 171-181)

Later, Sasaki's wife, Ruth Fuller Sasaki, would play an important role in spreading Zen. In 1958 she would be ordained at Daitoku-ji, a prestigious temple of the Rinzai sect of Zen in Kyoto. Her son-in-law (via a daughter from her first marriage) Alan Watts would meet Zen through the Sasakis (FIELDS, 186-192) and would become an important popularizer of Zen, Vedanta, and Taoism. Meanwhile, Senzaki's student Robert Aitken (FIELDS, 200) would do important work connecting Zen with the peace movement. (FIELDS, 253, 256)

But let's stick with the 1930s for now. In 1934, Dwight Goddard – an American who had been a Christian missionary and a mechanical engineer, who had studied Zen in Kyoto, and who introduced the Sasaki to his future wife (AITKEN, FOREWARD, XIII-XV) – founded a group called the "Followers of Buddha," but it quickly foundered. Goddard fared better in publishing, and his 1932 collection of sutras, *The Buddhist Bible*, became a success. (FIELDS, 184-186)

The development of Zen in the U.S., and the spiritual quest in general, was interrupted by World War II. Both Sanzaki and Sasaki were among the more than 100,000 Japanese-Americans, citizens and non-citizens, forced into the infamous concentration camps. (FIELDS, 191, 193)

After the war, most Americans of the "G.I. Generation" just wanted to turn inward and live a quiet, normal life. But among those who had grown up with the war, the demographic group between the G.I.s and the Baby Boomers, dissatisfaction was more common. The conformity, consumerism, and ongoing racism of post-war society, plus the growing consciousness of the threats of ecological devastation from pollution and of annihilation by nuclear war, prompted a search for alternative ways of living.

Some looked back to a "simpler" time, and the back-to-the-land movement picked up momentum. But when the forces of the real estate market co-opted the "escape the cities!" meme, the result was the sprawl of the suburbs.

Some looked to other cultures for a model. White hipsters, for example, looked to African-American culture, especially jazz. It was through the culture around jazz that cannabis use first became widespread, and introduced many to a new mode of thinking.

The writers of the "Beat Generation" (including, for our purposes, the associated "San Francisco Renaissance") emerged from that "hip" milieu, starting around 1944 when Jack Kerouac, Allen Ginsberg, and William Burroughs met in New York City. The label "Beat" originally came from the feeling of being "beat up" and "beat down," but later Kerouac re-purposed it, linking it to the word "beatific." (PROTHERO, 11-13)

The Beats were saddled with a reputation as nihilists – clearly, anyone who rejected the wonders of post-war America must have been a pinko commie who hated all that was good in the world. But in truth they were trying to affirm life, trying to say "yes" to a spiritual impulse that their society was burying under television and tranquilizers. In Kerouac's words: "I want to speak *for* things. For the crucifix I speak out, for the Star of Israel I speak out, for the divinest man who ever lived who was German (Bach) I speak out, for sweet Mohammad I speak out, for Buddha I speak out, for Lao-tse and Chuang-tse I speak out." (QUOTED AT PROTHERO, 8) They may have understood the feeling of being "starving hysterical naked," but they were also "burning for the ancient heavenly connection to the starry dynamo in the machinery of night." (GINSBERG, 9)

The poets of the Beat movement connected to Buddhism by looking both backward in time and abroad in space. Philip Whalen was introduced to Buddhism as a boy in the 1940s through the books of the Theosophists. (PROTHERO, 2) Kerouac sought out Eastern philosophy after reading Thoreau (SUITER, 164; PROTHERO, 1) and fell in love with Goddard's *A Buddhist Bible*, (SUITER, 166) while Gary Snyder came to an interest in Zen through the works of D.T. Suzuki. (SUITER, 18)

Snyder, in particular, played a key role. His parents had

been part of the back to the land movement during the Depression, and he grew up on the edge of the forest and on the edge of poverty. (LANGFORD, 6-8) His outlook was shaped to a large degree by Ernest Thompson Seton's Woodcraft ideals: "The biggest probable childhood influence on me," he said, "was Ernest Thompson Seton and his book of Indian woodcrafts." (QUOTED AT LANGFORD, 10) Snyder saw in Seton a sort of revolutionary who changed "the myth of the white man" because he was "on the side of nature, on the side of the Indians, on the side of the unconscious, on the side of the primitive." (ALMON, 6-7)

This interest in Native America culture and woodcraft influenced both his poetry and his Zen – when he organized a meditation retreat in December 1958, he replaced the traditional *kinhin*, walking meditation, with a nighttime run through the woods, leaping over boulders and crashing through the undergrowth! (SUITER, 242)

When Snyder met Kerouac he introduced him to Zen – and hiking and camping and mountaineering. Inspired by Snyder's wilderness ways, Kerouac spent a summer as a fire lookout in the Cascades, a sort of mountain hermitage. (SUITER, 179, 198-204) His time there and his friendship with Snyder inspired Kerouac's 1958 novel *The Dharma Bums*, the book that first brought Buddhist ideas to prominence in American popular culture. (Closing part of the historical loop, on the day that *The Dharma Bums* was published, Kerouac visited D.T. Suzuki for an impromptu tea and haiku session. (FIELDS, 223))

While the Beats brought Buddhist, especially Zen, ideas to a new popularity, their practice was unconventional and idiosyncratic. (At least, at first: after his meeting with Kerouac, Gary Snyder went to Japan to study Zen, while in the 1970s Phillip Whalen became a bona fide Zen monk, and Ginsberg a student of the Tibetan lama Chögyam Trungpa – about whom we'll have more to say later.) Alan Watts teased out the relationship in a brilliant 1958 piece in the *Chicago Review* titled "Beat Zen, Square Zen, and Zen." He contrasted the lawless, subjective, sometimes overly self-conscious "beat Zen," with the "square Zen" of rigid discipline, "a quest for the *right* spiritual experience, for a *satori* which will receive the stamp (*inka*) of approved and established authority. There will even be a certificates to hang on the wall." He concluded that either path could work, as the true experience at the heart of Zen was robust enough to not be damaged by either sort of silliness. (WATTS, "BEAT

ZEN," 19-22)

While *The Dharma Bums* forever associated Kerouac with Zen in the pop-culture mind, he actually thought Zen overly harsh and was more drawn to a diffuse sort of Mahāyāna, centered around compassion. His alter-ego in *The Dharma Bums*, Ray Smith, identifies himself as "not a Zen Buddhist...an oldfashioned dreamy Hinayana coward of later Mahayanism," and says Zen is "*mean*....All those Zen masters throwing young kids in the mud because they can't answer their silly word questions." (KEROUAC, 13) Kerouac's insistence on the primacy of compassion is reflected in a passage where Smith describes a prayer he has created:

> "I sit down and say, and I run all my friends and relatives and enemies one by one in this, without entertaining any angers or gratitudes or anything, and I say, like 'Japhy Ryder, equally empty, equally to be loved, equally a coming Buddha,' then I run on, say to 'David O. Selznick, equally empty, equally to be loved, equally a coming Buddha' though I don't use names like David O. Selznick, just people I know because when I say the words 'equally a coming Buddha' I want to be thinking of their eyes, like you take Morley, his blue eyes behind those glasses, when you think 'equally a coming Buddha' you think of those eyes and you really do suddenly see the true secret serenity and the truth of his coming Buddhahood. Then you think of your enemy's eyes." (KEROUAC, 68-69)

Around the same time in the 1950s that Kerouac was helping bring Buddhism to popular culture, three young men in southern California – Gregory Hill, Kerry Thornley, and Bob Newport – were turning to yet another alternative to the cultural and religious mainstream: salvation through absolute nonsense. Inspired in part by an interest in Zen (BENARES, HANDFUL, 61) and its tales of lunatic masters who refused to behave respectably, they created Discordianism, a spoof religion that grew into an artistic/philosophical movement that eventually included the writers Camden Benares and Robert Anton Wilson.

The Discordians argue – and the seriousness of the

argument depends on the Discordian and on the circumstances – that Eris, the Greek goddess of discord and confusion, is the one true divine power in the universe. Eris is best known to students of mythology for her wedding gift of the golden apple inscribed "Kallisti" ("For the Prettiest One"): Hera, Aphrodite, and Athena squabbled over it – each claiming to be the "prettiest" – until their scheming ended up starting the Trojan War. (Note that in standard versions of the tale Eris gets the blame, but she wasn't one of the ones bribing the judge to win a beauty contest!)

The argument that Eris is the supreme being has some strong points – after all, *somebody* had to put all this chaos here! And any group raising a fuss about a Goddess back in the 1950s is noteworthy.

This "Non-prophet Irreligious Disorganization" has become the sacred clowns of the Pagan movement, the safety valve that helps protect it against "the Curse of Greyface" – the idea that life is Serious Business and that Order must be preserved above all. (ADLER, 328-334) At any sufficiently large Pagan event, you will hear someone yell "Hail Eris!" or "Kallisti!" – paying their respects to the forces of chaos.

The Discordian influence on the 1960s counter-culture is a strange, largely unexplored historical territory. In 1968 Robert Anton Wilson, an early convert to Discordianism and an editor at *Playboy*, conspired with Thornley to put a letter and answer into the *Playboy* Forum advancing the theory that the "Bavarian Illuminati" were behind the recent wave of political assassinations, (GORIGHTLY, 140) helping fuel the fad for conspiracy theories.

It has been also been claimed that the Discordians helped turn the "V" hand gesture from "V for victory" to the iconic "peace sign": they associated it, via Roman numerals, with the sacred number – sacred to Discordians, anyway – five (MALACLYPSE, 33). Of course, as this claim comes from Discordians, it should be taken with heaping amounts of salt.

The gesture was popularized in Japan in the 1970s, and now you'll see little old ladies getting their picture taken at Buddhist temples and Shinto shrines, flashing this Discordian symbol. Hail Eris, indeed!

But the oddest part of the tale belongs to the Discordian Society's co-founder Kerry Thornley. He served together with Lee Harvey Oswald in the Marine Corps; he found Oswald a fascinating character and, partly inspired by Oswald's defection to the USSR, started a novel, *The Idle Warriors*. (GORIGHTLY, 34, 37-38) This made Thornley the only author to write about Oswald *before* the JFK assassination and brought him to the attention of the Warren Commission and, later, of New Orleans D.A. Jim Garrison.

Some conspiracy theorists believe that Thornley might have been "second Oswald," or otherwise involved in the assassination. Sucked into the weirdness vortex, for a time he became a genuine paranoid. (GORIGHTLY, 192-204)

Such can be the risks of dealing with Eris. As Thornley later told Greg Hill, "[I]f I had realized that all of this was going to come *true*, I would have chosen Venus." (QUOTED AT ADLER, 336)

Another group that started out as a joke and took on an unexpected depth was the Reformed Druids of North America (RDNA), formed at Carleton College, Minnesota, in 1963. It was created as a humorous protest against a requirement for students to attend religious services and had no intention of being an actual alternative religion. Its members were mostly members of mainstream religions who just happened to have a certain sense of humor and an anti-authoritarian streak.

But to the surprise of its founders, the RDNA persisted after the requirement was lifted and eventually gave birth to the New Reformed Druids of North America, whose interest in Celtic ways took a definitely Pagan direction. Eventually, out of the NRDNA evolved Ár nDraíocht Féin (ADF), an influential Druid group founded by Issac Bonewits (ADLER, 321-326) that has done much to promote pre-Christian Celtic spirituality.

While the RDNA and the Discordians made up their own religions in the search for alternative ways of living, others made up entire worlds. In the 1960s, the best work of the science fiction and fantasy genres began to mature from pulp adventure tales to deeper explorations of cultures that never were – and in so doing cast a critical eye on our own society.

Tolkien's *Lord of the Rings*, published in a popular paperback edition in the U.S. in 1965, became a touchstone of the counter-culture. His "Middle Earth" was invented in the waning days of the First World War, and the Shire of his hobbits is a glorification of pastoral English village life. The hobbits ally with forest-dwelling elves, with dwarves who live under the mountains, and even with walking trees, to preserve their way of life against an enemy who embodies industrialization. Tolkien's work echoes the Romantic movement's elevation of the pastoral over the urban, and the widespread longing in post-World War I

England to return to a "simpler" time.

Ursula Le Guin's 1968 novel *A Wizard of Earthsea* gave readers a more human and sympathetic wizard than Tolkien's Gandalf.* Its hero, Ged, works toward balance and harmony rather than a military triumph of "good" over "evil".

Le Guin's work is influenced by her Taoist, feminist, and multi-cultural outlook. Besides the *Earthsea* fantasy novels, her notable works include *The Left Hand of Darkness*, which explores gender issues by imagining a race of people whose biological gender changes over time, and *The Dispossessed*, an ambiguously utopian novel about an anarchic society without rulers or property. Literary critic and theorist Robert Scholes has said that she "works not with a theology but with an ecology, a cosmology, a reverence for the universe as a self-regulating structure...it is a deeper view, closer to the great pre-Christian mythologies of this world."† (QUOTED AT ADLER, 562)

Robert A. Heinlein's 1961 novel *Stranger in a Strange Land* told the tale of a Valentine Michael Smith, a human being born on Mars and raised by the indigenous Martians. When he comes to Earth as a young adult, he brings the Martians' religious practices with him and founds the Church of All Worlds to spread them. Their practices include the ritual of "sharing water" – critical on a desert planet like Mars – and the notion of "grokking," knowing someone or something so deeply that observer and observed unite. Tim Zell (who later went by the name Oberon Zell-Ravenheart) and a few co-conspirators took the novel as inspiration and founded a real Church of All Worlds in 1968. (ADLER, 289-293)

In a more pop-culture vein, *Star Trek* (1966 to 1969) gave viewers the elfin-eared Vulcan Mr. Spock, who projected a logical detachment from destructive emotions while engaging in

---

* Knowledgeable readers of Tolkien know that Gandalf is actually an Istari, a being something like an angel in Tolkien's cosmology.

† *A Wizard of Earthsea* is perhaps my all time favorite novel, one of those "young adult" novels that a reader can return to decade after decade and discover more with each reading. I cannot recommend it highly enough. The recent television miniseries that claimed to be based on the *Earthsea* novels had little connection, and was disavowed by Le Guin. Its creators should be keel-hauled.

hypnotic, telepathic "mind melds" – a sort of Space Age Merlin to Kirk's King Arthur.

Star Trek's attitude toward religion was not one where gods fared well. In the (second) pilot episode "Where No Man Has Gone Before," after an encounter with a mysterious energy field a crew member starts to develop god-like powers, and Captain Kirk has to kill him. In a later episode, "Who Mourns for Adonais?", Kirk and the crew actually knock off Apollo, who turns out to be an alien being who visited Earth thousands of years ago. Several cultures have computers that the locals think of as being gods – Kirk short-circuits them or blows them up.

Even though military hierarchy is strictly maintained on the ship, *Star Trek* radically overthrew the cosmic hierarchy of the Judeo-Christian tradition, and gave us something more in the Greco-Roman style: men (and women and Vulcans) who can strive with gods.

The overlap between science fiction fandom and the Pagan movement remains strong to this day: both are cultures that respect bold imagination.*

But an even stranger contributor to the counter-culture than science fiction was the experience and the visions of "psychonauts" who experimented with the "psychedelics" or "entheogens" peyote, mescaline, LSD and psilocybin.

Peyote is an ancient ceremonial intoxicant of Native American cultures, whose use was promoted by Havelock Ellis as early as the 1890s. (STEVENS, 7) The main active alkaloid, mescaline, was isolated in the 1890s, synthesized in the 1910s, and popularized by Aldous Huxley in his 1954 book *The Doors of Perception*. (STEVENS, 49) Peyote and mescaline were popular with the Beats; Ginsberg's poem "Howl" was partially inspired by a 1955 peyote vision. (STEVENS, 113)

Psilocybin, as found in "magic mushrooms," is another ancient psychedelic. It was used in Native American cultures, and popularized by Timothy Leary starting in 1960. (STEVENS, 122, 136) It also makes a lightly fictionalized appearance as the "*moksha-*

---

* Of course, then there's that other religion that came out of science fiction: Scientology. Which shows the danger of taking suspension of disbelief too far. Really, "body thetans" resulting from frozen aliens being dropped into volcanoes and blown up with H-bombs?

medicine" in Huxley's last novel, *Island*. Published in 1962 and informed by his experience with psychedelics as well as decades of thought on education, psychology, art, the nature of creativity, and metaphysics, *Island* is Huxley's utopian counterpoint to his *Brave New World*, his attempt to portray a radically sane society. (STEVENS, 141) It was a book that many in the psychedelic movement cited, (STEVENS, 184, 193) though how much they actually understood and absorbed from it is questionable.

But it was LSD, first created by Albert Hoffman in 1943, (STEVENS, 4) that made the movement. By 1959 LSD was being used by psychotherapists, and got a lot of attention when it was used by high-priced Beverly Hills therapists treating celebrities like Cary Grant. (STEVENS, 65)

By 1962, Leary had gotten ahold of LSD (STEVENS, 163) – or it had gotten ahold of him – and the avalanche began.

The experiences of the psychonauts were often similar to the states of mind described in some forms of Hinduism and in esoteric styles of Buddhism. This inspired a great deal of interest in these forms of Eastern philosophy. Huxley and Leary, for example, both had a fascination with the *Bardo Thodol*, the *Tibetan Book of the Dead*. (STEVENS, 186) Leary's research partner Richard Alpert went to India to study Hinduism and became a convert, changing his name to Ram Dass. Images of Hindu and Tibetan deities became prominent in the psychedelic subculture. (STEVENS, 350)

The same deities, in different masks, can be found in Japanese Buddhism, even in Zen. But unlike the psychedelic movement, Zen had always taught that visions – whether of heavenly pleasure-realms or of agonizing hells – that arose during meditation were to be let go of without attachment. (FIELDS, 250) It was a system grounded enough to be neither much excited nor disturbed by all the psychedelic hubbub.

But that is not to say it stayed apart. Zen and the psychedelic movement came together in 1967 at the first "Human Be-In" in San Francisco. Gary Snyder read his poems, and Zen master Shunryu Suzuki, who had come to the U.S. to spread the Sōtō school of Zen, made an appearance, mutely holding up a single flower. Allen Ginsberg chanted the Prajñāpāramitā (Heart) Sutra. (FIELDS, 249) Richard Alpert and Timothy Leary were there; Leary spoke about getting humans out of cities and back to a tribal or village organization, and urged the crowd to tune in, turn on, and drop out. (STEVENS, 331)

Shortly after the Be-In, the San Francisco *Oracle* (Haight-

Ashbury's underground newspaper) gathered Leary, Ginsberg, Snyder, and Alan Watts for a discussion of what it all meant. Leary saw humanity splitting into two cultures, one organized as a dehumanized anthill or beehive while the drop-outs formed an independent tribal society. Watts resolved to be a bridge-builder between the anxious "squares" and the "drop-outs."

But Snyder looked forward to a long-term social evolution: "The children of the ants are going to be tribal people....We're going to get the kids, and it's going to take about three generations." In his view the psychedelic movement was merely an acceleration of a trend away from the consumer society and toward something more contemplative. (STEVENS, 331-333)

By this point, the alert reader may have noticed something about the historical characters mentioned: very few women. Perhaps this made the final contributor to the countercultural melange more wild and way-out than even science fiction or psychedelic visions. Feminism – the idea that the half of the human race that had been largely ignored for most of history might, just might, be worthy of equal respect and have some worthwhile ideas to contribute – finally started to gain traction in the 1960s.

The ritual magic tradition of the Golden Dawn had been open to women on an equal basis, and Gardner's Wicca continued that and went further. It made Goddess imagery more prominent, and redeemed the term "witch" from the picture of the wicked old crone to a wise practitioner of an ancient craft. (In Gardner's usage, "witch" is a gender-neutral word.)

Some American feminists seized on the myth of the witch, and especially the notion of the "burning times": the idea (from the inaccurate theories of Margaret Murray) that millions of women in Europe had been executed for practicing a pre-Christian religion. Witches became heroes to many in the women's movement.

For example, from the 1968 manifesto of WITCH (the "Women's International Terrorist Conspiracy from Hell," though the meaning of the acronym changed many times): "Witches have always been women who dared to be: groovy, courageous, aggressive, intelligent, nonconformist, explorative, curious, independent, sexually liberated, revolutionary. (This possibly explains why nine million of them have been burned.)" (ADLER, 179)

Feminism and American Paganism have become so closely related that the 1996 edition of Margot Adler's *Drawing Down the*

Moon – the best general book extant on the Pagan movement – is labeled by its publisher as belonging under two categories, "Religion" and "Women's Studies."

So this was the environment of the late 1960s: the anti-war, feminist, anti-racist, and ecological movements, all simmering together with a heaping helping of sex, drugs, and rock and roll.

Gardnerian Wicca had started to leak into the U.S. via books during the 1950s, but it officially came over when Rosemary and Ray Buckland founded a Gardnerian coven in 1964. (ADLER, 118) This pro-nature, goddess-oriented, anti-dogmatic religion proved to be highly compatible with the counter-culture.

More, its claim of ancient origin was likely comforting to many who felt adrift – what better response to critics who charged that the counter-culture had "no respect for tradition," than to adopt a religious tradition that claimed to pre-date that of the critics?

Wicca was like a seed crystal dropped into this supersaturated environment. A new sort of religious or spiritual movement crystallized around it, including it but taking many elements also from the surrounding solution.

It was Kerry Thornley, co-founder of the Discordian Society, and Tim Zell, of the Church of All Worlds, who gave the new thing a name. Thornley had joined Kerista, "a sexually swinging psychedelic tribe," and wrote in the group's newspaper, *Kerista Swinger*, "[L]et us look at the jobs of the far less intellectual, but far more constructively functional religions of old. These were the 'pagan' religions – the religions that survive to this day in England and the United States as 'witchcraft.'" (ADLER, 294; GORIGHTLY 73)

Margot Adler credits this as the first use in the U.S. of "Pagan" to describe past and present nature religions. (ADLER, 294) (For the record, Thornley said his influence on the movement had been exaggerated. (GORIGHTLY, 227)) Tim Zell picked up Thornley's use of the word, and by 1968 was spreading it in the Church of All Worlds newsletter, *Green Egg*. (ADLER, 289-295)

And from there, we have a Pagan movement.

The Way of the Kami

The small city of Nara, about fifteen miles from Kyoto, was Japan's first permanent capital. (Prior to that, the capital was moved with every new Emperor.) It contains an amazing eight UNESCO World Heritage sites, and dozens of places and objects designated National Treasures by the Japanese government.

In less than an hour you can walk from one World Heritage site, the Daibutsu at Tōdai-ji temple, one of the largest bronze statues in the world; through Nara Park with its sacred deer and stone lanterns; to another World Heritage site, the Kasuga Grand Shrine, one of the preeminent Shintō shrines; and then a little further on, at Shin Yakushi-ji, the "new" Medicine Buddha temple – "new" in the sense that it was built in 747 CE, as opposed to the Yakushi-ji founded in 680 – you can see the designated National Treasures there, the statues of the Medicine Buddha and the "Twelve Divine Generals" that drive disease out of the body.

For someone interested in the spirituality of Japan, Nara is a must-see, and I've managed to visit several times. When I saw that the National Museum there was going to have an exhibit on "Shintō Gods and Buddhist Deities," about religious syncretism in Japanese art, I knew I would have to check it out.

Buddhism was first introduced to Japan in 577 (BAYS, 90), but at first did not have much influence on the worship of *kami*, the spirits and deities of the native religion, Shintō. It was not until the Nara period (710-784) that Buddhism was emphasized by the state, as part of an effort to emulate Chinese culture and government. To make it more palatable to the people, efforts were made to incorporate kami worship into Buddhism. This began a syncretism that combined Buddhist deities with the kami of Shintō. (NARA NATIONAL MUSEUM, 333)

Statues were never made of the kami before this point, but the practice was adopted from Buddhism during the Nara and Heian periods (784-1185). (Interestingly, Buddhist art did not make representations of the Buddha until it picked up the practice of making religious statues from the Greek culture spread by the armies of Alexander (FIELDS, 16) – so in making statues of the kami, followers of Shintō were adopting an ancient Greek religious practice!)

Some kami were said to venerate Buddhism, and so many statues portrayed the kami as Buddhist monks, or as Buddhist or Taoist deities. (NARA NATIONAL MUSEUM, 331) It is another wonderful example of the way in which Japan has managed to take foreign influences and turn them into something uniquely Japanese.

Inspired by the exhibit, I decided to pay a visit to the Kasuga shrine, a major center of Shintō. I'd learned, at the museum, that this was regarded as one of the places the kami were said to have come to Earth, so – why not? I'd walked by it before, but this time I paid the small admission fee to actually enter the shine area, or at least the part of it open to tourists and worshipers. Like most large Shintō shrines, the inner sanctum is not open to ordinary visitors. Still, what I saw was pretty.

Afterward, I decided to walk back over into the hills behind the shrine a bit, just to enjoy the woods. Here I had a most amazing "coincidental" meeting.

As I walked up the path, I heard the music of a high-pitched flute (not the mellow *shakuhachi* with which I was familiar, but something much more penetrating) from up the hill a bit. Following the direction of the sounds, I came to a small side shrine where I found a Japanese gentleman talking about Shintō to a family of American tourists (who, as it turned out, were from my home state of Maryland).

This gentleman, "Kaz," turned out to be a Shintō priest.[*] He had been playing the *ryūteki*, "dragon flute," which had attracted us. We were very fortunate to meet a Shintō priest who had lived in the U.S. for several years and knew our language and culture, and who had both the desire and ability to explain his religion to us.

Kaz gave us all a little lesson in basic Shintō ideas – the most important of which, he said, was gratitude to the kami. He taught us the simple but precise bowing ritual by which this gratitude is expressed. It's just three bows and two hand claps, but each movement has to be just so. And the pauses, the stillnesses, are very important – these are the spaces where the

---

[*] Showing the self-effacement that is so valued in Japanese culture, Kaz has asked me not to use his full name here. I am extremely grateful to him for the time he spent with me, his openness, and his patience with me (despite my errors of etiquette).

divine can enter.

The sun was going down soon, and the tourist family had to be on their way. Kaz and I talked a bit longer, and he graciously agreed to meet me a few weeks later to talk more about Shintō.

* * *

Shintō, Japan's native religion, is important to the themes we're exploring for several reasons. Not only is it an ancient nature-centered religion that has survived in an industrial culture, but it occupies a special position in the Paleolithic/Neolithic dynamic that we've discussed.

Some of Shintō's roots go back several thousand years to the Jōmon people, (SHIMAZONO, 281; SHIVELY 329, 358) a culture right on the cusp of the Neolithic transformation. Until the end of the Jōmon period and the start of the Yayoi, around 400 or 300 BCE, Japanese culture evolved without the influence of large-scale crop cultivation (VARLEY, 2-5) – the "mandala" of farming culture, in Joseph Campbell's conception. (CAMPBELL, 130, 140-143, 151-153) Some of the Jōmon culture's shamanic approach to religion still comes through in contemporary Shintō.

According to Shintō Grand Master Motohisa Yamakage,

> Shinto, then, has no founder, no doctrine, no commandments, no idols, and no organization. What it does have are ambiguous characteristics like sympathy and silent experience. This is the very reason why it has often been considered a non-religion by Japanese scholars as well as foreign intellectuals. Japan's unique historical circumstances and cultural background explain the development of Shinto at the intuitive rather than overtly intellectually level. (YAMAKAGE, 51)

The "ambiguous characteristics" that Yamakage mentions are those found in contemplation of the natural world, and are just what is so badly needed today. These internal experiences are hard to express in words but are much more satisfactory to basic human needs than the doctrines of more organized and dogmatic religions.

Shintō shrines do not hold regular devotional services. Unlike churches or synagogues or mosques, they are not built around a meeting hall. While people congregate for festivals and celebrations, and there may be special rituals conducted for a group, most of the time adherents visit to pray individually or with a few friends or family members. There's no Shintō equivalent of a Catholic mass.

If you ask several Shintōists about their beliefs you will get widely varying answers. (In this if in nothing else, it has something in common with the Pagan movement!) Jean Herbert of the University of Geneva was one of the few Westerners so far to make a deep study of Shintō: he noted, "I met over one thousand Shinto priests and Shintoists, and I never heard the same words from each of them. In Shinto, people don't talk in the same pattern. They neither need nor are obligated to talk in the same fashion." (QUOTED AT YAMAKAGE, 40)

Yet he continues (again, in a manner reminiscent of Paganism), "...when I linked everybody's sayings together, I can see one philosophy and one set of philosophical principles emerging. We cannot say, then, that Shinto is underdeveloped."
(QUOTED AT YAMAKAGE, 41)

Shintō has influenced and has been influenced by Japanese Buddhism, having (mostly) peacefully co-existed with it since the sixth century. There are often small Shintō shrines on the grounds of Buddhist temples, and during the New Year's celebration you can see many people at Buddhist temples carrying *hama-ya* (sacred arrow) talismans that they just obtained at the local Shintō shrine.

Writing, and thus history, came relatively late to Japan, and was brought over by the same Chinese and Korean envoys who brought Buddhism, Taoism, and Confucianism. Because of this there is little historical record of what Shintō looked like before the influence of these foreign religions. But for them to have become as well-mixed as they did, there must have been remarkable compatibility right from the start.

Over the centuries, Shintō did develop organization, elaborate rituals, and a priestly class. This organized form is often called "Shrine Shintō." And in the nineteenth century, in the wake of Perry's "Black Ships" steaming into Tokyo Bay and forcing Japanese ports open to U.S. trade, leaders who sought to strengthen Japan turned religion to political ends and developed "State Shintō." This is when the role of the Emperor changed from a sort of high priest to a supposed living god. This aberration would last for several generations, coming to a head seven decades later as the U.S. and Japan struggled for control of the Pacific, leading to the U.S. embargo of Japan, the attack on Pearl Harbor, the horrors of the Pacific theater of World War II, and the first atomic bombings. It is most unfortunate that in the minds of many people these are the associations that Shintō carries, even though they represent a small and distorted fraction of its long history.

Fortunately "Ko Shintō," ancient Shintō, has survived in folkways and in family traditions, and seems to be making something of a comeback.

* * *

A few weeks after our first meeting, Kaz and I met again, and he was kind enough to try to explain some Shintō concepts to me. Our discussion was free-flowing, rather than in the form of a question and answer interview. But I have tried to take from our talk some excerpts that illustrate one practitioner's ideas of Shintō. Please note that Kaz's fluency in English is truly excellent. Because of the subtlety of the topics under discussion, I did not want to risk introducing distortion, and so have done less cleaning up than would normally be done in a transcript.

On the role of intellect: "You don't need any knowledge to practice Shintōism. Kami is inside you. They don't have the words. From the beginning there's no human words. Then humans became so intelligent, that they want to know. They want to practice."

On religious universalism: "Taoism [can] get along very well with Shintōism, I believe, because they have the same concepts. Great teachers in history, they say the same thing, in different words."

On ethical teachings: "Shintōism doesn't have commandments. But Shintōism has pointers. It's Shin-tō-ism – the 'tō', 'way'.* But it's up to you if you go that way or if you go the other way. But if you are against the law of nature, or the kami, you will be notified by harsh situations."

Q: *When you were a child, were you taught about Shintō?*

---

* "Tō" is another pronunciation of "dō," meaning "way," "road," or "path" – as in jūdō, the "soft way" or "gentle way." It is the same character pronounced "Tao" in Chinese.

A: "It's part of your life. People don't recognize Shintō because it's part of their own culture. So we...nowadays, we're so influenced by foreign stuff, especially Western culture, and even the parents cannot teach the children at home. The way you behave, the things you say, the mannerisms, it's all part of Shintōism in this country. But they don't discern it as Shintōism. If it's part of your life, you don't have to say it's Shintōism every time.

"The word Shintōism, or Shintō, is quite new, compared with the length of the existence of Shintōism, which is more than 10,000 years at least. It's part of everyday life."

Q: *Do you talk to children about kami [to teach them about Shintō]? Or is it just sort of, "do things this way"?*

A: "I had a chance to talk with students who were visiting Kasuga Taisho [Grand Shrine]... I play [my] flute, they hear it at a distance, they come over, they ask me what the instrument is, and I say this is this, this is that, and I started talking about shrines, and Shintōism, so that they can have some familiarity. Instead of preaching, they don't want to [be] preach[ed at]. They are curious, too, inside their mind... [T]he [Japanese] constitution prohibits, in a public place, to teach Shintōism. They consider it as a religion."

Q: *You think that a lot was lost, building up for the wars?*

A: "They abused Shintōism. To control the people. The people become very allergic to anything religious, anything which has the looks of religion. Though they want the spiritual work, spiritual guidelines, they cannot trust anything. They are lost.

"But now there's a [revival] movement. I feel that they want to practice, they want to regain confidence [in] the Japanese [way]."

On magic and ego: "[If you reach the point where] you almost completely understand who you are, what's your mission in life, then you start your second life. That's when you become totally harmonized with the natural force, and then many things come easily to you. Because you are working on your spiritual mission, [your] true mission, so the kami is behind you. Once you become spiritually aligned, you are part of nature. In an extreme sense, you become a magician, a person who commands nature to give you what you want. But until you reach that part, you go through your ego-created life. But once your ego gives in to your spirit, then you become the true you."

On Shintō and Buddhism: "Kami and *hotoke*, or Buddhism, are two sides of the same coin in this country. Buddhas [are] figures of sacred existence. The other side, that's kami. That's probably a created concept, but it has some truth in it. Kami doesn't have any personalized figure. It's so hard to grasp what kami is, because it's just a natural force. So, Buddhism came to Japan, helped the Japanese understand what the natural force is, through the personalized figure."

On the popularity of Christian-style wedding ceremonies in Japan: "[For] one day, they become Christian...I used to laugh at them, for being just one-day Christians. But if I look a different way, they are so open-minded about religion. They can believe in god in Christianity, they can believe in god in Judaism, it doesn't bother them. I feel that Shintōism contains the concept, 'respect everything'.... Anything which believes in only one god, their god, that's very narrow minded. It causes war or conflict.... 'If I'm right, you're wrong', 'This, or that.' But in Shintōism, 'this, and that, and that.'"

On freedom of religion and the role of the Emperor: "Shintōism is not a religion. But if I call it religion, separation of religion and politics creates a fundamental disruption in the Japanese political system. Because religious ceremony, or the belief in kami, was part of the political system. When Japan formed a single nation, in this place, Nara, we call this *Yamato*... Yamato stands for the origin of Japan, Japan as a country...So when they started it as *Yamato Chotei*, Yamato government, the political system was based on the Chinese system.... Back then, every political activity was kami-centered. So that they tried to be harmonized with the kami's mind, which is nature's mind... The emperor was the head priest, who connected the populace, ordinary people, with kami. That was the emperor's main function...[a] figure of authority, not power. The Emperor didn't really have power. They [only] apparently have power... Now, today, it's written into the Constitution that the Emperor is a symbol of the Japanese people. But in a way, it was the same back then. Because authority lasts forever, but power does not."

On *harai* (spiritual purification) and awareness: "[If you can say] 'Oh, I'm honest, trust me,' this means you are part dishonest – you realize you are dishonest, right? People [who are] completely honest are in an absolute situation, [they have] nothing to compare with. That's why they don't realize they are honest, themselves.... On the other hand, if [someone says], 'Oh,

I'm so selfish,' the person has realized what generous mind is....
[When] people say 'I'm sorry, I'm so self-centered' or 'I'm so
arrogant' – now, you are healed, I say, because you know, you've
felt the other side. All that person has to do is increase that part.
[But] 'Oh, I'm so kind', those people who keep saying that...that
person is yet to grow. They haven't identified the problem.

"Awareness [relates to] Shintō purification and cleansing
[rituals]. Purification and cleansing does not only mean your
physical body, it also means your spirit, the mind, the way you
think. Harai means cleansing, it's the closest translation I can
think of.... Harai is like, wash with divine force. Wash yourself.
But it also means – it means many things – it means awareness.
Awareness of your misaligned consciousness. Without awareness
of your misalignment, you never be cleansed. People have
awareness, [they think] 'yeah, I'm doing wrong'. But many
people disregard it, because of their pride. Because they care
about the way they look, or stupid egoistic mind which bothers
them. That's why they try to maintain the status quo, who they
are, the way they have been – which is twisted. But true
cleansing, in this sense, occurs, when you have awareness and re-
align yourself. That's the complete cleansing....awareness alone is
not enough, doesn't suffice. Awareness, and re-alignment."

On strictness of ritual: "Shintōism doesn't associate with
the painful rituals...it detests the painful *shugyō* [training] which
harms your body. The physical body is so important to your
mission.... However, Shintōism asks, requires, strictness in
following the procedure. Strictness of you being aligned with
nature. If you are off a bit, you come back to it again. But it
doesn't have to be painful. You may feel pain in doing that again,
over and over, but doesn't involve physical pain.... Damaging
your body is against nature."

On this life versus the afterlife: "After you die you become
completely consciousness, pure energy. And energy [beings go]
to where they are comfortable. It's like a law of physics: same
vibrations attract same vibrations. So after you're dead you go to
the absolute world....You get together with other spirits with
similar ideas. They cannot teach each other.

"Here, we have teachers, masters, as well as people who
are [ignorant...the ignorant can realize that others know more]
and they get the teaching. That's the advantage of this mixed up
third-dimensional physical world. After you die, you're pure
energy, you go to where you belong to. Where it takes them long,

long time before they get awareness....Your personal spiritual growth is much faster in this third-dimensional world, because you can meet the person who otherwise you wouldn't be able to see, to get their teaching."

On the role of Buddhism: "When I look at the Japanese [Buddhist] monks' value.... They are here to take care of those lost spirits. Shintōism wasn't very interested in the lost spirits. They assume every ancestor who's dead becomes kami.

"Sometimes kami can get lost, and those kami who get lost, become kami who do a rampage in this world, cause disasters or accidents. They call that *magatsu* kami.... Magatsu means "twisted." I think when the Buddhist monks were brought in, imported from China to Nara, they probably found their way to survive in Japan by taking care of magatsu spirits."

Kaz also tried to explain to me some of the esoteric aspects of the prayer ritual he had taught me when we first met. "Nature, or anything outside of your consciousness, is a mirror of yourself, of your mind. That reflects what you are, who you are, what you're thinking about in your mind. Sometimes you see trees and mountains and animals, and say they look happy, they are so cheerful – when you are cheerful and happy. But when you lost your girlfriend, and become so sad, everything looks so dark and sad. That's a reflection of your mind, because they are neutral...just they way they are. But we interpret – 'oh, this tree looks sad.' Anything outside of you, perceived by the [senses], through your mind, and you interpret it. Even the way people say [things] – when you're angry, anything people say sounds angry. And you react to that, instead of respond. In Shintōism, nature is considered the mirror."

The basic Shintō prayer ritual that Kaz taught me involved bowing and clapping the hands. Usually it's said that the bowing is to show respect, and clapping the hands is to "wake up" the kami. But Kaz had a deeper, very lovely interpretation. Part of this was based on a relationship between the elements of fire and water and a correspondence with left and right, respectively. *Hidari*, "left," contains the word *hi*, which can mean fire, and *migi*, "right," contains *mi*, as in *mizu*, "water." The character *hi* can also be read as *ka* – thus in the left and right hands coming together there is fire and water meeting, and the syllables *ka-mi*.

"[Clapping hands] is lateral movement, lateral greeting. Bowing is longitudinal. It's a cross. Anything on this earth is a thread: to make a surface, or something you can see, [it has to be composed of horizontal and vertical threads]. So bowing this way, clapping this way, we are making the nature, representing nature.

"If you put water...on the ground...[it] spreads [horizontally]. Fire goes [vertically]. Water, fire. Ka-mi. Everything you would try to express, the basic elements of the universe with your true body. That's Shintōism.

"...Showing the nature, or trying to be the nature – at the same time, your mind is nothing but gratitude. Thank you. Thank you. Thank you. While I'm living as a human being, I can learn the lesson quickly and grow quickly. Thank you so much, to the nature. That's Japanese ancient wisdom."

* * *

A few weeks later, I had wonderful opportunity to observe Kaz teaching a harai ritual to group of acolytes. The instruction was all about the details of the ritual, and not at all (so far as I could tell from my limited understanding) about belief, dogma, or catechism.

In an e-mail message to me, Kaz explained the importance of harai:

> Lastly, the core of the Shintoism is "harae" or "harai" that is simply translated as "purification" or "cleansing" in English; however, "harae" or "harai" means more than that in Japanese, especially in a view of spirits of language. All of my Shinto teachers said, "Shinto begins with harai and ends with harai." Please do keep the following in your mind, "harai" refers awareness inside you that you are off the "way" that is a way to Kami's heart or essence. Well-established individuals often demonstrate their spirituality of "harai" devoid of his/her ego or selfishness. Often they listen to what others want to say sincerely, I mean "truly" sincerely. Most people do not have this attitude. This is an important key to "harai". Enough said about the concept in English. Please do experience or feel it yourself to get the wisdom.

And this, perhaps, is the most useful and valuable lesson that Shintō has for us. For a durable spiritual path, one that can last for thousands of years, what is needed is not belief or dogma, but a sincere practice that helps people experience personal transformation.

Why Buddha Touched the Earth

A statue of Jizō, in Minō, Ōsaka, Japan

There's one character in Japanese Buddhism who is perhaps seen more frequently than Daruma (Bodhidharma) or Kannon (the Japanese name for Kuan Yin) – maybe even more than the Buddha himself, depending on how you count. His name is Jizō, and he is a special guardian of children (and therefore also of expectant or hopeful mothers), of firefighters, and of travelers. Because of his association with travelers, Jizō statues are often found along the road, out in the open rather than cooped up in temples. It's helped make him a very accessible deity.

Jizō watches over those traveling not just earthly roads, but all the paths through the "six realms" of existence, especially hell realms.

The idea of hells doesn't seem to be part of the Buddha's original teachings. While he used the Hindu concept of reincarnation as a teaching tool, the Buddha didn't have much to say about the afterlife: it wasn't relevant or helpful to his goal of relieving human suffering. And notions of an afterlife don't mesh all that well with the ideas of anātman and śūnyatā, "no-self" and "emptiness." If the "self" is an illusion, if "I" am a character in the story my mind is telling, what is there to live on in a heaven or to be reborn?

But Mahāyāna Buddhism never met an idea, myth, or metaphor that it didn't like. In the centuries after the Buddha's death, Mahāyāna teachers and adherents began to include and adapt their cultures' notions of reincarnation into their versions of Buddhism. After a while, the view evolved that there were six paths of reincarnation to which a person might be subjected. One might be reborn in the pleasure realms of the gods, or as a "titan" (or "wrathful demigod"), as a human, as an animal, as a "hungry ghost," or into a hell realm. But none of these are permanent. The pleasure realms are a stagnating gilded cage that eventually breaks open, the hells a temporary sentence.

Jizō's great vow is that he will not enter Nirvana so long as any being is in hell – an "I am not free so long as any man is enslaved" sort of sentiment. He descends into the hell realms to aid and comfort and teach the dammed. In the Mahāyāna mythology, no sentient being will be thrown away, no one is left behind. With bodhisattvas like Jizō guiding us, we all make it to enlightenment, though it might take billions of years. It's a lovely thought.

Jizō's association with firefighters stems fairly straightforwardly from his mission to descend into hell realms and rescue those in need. Surprisingly, his connection with children also comes from a hell myth, one about the afterlife of children who die young. According to the legend the spirits of these children are stuck on the banks of the river Sai, a sort of Buddhist version of the river Styx. Since they died young they had no opportunity to accumulate enough merit to move on, and so they are condemned to stay on the riverbank and pile up stones to build little stūpas, which are knocked down by demons every evening. Only Jizō offers them protection and aid. (BAYS, 63)

Because of this association with children who have died, there is a common memorial ritual of clothing Jizō statues in bibs or other children's clothes, or leaving toys or other items with a statue. Seeing these offerings at roadside Jizō shines has moved me to tears more than once.

Jizō is not an invention of Japanese Buddhism; he goes all the way back to India, where she was known as Kṣitigarbha. No, that's not a typo; a gender change occurred during her/his migration. It's not unprecedented: the male bodhisattva Avalokiteśvara became the goddess Kuan Yin in China. Kṣitigarbha was definitely female, while Jizō is mostly – but not exclusively (BAYS, 81-82) – portrayed as male.

"Earth Store Bodhisattva"

But it seems that Jizō/Kṣitigarbha never made as much of a splash on the Asian mainland as he/she did here in Japan. (His success in Japan might be due to his association with the dead, as Buddhism first found its way into Japanese culture by providing rituals relating to death and the afterlife.) So I hadn't heard of Jizō until my first visit, and even then all I learned was that he was a Buddhist figure seen as a guardian of children.

My ignorance turned out to be ironic.

For about 15 years, I've had a Buddhist wall hanging that I bought from a vendor in the parking lot at a Grateful Dead show. I was told at the time that the Chinese characters in an upper corner read "Earth Buddha."

As someone interested in both Buddhism and in Earth-oriented Pagan religion, I thought that was pretty cool. This "Earth Buddha" was my first hint that there might be some deeper connection between Paganism and Buddhism.

When I had managed to teach myself a tiny bit about kanji, I tried looking up the characters that label this painting. Four characters: the first is indeed "earth," the last two were "bodhisattva" (or "bosatsu" in their Japanese reading). The second character, though, I couldn't quite figure out. Still, "Earth (mumble) Bodhisattva" was good enough.

There my knowledge stopped for a few years. But during a visit to the National Museum in Nara, I found a few Jizō statues on display. The exhibit mentioned Jizō's role as a guardian of travelers, and being a traveler far from home I set out to learn more about him.

I was particularly struck when I read that Jizō is portrayed carrying a monk's staff, which he uses to pry open the gates of hell, and a gem that lights the way. Hey, I thought, the "Earth Buddha" in my painting has a staff, and a sphere that might be a gem...

Then I took a look at the kanji for his name. Jizō Bosatsu means "Earth-Store" or "Earth-Womb" Bodhisattva. Yes, I'd had Jizō hanging on my wall all these years and not known it. (The depiction that I have is more of a Chinese style, so I don't feel too bad for not recognizing him/her right away in Japan.)

If the Earth Store Bodhisattva was just a Buddhist Earth spirit who protected the vulnerable, he/she would already be of interest to Pagans. But the story goes deeper.

According to the legendary accounts of the Buddha's enlightenment, as he sat in meditation, Siddhartha was challenged by the demon Māra, the lord of illusion. Māra tried tempting and threatening the Buddha, and when that failed Māra tried pressing an argument that the accolades of his army proved that he had a better claim of spiritual leadership than the solitary Buddha.

Here's how Buddhist scholar Paul Carus tells the story:

> Mara caused a whirlwind to blow, but in vain; he caused a rain-storm to come in order to drown the Buddha, but not a drop wetted his robes; he caused a shower of rocks to come down, but the rocks changed into bouquets; he caused a shower of weapons – swords, spears, and arrows – to rush against him, but they became celestial flowers; he caused a shower of live coals to come down from the sky, but they, too, fell down harmless. In the same way hot ashes, a shower of sand, and a shower of mud were transmuted into celestial ointments. At last he caused a darkness, but the darkness disappeared before Buddha, as the night vanishes before the sun. Mara shouted: "Siddhattha, arise from the seat. It does not belong to you. It belongs to me." Buddha replied: "Mara, you have not fulfilled the ten perfections. This seat does not belong to you, but to me, who have fulfilled the ten perfections." Mara denied Buddha's assertion and called upon his army as witnesses, while

> Buddha declared: "I have no animate witnesses present;" but, stretching out his right hand towards the mighty earth, he said: "Will you bear me witness?" And the mighty earth thundered: "I bear you witness." And Mara's elephant fell upon its knees, and all the followers of Mara fled away in all directions. When the hosts of the gods saw the army of Mara flee, they cried out: "Mara is defeated! Prince Siddhattha has conquered! Let us celebrate the victory!" (CARUS, 111-112)

This moment is a favorite subject of Buddhist art. Many sculptures and paintings depict the Buddha reaching down to touch and invoke the earth.

In Carus's version, the Buddha's witness is merely "the earth," without personification. But in other versions of the tale, the earth is represented by the goddess Prithivī. In the Lalitavistara, for example, the story goes that she rose up halfway out of the ground and testified to the purity of the Buddha. (SHAW, 17, 20)

Prithivī is an ancient goddess, long pre-dating Buddhism: she's mentioned in the Rig Veda, one of the oldest extant religious texts. She is the "Womb of the World," the "Source of Everything," "All Nourishing," "Mother of Plants." She is also proof against lies, "founded on truth" and cannot be deceived. (SHAW, 18) Certainly a good witness to have on your side.

Some scholars believe that the bodhisattva Kṣitigarbha developed out of Prithivī. (BAYS, 81; LEIGHTON, 222) And in the account of nineteenth-century Buddhist scholar Samuel Beal, it was Kṣitigarbha who testified for the Buddha. (GETTY, 90)

Let's ponder this for a moment. According to the mythology of Mahāyāna Buddhism, the Buddha's spiritual authority derives from an earth deity – an earth goddess, no less.

If we consider the connection between earth religions and agriculture, then it is not surprising and not by chance that in the mythical biographies, the young Buddha-to-be first experienced a state of meditation while watching the rituals of the spring plowing (BEAL, 73-74; HAHN OLD PATH, 45-48; WARREN 53-55).

Compare this connection to the earth with the Abrahamic religions. Jesus, Moses, and Mohammad all claimed the authority of the sky god (the "god of heaven") Jehovah. And in the classic

Greco-Roman pantheon, the chief of the gods is thunderbolt-hurling sky god Zeus/Jupiter. Even Shintō has as its foremost kami Amaterasu, a sun goddess. All sky religions, hierarchical and, except for Shintō, patriarchal.

But Buddhism is – at least by this bit of mythology – an earth religion! When challenged, when in doubt, the Buddha did not appeal to a higher power, but reached down for support.

But perhaps we're reading too much supernaturalism into it.

Another interpretation of the Buddha's touching the earth was suggested to me by my friend Eric Wiegmann, who spent several years as a monk in a Tibetan Buddhist tradition. As he discovered, after excessively long periods of meditation it's quite possible to become both mentally disoriented and physically dizzy. Can we imagine that Siddhartha was lightheaded, and just reached down to the ground to steady himself?

The comedian Steven Wright, known for expressing a wonderfully quirky off-center point of view, has a bit that goes "You know how it feels when you're leaning back on a chair, and you lean too far back, and you almost fall over backwards, but then you catch yourself at the last second? I feel like that all the time." (O'BRIEN) What if that's how the Buddha felt?

Meditation practitioners who overdo it can fall over – and not just physically. If you don't catch yourself it's possible to become detached and withdrawn, to lose track of your connection with the world. The Japanese even have a word for it: *Zenbyō*, "Zen sickness."

And then, rather than being a way of cutting through illusion, meditation becomes another attachment, another false escape which can be cured only by falling back to Earth. As the twentieth century Zen master Seung Sahn wrote, "So much sufferings [sic] in Nirvana castles. So joyous to sink into this world." (SAHN, TEACHING LETTERS, 217)

The Beatles song "Dear Prudence" is based on such a case, or at least what John Lennon, that old Zen Pagan, perceived to be one. Prudence Farrow, sister of the famous actress Mia Farrow, was training with the Maharishi Mahesh Yogi at the same time that the Beatles were. Farrow stayed secluded in her room meditating all the time, rather than interacting with the other students. In Lennon's words,

All the people around her were very worried

> because she was going insane. So we sang to her.
>
> They selected me and George to try and bring her out because she would trust us. She went completely mental. If she'd been in the West they would have put her away. We got her out of the house. She'd been locked in for three weeks and wouldn't come out, trying to reach God quicker than anybody else. That was the competition in Maharishi's camp: who was going to get cosmic first. (What I didn't know was I was already cosmic.) ^(BEATLES, 284)

To use an analogy, one of the greatest dangers that pilots of small aircraft face is getting lost in clouds such that they forget in which direction the ground lies. Could it be that as he sat under the Bo tree, Siddhartha was lost, in mental space rather than airspace, and put his hand down to the ground to re-orient himself?

In that moment, moving from total confusion to feeling the ground under him, he might have experienced an instant of the clarity that Zen calls *mushin*, "no mind. "* Joseph Campbell explains this "no mind" as follows:

> [W]e might say that when a situation or phenomenon evokes in us a *sense of existence* (instead of some reference to the possibility of an *assurance of meaning*) we have had an experience of this kind. The sense of existence evoked may be shallow or profound, more or less intense, according to our capacity or readiness; but even a brief shock (say, for example, when discovering the moon over city roofs or hearing a sharp bird cry at night) can yield an experience of the order of no-mind: that is to say, the poetical order, the order of art. When this occurs, our own reality-beyond-meaning is awakened (or perhaps better: we are

---

* Of course, "explaining" mushin is a hopeless, paradoxical, inherently contradictory thing to attempt!

awakened to our own reality-beyond-meaning)...One moment later, and we have classified the experience, and may be having utterable thoughts and describable feelings about it – thoughts and feelings that are in the public domain, and they will be either sentimental or profound, according to our education. But according to our life, we have had, for an instant, a sense of existence: a moment of unevaluated, unimpeded, lyric life – antecedent to both thought and feeling; such as never can be communicated by means of empirically verifiable propositions, but only suggested by art. (CAMPBELL, 186)

Imagine it this way: Siddhartha, dizzy and confused, even despairing a little bit. He's consulted the best spiritual teachers around, to no avail. He's starting to wonder if he's completely off-track. He's pushed his body to the limit, almost died, with nothing to show for it, and he's still recovering from that bad idea. With nothing else to go on, he meditates and meditates and meditates until he's chased himself in circles.

He starts to lose it. He gets dizzy and puts his hand down to steady himself. He feels the ground, the earth, the cool rich living soil under his hand, always supporting him and all beings, giving him orientation. The circle breaks, and he comes to, like a sleeper suddenly doused with cold water. Ah! Down is down, up is up. You can't fall off the earth. Nothing to fear. Here I am. So simple. Ah!

Ah!

A spiritual seeker, like an electrical circuit, must be well grounded in order to prevent dangerous currents from flowing. But from the ceremonial magic movement of the late 1800s and early 1900s, through the psychedelic movement of the 1960s, to today's "New Age" and "personal growth" movements, many people have lost that vital connection. Even, sadly, in parts of the supposedly Earth-centered Pagan movement, there are many who need a good solid grounding.

Let us then consider Jizō, Kṣitigarbha, or Prithivī – or, if you prefer, Gaia, Isis, or Astarte, the Earth spirit by whatever name – as a personification of that moment of clarity that comes from touching the earth, grounding away all delusion and self-doubt, knowing our intimate connection and oneness with the living planet.

If this was the power that the Buddha appealed to in his hour of need, then it ought to be good enough for the rest of us.

How Shall We Live?

One of the social perks of being an American in Japan is that many people want to practice their English on you. Strangers will come up and start conversations, buy you drinks or even dinner, just to chat.

You get to meet a wide cross-section of people this way. Usually it's just small-talk, "Hello," "Where are you from?", and so on. But one Osaka businessman gave me an interesting lesson in ethics along with a round of drinks.

I had come to a jazz club (called, charmingly, "Rugtime") to see my friend Eric's band play. Eric is a former Buddhist monk and acupuncturist, current elementary school vice-principal and drummer in several bands – one of the most interesting people I could ever hope to know. During a break he and I were chatting, and an older Nihonjin gentleman approached us and asked in (extremely good) English if he could buy us drinks. We of course readily assented.

We engaged in some of the usual small-talk, and our new friend asked us our impression of Osaka.

Osaka has a unique place in Japanese culture. It's known as the home of both gangsters and comedians, and for its unique dialect. It's the place where people cross the street against the light and park their bicycles right under the signs that say "No Bike Parking" – compared to other Japanese cities, that's wild behavior.

The city has always been a mercantile hub, and because its merchants were key to keeping the economy humming during the feudal era and the centuries of Japan's isolation, they were granted a little extra latitude. So Osaka never quite fell fully into line with the social norms enforced in Tokyo.

I tried to explain to this gentleman how I liked Osaka's energy, its hustle, its willingness to make a deal and get down to business.

His eyes lit up. "Yes, yes! Let's do business. Make everybody happy!"

The idea that a business transaction should leave everybody involved happy is something that we rarely hear these days, drowned out by talk of quarterly profits and shareholder value. But going deeper and considering not just the customer's satisfaction, but the effects of our business dealings on the broader world, we see what Dickens's ghostly character Jacob Marley learned only after his death and related to Ebenezer Scrooge: Mankind was his business.

In Buddhism, this is the concept of "right livelihood," a big part of the Buddha's ethical teachings.

To bring up the topic of ethics often makes us cringe. Most of us have been soaked in supernaturalist ethical systems that threaten or tantalize us with divine punishment or reward, either in this life or in an afterlife. And so once we get beyond the idea that God or Goddess is going to spank us if we are naughty or give us candy if we're good, we tend to tune out any deep ethical talk. We know that killing and stealing and the like are wrong, and we don't feel that we need to examine the topic much further.

For example, for ethical guidance many Pagans rely on some version of the Wiccan Rede: "An it harm none, do what ye will." But without deeply considering what does harm, and without a true understanding our will, the Rede doesn't offer much guidance.

And as Buddhism has entered the West, there has often been a focus on meditation and on theory, without much consideration of the fundamentals of ethical behavior. But without that consideration, Western Buddhism is in danger of becoming little more than a feel-good system of psychobabble.

Rather than being a set of divinely dictated rules, ethics – when done right – is a philosophical discipline that calls us to deeply contemplate the question, "How shall we live?" It asks us to consider the long-term and subtle consequences of our actions, on others and on ourselves, and is a necessary foundation for a spiritual life.

There are three elements of the Buddha's "Eightfold Path" that directly address ethics: right speech, right action, and right livelihood. In those spheres of activity – essentially, anything that involves our interactions with others – the Buddha called on us to refrain from what he thought were harmful and dangerous behaviors. The minimum recommendations are found in the "thou shalt nots" of the precepts, known in Pali as the *pansil* ("five practices"). Those who formally convert to Buddhism vow to undertake to refrain from:

1. taking life (generally understood to refer to harming others in general)
2. taking that which is not freely given
3. sexual misconduct (in some versions, to refrain more generally from "abuse of the senses")
4. false speech, and
5. using intoxicants that cloud the mind

Some Buddhists – especially those who grow up in a Buddhist culture – take a lawyerly approach to the pansil, looking for loopholes. This is a natural reaction if they are seen as rules imposed by outside authority. But if we understand them as foundational practices for personal development, then cheating the spirit of the pansil is only cheating oneself.

Toward this end, I sometimes think that the soul of the pansil can be summarized in two rules:

1. Don't make trouble.
2. Don't settle for cheap thrills.

The motivation here is not fear of some divine punishment, but the creation of conditions that aid our practice. After all, it's difficult to engage in self-cultivation when you've got the whole town chasing after you because you stole some jewelry, used it to try to seduce a beautiful woman, and then beat up her husband when he objected. The "trouble" that you make will almost certainly come back around.

(We do have to look carefully at the line between "making trouble," and revealing trouble that already exists. For example, the 1960s lunch counter sit-ins, so important to the civil rights movement, certainly were troublesome for staff and management of these facilities, not to mention people who just wanted a quiet lunch. But the peaceful protesters were not causing trouble – they were revealing the trouble that was created by segregation.*)

Even if you could get away with stealing, violence, and illicit seduction – if you could keep it secret, perhaps, or if you

---

* Or consider the myth of the golden apple: Eris's gift doesn't make the trouble, it reveals the trouble latent in the jealousies, and willingness to cheat, of Aphrodite, Athena, and Hera.

had a position of power that no one could challenge – the mental habits formed by such action are directly opposed to those we're trying to build, those that can liberate us from suffering. If we seek after the "cheap thrills" of mindless sex or drug use,* or the adrenaline rush of violence or theft, we're agitating the very mind we're trying to calm.

But does this mean denying pleasure? In the Magandiya Sutta, the Buddha used a telling metaphor to explain: imagine a man suffering from leprosy, who can obtain a little temporary relief from the suffering of his disease by scorching his skin over a fire. Then imagine that the leper is cured. If he now scorched himself, it would not bring any sort of pleasure or relief, but would be intensely painful. (NANAMOLI, 611)

We might also consider the way that sweet foods cloy the tongue, and make it difficult to enjoy the subtle flavors of food. When I was a child, I thought that when I grew up I would eat candy all the time, but instead I find that I enjoy food much more when sweets are a rarity.

Can we imagine that, having refined his perceptions, the Buddha could enjoy something simple like sitting and watching the sun set, as much as you or I might enjoy a night of carnal delights? Imagine the benefits – free admission, no hangover the next morning.

Besides laying down the "don'ts" of the pansil, the Buddha recommended that we strive to cultivate the virtues known as the *pāramitās*, or "perfections":

1. Generosity
2. Virtue, or uprightness
3. Patience, or tolerance
4. Diligence, or effort – "gumption," if you will
5. Contemplation, or meditation (Dhyana)
6. Transcendental wisdom, or insight (Prajñā)

However, the psychological impact of recommending abstract virtues is different from pointing out the concrete negative consequences of "bad" behaviors.

---

* Which is not to imply that all sex, or drug use, is mindless.

If you tell me that lying and cheating is liable to come back to bite me in the rear end, or that getting drunk every night will interfere with the meditation practice I'm trying to cultivate, you're appealing to my own self-interest, and may well get through. But if you suggest that I really ought to try to be more generous and patient and so on, it immediately sets up a contrarian thought in my mind: if I need to become more generous, patient, etcetera, then I suppose I must by nature be a person not possessed of these qualities, and so I don't feel like being one, and therefore to hell with the whole thing. It may not be a wise or sensible train of thought, but it is a very common reaction.

This is what Lao Tzu (or some other Taoist philosopher using his name) referred to when he wrote, "If we could renounce our benevolence and discard our righteousness, the people would again become filial and kindly." (LEGGE, 62) Many Taoist stories follow the theme of a Taoist sage gently chiding a Confucian for too much moralism.

Zen absorbed from its Taoist forebearers this skepticism about the usefulness of moral preaching. Hui Neng, the Sixth Patriarch, cut through the tangles of ethical dilemmas with the characteristic Zen directness when he challenged another monk, "When you do not think good and when you do not think not-good, what is your true self?" (QUOTED AT EKAI, 29) The Third Patriarch, Seng Ts'an, was even more radical, stating that "The conflict between right and wrong / Is the sickness of the mind." (QUOTED AT SMULLYAN, 108)

And a famous story about the Zen master Hakuin tells how he helped a samurai cut through – almost literally – the ethical muddle with a direct illustration. The story is told in many sources with many variations, so this is my own rendering:

> The samurai Nobushige came to Hakuin and said, "I have heard some Buddhist teachers say that there is a hell, and some say that there is not. Please, tell me, is there a hell?"
>
> The master looked at him with disdain. "What a fool you are to ask such a question! And they say you are a great warrior! Why, you look like a total buffoon to me!"

Outraged, Nobushige drew his sword. "Impudent monk! I'll have your head for such insults!"

As the warrior drew back his arm for the death blow, Hakuin looked him in the eye and calmly said, "This, is hell."

Nobushige stopped, understanding the master's lesson. He sheathed his sword, and bowed deeply.

"And this," said the master, "is heaven."

Just telling Nobushige "If you're not nice, you'll end up in a hell of your own making," would not be enough. A generous, patient, and compassionate heart cannot be cultivated by rules, nor by supernatural threats and promises. The Taoist/Zen approach, instead, calls on us to get past our small egos and recognize our oneness with the Universe – including our oneness with other sentient creatures.

The cultivation of compassion is recommended because it helps free us from our egos, from our limited sense of self. As the Chinese sage Hsieh Wen-Ching said,

> The reason why a man has thousands of troubles is because he clings to the idea of self: therefore, he schemes and contrives in ten thousand different ways. He alone wants to be rich, he alone wants to be honored, he alone wants to be easy, he alone wants to be happy, he alone wants to enjoy life, he alone wants to be blessed with longevity; and to others' poverty, misery, danger, or suffering, he is altogether indifferent. It is for this reason that the life-will of others is disregarded and Heaven's Reason neglected. Only be cured of the disease of egotism, and your heart will be broadened even to the vastness of infinite space, so that wealth, honor, happiness, comfort, health, longevity could all be enjoyed with others. And, then, the will to live will have its way, everything will

> have its natural longings satisfied, and Heaven's Reason will be displayed in an untold exuberance. (D.T. SUZUKI AND CARUS, 33)

We might summarize these ideas as a third point:

> 3. Try to do those things that bring out your compassionate and patient side.

The pāramitās, then, become less rules for behavior than signs that let us know when we're on the right track. Every human is a mix of enlightened and unenlightened ideas and behaviors, wise and selfish thoughts; our task is to decide which of the voices in our head to listen to, and which ones to politely thank for their input, but ultimately disregard.

So are these three principles enough? If we refrain from making trouble for others, if we avoid self-defeating cheap thrills, and if we continually try to open our hearts, will our behavior inevitably tend to the wise?

Well, no. There is one more thing required, a fourth principle – but one so fundamental that instead of numbering it fourth, I'm going to steal a trope from the science fiction of Isaac Asimov* and call it a Zeroth Rule of Ethics:

> 0. Get your facts and your thinking straight.

Much evil is done by those who think they're doing good work. The people who hanged the "witches" in Salem thought they were on the side of righteousness. In the pre-Civil War United States, many slave owners really believed that dark-skinned people were incapable of handling freedom and so slavery was in the best interests of the slave. Many terrorists and mass murderers are convinced that they are on the side of the angels.

To do right, you've got to think right, be an informed critical thinker.

But so often, organized religion works against this end,

---

* Asimov's *Robot* series of novels and short stories features his famous Three Laws of Robotics, which govern robots' behavior; later in the series, he introduces a "Zeroth Law" that has priority over even the First Law.

demanding that we disregard any information that conflicts with established dogma, and forbidding questioning or criticizing of ecclesiastical authority.

Transcendental love can take us beyond ethics, and transcendental wisdom can take us beyond reason. But to get *beyond* something, you must go *through* it. If you're going to put aside rules and rely on your own character, you'd better make sure your character is of exceeding quality first – as Bob Dylan put it, "To live outside the law, you must be honest."

Understanding that compassion is the means of getting beyond ourselves for spiritual growth, that ethical behavior is the way to cultivate compassion, and that critical thinking is a necessary component of ethics, we can and must reject any path that calls on us to substitute faith or the dictates of authority for reason or compassion. There's no shortcut, no way to avoid the necessity of thinking hard and living right.

How to Sit Down and Shut Up

It was in seventh grade, when I was eleven or twelve years old, that my English teacher Alan Reese introduced the class to what he called "breathing exercises." I can't remember if he was trying to get us to unleash our creative potential, or to get a bunch of rowdy kids to be quiet for a few minutes; perhaps a bit of both. But as I recall, the instructions were simple. Sit up straight, but don't strain or become stiff. Breathe slowly and deeply, all the way down into your belly as you breathe in through your nose, and then fully exhale. Count your breaths, up to eight, and then go back to one. Anything else that comes into your mind besides the breath and the count, let it go. If you lose count, start over again at one.

A few years later, in my karate class we received instruction in basic Zen meditation. Sit in the *seiza* kneeling position, back straight but not stiff, as if pushing up with the top of the head. Breathe fully and deeply, all the way down into the *hara*, the belly. Focus on the breath and let any other thoughts that arise come and go, neither clinging to nor avoiding them.

And I realized that in his "breathing exercises," Mr. Reese had snuck meditation practice in on us – and that it was not anything mysterious or esoteric, not the big deal it's sometimes portrayed.

Why meditate? Popular how-to books cite a number of benefits for various types of meditation, but from the perspective of Zen it's a dangerous distraction to speak of a goal or direction. If you set out with some goal, you will find it – you will do the same sort of mental filtering that makes the Law of Fives work, and will miss the experience of mindfulness.

Even to speak of mindfulness or direct insight can be saying too much, lest we attach to our ideas of these things rather than having an experience. This is why the Buddha held up that flower…

But on the other hand, we need some motivation to get started. The essence of Zen is direct insight into reality, seeing things as they are without surrounding them with mental constructions. Zen style meditation is nothing other than taking time to practice this perception. Gary Snyder calls it "spending quality time with your own mind," (SNYDER, 115) which I think is a wonderful summary. And the karate master and meditation teacher Tadashi Nakamura says, "Everyone takes it for granted that without fail we will cleanse our bodies daily, scrubbing this, grooming that. By the same token we should clean our minds regularly, letting go of that which we don't need so that that which has meaning can rise to the surface." (NAKAMURA, 2)

That's probably about as much as we can safely say about "why." But we can talk about "how," about technique, what to do with the body and the conscious mind, and so this will be our focus here.

We can divide the practice of meditation into four aspects: circumstances, posture, breathing, and cognition.

Circumstances

You don't need much to do *zazen*, seated meditation in the fashion of Zen. You don't need any esoteric knowledge or to memorize any prayers. You don't need a guru to give you a mantra. You don't need any sort of altar, or prayer beads, or a statue of the Buddha. If you like having these things around, knock yourself out, but they have no more to do with the core of Zen than a velvet Elvis does. You don't need special meditation cushions – if you use a posture where cushions are useful, the pillow you use beneath your head at night will do quite well, or you could fold a blanket or wad up some of your laundry.

All you need is the ability to breathe, and a few minutes of relative quiet without interruption.

The most important thing about zazen is to actually do it. Sitting for even five minutes every day and sticking with it, is going to be much more useful than that hour of meditation you intend to do each day, but "fall off the cushion" in the first week. We each have to find our own set of circumstances that will allow us to establish the habit.

"Full lotus"

For example, it seems that many Buddhist teachers are morning people. They are always talking about doing zazen first thing in the morning, getting up early to meditate before starting the work day. I tried several times to make this a habit, before finally accepting that I'm not a morning person, and that the snooze button would always win over zazen. I found that it was pointless to fight my own nature – which, after all, was the very thing I was supposed to be observing. It works far better for me to stay up a little later and sit before going to bed, than to try to commit to a morning meditation.

If you can do both morning and evening, wonderful. Some recommend the dinner hour, when, if you live in a large city, the bustle tends to slow after the homeward rush. Whichever time works best for you is fine.

Depending on the time you choose, you may want to turn off your phone. You might want to dim the lights, but it's not strictly necessary. If you live with other people, ask for their help in getting a few minutes of quiet. If you live with kids or animals, see to their needs before you try to sit.

Posture

Meditation can be done while sitting or standing or walking. Indeed, as the Zen arts such as *budō* (martial arts), *chadō* (the Way of Tea), *sumi-e* (ink painting), and *ikebana* (flower arranging) show, any task from swinging a sword to putting flowers in a vase can be approached meditatively. But isolating the core of the thing by seated practice can be very useful.

Seated practice can be done in one of the cross-legged positions, in the kneeling-like seiza position, or even sitting on a chair. Whichever is used, a seated meditation posture must be stable and balanced, so that muscular tension is not needed to stay upright. It must allow for proper breathing, with the belly able to move in and out. And it must not tend to put the meditator to sleep!

"Half lotus"

The classic cross-legged posture is the famous "lotus" position (*kekka fuza* in Japanese, *padmasana* in Sanskrit), where both feet are placed on the opposite thighs. The half-lotus (*hanka fuza* or *ardha padmasana*), where only one foot is pulled up, is an alternative for the less flexible. Also used are the "Indian style" or "tailor fashion," where the feet are tucked under the legs, and the "Burmese" posture where the bent legs rest entirely on the floor or cushion.

The classic texts say that the half-lotus should be done with the left leg on top of the right, and the full lotus with the right foot placed on the left thigh first. However some modern teachers recommend alternating, to reduce the strain on the body.

Optimal use of cross-legged sitting for meditation requires some sort of cushion underneath the buttocks, so that the body doesn't tend to tilt backwards and the hips can be higher than the knees, allowing for deep diaphragmatic or "belly" breathing. In formal practice settings a traditional *zafu* (round pillow) or *zabuton* (rectangular cushion) is often used, and yoga and Buddhist magazines are full of ads for meditation cushions. Having a special cushion can be nice for ritual purposes of setting intent, but there's usually no reason that an ordinary bed pillow or two won't do. (Though if you use soft pillows, you may have to fold them over in half.)

Using the lotus, or even half-lotus, position can be difficult. But remember that one component of the Eightfold Path is Right Effort. On the other hand, it's of no benefit to damage your body by forcing it beyond its limits, as students of some of the harsher schools of Zen have been known to do. The ideal practice is neither too tight not too loose – like tuning a stringed instrument. A slack string will not sound, while one wound too tight will shriek until it breaks.

Seiza

Seiza is the formal Japanese way of sitting, very commonly used in martial arts dojos. One kneels on both knees, puts the tops of the feet on the floor, then sits back on the heels. Many people find this to be remarkably uncomfortable! It does become less difficult with practice, and is a bit easier if you cross the feet, the right instep on the left sole. Crossing the feet is less formal and a bit of a cheat, but I've seen it done in Japan. Seiza has the advantage that the knees are naturally lower than the hips, without the use of any cushion. A special low tilted bench can be used with this posture.

If you have back or knee problems – or if you'd like to sit meditation in a public place, like a doctor's waiting room, without being a spectacle – you can do meditation seated in an ordinary chair. If you are using a chair at home, you may wish to tilt it forward slightly by raising the back legs. (Not recommended with a wheeled office chair, obviously.) Sit forward a bit, without leaning against the chair back, and with both feet on the floor. I prefer to sit near the edge so that my knees can be lower then my hips and the posture becomes more like seiza, but this will vary depending on build and your reason for using a chair.

In any posture, the goal is to properly align the body so that the muscular effort needed to stay upright is minimal. With this, we can become aware of how much excess tension we carry, and thereby become aware of the mental habits that generate it.

The stability and balance of a posture comes from the alignment of the pelvis and of the spine. Obviously the pelvis must not be tilted to one side or the other; to help center yourself, you can gently rock from side to side a few times as you settle into position, gradually coming to rest upright in the center. Many of us have a tendency to tilt the pelvis forward or backward. Imagine the pelvis as a bowl, in which the intestines and other organs sit. Don't tilt the bowl backward or forward, but let it be level.

From the stable base of the pelvis, the bones of the spine must be stacked, leaning neither to the side, front, nor back. But the spine has a natural S-curve when viewed from the side. Do not try to make it straight, in fact you want to pay special attention to the inward curve of the lower back. Think instead of making the spine long. Imagine yourself in a low room, and push up slightly with the crown of your head to touch the ceiling.

The ears should be in line with the shoulders. If you tend to jut your head forward – as many of us do these days, a habit formed by hours hunched over computers – draw the chin slightly inward, so that the head rests aligned on the top of the spine. Let the shoulders expand to the sides and hang down off of the framework of the spine, and let the arms be slightly away from the body: imagine that you have eggs under each arm, and don't break them!

In formal Zen practice the hands are placed in the "cosmic mudra," called in Japanese *ho-in*: the hands cupped, palm up, left resting in the right and thumbs lightly touching, and held against the lower abdomen. The hands are below the navel, at the area known to qi gong practitioners as the *dantien* and to martial artists in Japanese styles as the *tanden*, with the thumbs at navel height. If you are sitting on the sly in public, you might just rest your hands on your thighs.

Besides helping to bring attention to the belly, and thus to proper breathing, this mudra can act as a feedback mechanism. Do the thumbs press tightly together with tension? Or do the hands tend to slump and laxly tilt forward?

Place the tip of tongue against the roof of the mouth, just behind the front teeth. In the energetics of Chinese and Japanese traditional medicine, this connects two major energy channels; more practically, it helps keep saliva from building up in the mouth. Direct the eyes to a spot on the floor about three feet in front of you, and close them halfway. (Traditional Sōtō style, you sit facing a wall – that's fine too.) Do not close the eyes completely – Zen style meditation is not about withdrawing awareness from the outside world.

Breathing

The desired breath during meditation is slow and full. Many of us tend to breath much more rapidly and shallowly than is physiologically ideal, often involving only the upper part of lungs. A proper breath uses the diaphragm and the abdominal and lower back muscles, as well as the intercostal muscles, to completely expand and then empty the lungs.

The focus is on the belly, or the *hara* as it's called in Japanese. When the diaphragm pulls down to expand the lungs, the belly naturally pushes out. Did you ever stand in front of a mirror as a kid and puff your belly out? Same thing! (As adults, we tend to spend our effort pulling that belly in instead, a habit that can be difficult to let go of.) You may have to adjust your clothing to allow this.

So imagine that your belly is a water balloon. As you slowly breathe in through the nose, fill the belly balloon from the bottom up, naturally expanding to the front, back, and sides. As you exhale, gently squeeze the balloon starting from the bottom, allowing the belly to move inwards so that all the air is expelled. Exhalation should be the active phase of the breath, taking about twice as long as inhalation.

However, ultimately the practice of meditation is less about controlling the breath than watching it, being aware of it (along with everything else). How you are breathing when you sit is how you are breathing in that moment. Don't feel that you're "doing it wrong" if your breathing is shallow.

Cognition

In some forms of meditation, the objective is to remove awareness from the external world and to focus entirely on mental constructions. But this is not the way of Zen. The American Zen teacher Charlotte Joko Beck writes,

> Once we have assumed our best posture (which should be balanced, easy) we just sit there, we do zazen. What do I mean by "just sit there"?

> It's the most demanding of all activities. Usually in meditation we don't shut our eyes. But right now I'd like you to shut your eyes and just *sit* there. What's going on? All sorts of things. A tiny twitch in your left shoulder; a pressure in your side…Notice your face for a moment. Feel it. Is it tense anywhere? Around the mouth, around the forehead? Now move down a bit. Notice your neck, just feel it. Then your shoulders, your back, chest, abdominal area, your arms, thighs. Keep feeling whatever you find. And feel your breath as it comes and goes. Don't try to control it, just feel it. Our first instinct is to try to control the breath. Just let your breath be as it is. It may be high in your chest, it may be low. It may feel tense. Just experience it as it is. Now just feel all of that. If a car goes by outside, hear it. If a plane flies over, notice that. You might hear a refrigerator going on and off. Just be that. That's all you have to do, absolutely all you have to do: experience that, and just stay with it. Now you can open your eyes.
>
> If you can just do that for three minutes, that's miraculous. Usually after about a minute we begin to think. Our interest in just being with reality (which is what we have just done) is very low. (BECK, 25-26)

To do zazen is to watch the mind at work as it creates the reality we experience. Ideally, we can view and accept whatever sensations or thoughts arise without clinging to any of them, viewing them from a safe detachment as if they were images on a movie screen. But because our natural interest in "just being with reality" is low, we can use a few tricks to keep us on task, so that meditation time doesn't become daydreaming time. You don't have to use any of these tricks – if on any given day you're feeling especially enlightened and are able to *just sit*, by all means, go for it.

Counting the breaths

Perhaps the most common trick taught to novice meditators is the one that Mr. Reese taught me all those years ago: counting the breaths. Count each exhalation: one, two, three, up to the tenth breath, then start again at one. (Some people prefer to count to eight, a number with auspicious meaning in the Chinese culture where Ch'an/Zen originated; this may have a slight advantage of being a little less automatic.) If – or rather, when – you lose track, or count past ten, or find that you've gone off into distraction, let go of whatever thought you have grabbed on to and start over at one. If that thought comes back, let it go again; repeat as needed.

How do we let go of these thoughts? We don't want to attempt to suppress them – that is just another form of attachment. The thing that you refuse to look at binds you just as much as the thing you can't tear your eyes away from.

Instead we want to acknowledge that any thought that arises is a part of us, and welcome it without shame or pride. Perhaps an angry thought comes up. We might say, "Ah, anger. Anger is a very important energy that can motivate us to action. But I am being angry about something in the past, and I am focusing on being in the present. Thank you for your advice, anger. But now is not the time for action on that, so we will let that rest for now." And then return to the present.

Or perhaps a sexual thought arises: "Oh, sexuality. Without sex, we wouldn't be here; the red thread of passion is not to be neglected. But this is not something in the here and now; I am having a fantasy about something that might or might not happen in the future." And return to the present.

Emotional pain can come up while sitting. Paradoxically, this can result from the letting go of muscular tension. We sometimes armor ourselves against emotional pain by shunting it aside, storing it in the muscles as tension. When we sit and become aware of it, that tension will often release – and the delayed emotional pain will come up. This is part of the process, and need not be feared. If you have been holding on to a big pain for a while, this can be difficult. Take it a little bit at a time, and do not be reluctant to get help from friends, teachers, or healers if you need support.

The pain must be released from the muscles and processed by the mind, before we can be free of it. Identify the pain, remind yourself that its cause is in the past, not in the present, and return

to your breath in the present moment.
That is the wonderful, powerful thing about the breath: it is always in the present tense. Thinking about past breaths, or speculating about future ones, will leave us suffocating. We have to breathe in the now.

Some days your breath count may never make it past two or three, before you become distracted. That's fine. That's where you are that day. Don't feel you are "doing it wrong" if you are distracted – if you note "Ah, I am distracted today," you have seen something true.

Chanting

Chanting is found in most forms of Buddhism, including Zen, as a group practice. But one can use a silent chant, repeating the words to oneself, as an aid to meditation, though it's not usually used this way in traditional formal Zen practice.

Unlike some forms of practice, in Zen the objective is not to use the chant to "trance out" into some state of bliss. Like counting the breaths, it is a way to detect when we've gone off into distraction. When we lose our place, or find that the chant has stopped, we know it's time to cut loose from whatever thought is dragging us behind it, and start again. In a sense, we're taking the part of the mind that's always looking for distraction and feeding it the chant, stuffing it full until it lies down for a nap.

Using a chant is a more verbal and mental exercise than connecting with the breath, the most basic physiological process. But I have found it to be useful when my mind is exceptionally cluttered, or when I am upset and having difficulty letting go of sticky thoughts.

You could use any chant, Buddhist or not, for this purpose. I have two favorites that I like to use. First, the mantra from the Heart Sutra:

> Gate gate pāragate pārasamgate bodhi svāhā

which Thich Nhat Hanh translates to "gone, gone, gone all the way over, everyone gone to the other shore, svaha!" where "svaha" is a cry of joy like "Welcome!" or "Hallelujah!" (NHAT HANH, HEART, 50) I think that Beat poet Phillip Whalen's rendering in "Sourdough Mountain Lookout" catches it well:

> Gone
> Gone
> REALLY gone
> Into the cool
> O MAMA! (WHALEN, 45)

Second, the Enmei Jukku Kannon Gyō, the "Ten Verse Kannon Sutra for Timeless Life," an invocation of the Bodhisattva of compassion, Avalokiteśvara, also known as Kwan Yin, Kannon, and Kanzeon:

> Kanzeon
> namu butsu
> yo butsu u in
> yo butsu u en
> buppō sō en
> jō raku ga jō
> chō nen Kanzeon
> bo nen Kanzeon
> nen-nen jū shin ki
> nen nen fu ri shin

As translated by Robert Aitken:

> Kanzeon!
> I venerate the Buddha
> with the Buddha I have my source,
> with the Buddha I have affinity –
> affinity with Buddha, Dharma, Sangha,
> constancy, ease, assurance, purity.
> Morning my thought is Kanzeon,
> evenings my thought is Kanzeon,
> thought-after-thought arises in mind,
> thought after thought is not separate from mind
> (AITKEN, MORNING STAR, 106)

If you would like to try these on your own, I suggest searching the Internet for recordings of the chants.

Listening

Many years ago, my karate dojo held a beach training event in Ocean City, Maryland. After an evening workout that took us into the breakers, we had a meditation period, and our sensei had us lie in the wet sand and listen to all the sounds we could hear.

At first, I couldn't hear much. I was focused on being cold and wet and on the gritty sand everywhere inside my uniform. But as that settled, I heard the breakers crashing on the shore. Then I could hear some people down the beach a bit, talking. Then the person next to me, moving slightly and rustling in the sand. Then the traffic up on Coastal Highway, maybe 200 yards away.

After perhaps ten or fifteen minutes, near the end of the meditation, I finally became quiet enough in my own mind to become aware of a marvelous sound that had been there the whole time: the small soft sound of the breeze whistling against my own ears.

When we continually hear a sound, our mind filters it out. The same applies to sights and smells and all our other sensations. It makes sense from an evolutionary perspective: the things that stay the same are unlikely to be threats, so the things that are new and potentially dangerous are what get the attention of our survival-mind.

But this filtering is a distortion of reality. Cutting out the things that we see or hear again and again, we lose track of everyday miracles and take wonders for granted. (And this filtering can let threats effectively disguise themselves, just by seeming on the surface to be something familiar. The fact that Zen training helps counter this habitual filtering is part of the reason it's been useful to warriors and martial artists over the centuries.)

Deep listening shows us this filtering in action, as we become aware of sounds that have been present but blocked from our consciousness. Where using the breath puts us more in touch with our bodies, and meditation using a silent chant pulls us into the nature of words, listening meditation pulls us out into the world.

There are other forms of meditation used by Zen practitioners: koan practice, *kinhin* (walking mediation), *shikantaza* ("just sitting"), and of course the variety of meditative

Zen arts mentioned earlier. But it's less important what precise form meditation takes, than to actually *do* it, and to do it with determination and dedication. With that, even a "wrong" method can turn out right.

There is a wonderful story about this from the Korean Zen (Seon) tradition. Three centuries ago there was a monk called Sok Du, which means "Rock-head." As that name indicates, he was not the most intellectually brilliant fellow. But he had a great determination, and so even though the sutras were beyond him and even sitting meditation was too intellectually challenging, he stayed at the temple doing "working Zen" – laboring in the fields and in the kitchen.

When the master of the temple tried to help him out and asked if he had any questions, Sok Du said, "Well, Master, you are always talking about Buddha. What is Buddha?"

The Zen master answered, "Buddha is mind," which is a fairly stock Zen answer. But in Korean, "Buddha is mind" sounds a little bit like "Buddha is grass shoes." And that's what Sok Du heard.

Of course this puzzled him, but he was confused by this Zen stuff most of the time anyway. So he stuck with it. "Buddha is grass shoes. Buddha is grass shoes. What's that mean? I don't know, but that's what the master said. So Buddha is grass shoes." This was his thought, his meditation, all the time for three years. Buddha is grass shoes.

Then one day, he was out in the hills gathering firewood. As he walked down the path, he slipped and his straw sandals – his "grass shoes" – tore loose and flew up in the air! In that instant, he had an enlightenment experience.

He went rushing back to the master. "Master! Master! I understand!"

"Oh? Well then, what is Buddha?"

And Sok Du smacked the master on the head with his broken sandal!

"Is that all?" said the master (who was probably used to uppity monks trying to show enlightenment with outrageous behavior).

"My grass shoes are all broken!"

"Ah! Wonderful!" said the master, and burst out laughing.

(Sahn, Compass, 149; Sahn, Dropping Ashes, 83-84)

Knowing that intention and determination are more important than fine points of method, we don't have to wait for a perfect teacher or perfect circumstances or perfect understanding of technique. We can begin, right now.

Zen in the Art of Magic

While searching for the famous giant bronze Buddha called the Daibutsu in Kamakura, the old feudal capital just outside Tokyo, I stumbled across an ancient Shintō shrine, Zeniarai Benten. It is more formally known as Zeniarai Benzaiten Ugafuku Jinja – "coin washing shrine of Benzaiten / Ugafuku."

The full name is a wonderful example of the syncretism in Japanese religion: Benzaiten is the Japanese version of the Hindu/Buddhist goddess Sarasvatī, while Ugafuku is a Shintō deity of good fortune who became combined with her over the centuries.

The shrine is centered around a sacred spring. Go through the series of *torī* (symbolic Shintō gates) that mark the space as sacred and you enter a cave, decorated with hundreds of colorful strings of origami cranes, where water from the spring flows into a pool. Hundreds of thousands of people come here each year to wash their money in this water; the belief is that when this money is spent, it will come back to the spender many times over. Apparently it doesn't work if you hold on to the money; you have to spend it – a sort of magical economic stimulus plan.

Of course I washed all the cash I had with me, and soon spent it all except for a single five yen coin, which I kept as a souvenir. (The five yen coins have a hole through the center, making them perfect to wear as an amulet.)

On a few occasions at large Pagan festivals, I've used this coin as a tool to do a prosperity ritual, bringing a little bit of Shintō magic to the American Pagan scene.

The ritual goes like this: since I don't have water from Zeniarai Benten's spring, I'll fill a large container with water from the local source (the "sacred wells" of Camp Ramblewood or of the Brushwood Folklore Center, the locations where the Free Spirit Gathering and Starwood* are held). I'll talk about my trip to to Zeniarai Benten, about the shrine and about the money washing ritual done there, and discuss the concept of prosperity a little bit. I'll point out that prosperity is not something that is

---

* Starwood has moved to a new location since this was written.

realized individually, but something that happens on a community level as the financial energy flows around; the point of this ritual is to get that energy moving to the benefit of everyone.

I then talk about how all water is one, moved by the sun and the rain so that water of these wells interpenetrates that of the springs of Zeniarai Benten, and that:

> Sacredness is a matter of intention and agreement, nothing more and nothing less. This water is sacred because we agree that it is, because we agree to charge it with our "energy," however we may conceive of that – our thought, our will, our spirit, our life-force. My friends, is it your intention that this water be sacred?
>
> Then as a token, as a symbol, as a reminder of that agreement and as a focus of that intention, I place in this water a coin, washed in water from Zeniarai Benten, bringing us a spark of that magic, a whisper of its beat, a line of its poem.
>
> And now I ask you to set your personal intention for this ritual. Thinking of what we have discussed here today, what does prosperity mean to you? How will it specifically manifest in your life?
>
> And now, one by one, please come up and put your money in the basket. But this isn't a collection basket like you might find in a church somewhere, no – you're going to get that money back. But when you get it back, maybe you'll start to think of it a little differently. Maybe you'll start to think of money as not just being "yours" or "mine," but as part of an energy that we all share, an energy that has to keep flowing to be useful – flowing just like water.
>
> Put your money in the basket, set your intention, and let's do some money laundering.

After each person has performed the money washing ritual, I thank them for their attendance and participation, remind everyone again about the concept of prosperity as moving energy, and that the money has to be spent – and that there are many vendors at the festival who would be happy to help with that!

This is a very simple ritual, with a straightforward intention. But it illustrates all of the key components of magic. Let's take a closer look.

* * *

"Intention is the glue and play is the spark." – Billy Bardo

As we discussed previously, Zen-style meditation is meant to cultivate direct perception without mental filtering and analysis. But this is not how the mind usually works. The brain is a story-telling, model-making machine, with a sad tendency to tell stories of pain. While the meditative approach to dealing with bad brain stories is to attempt to quiet the mind by letting it talk itself out, another way is to try to lead it into new, more positive and beneficial story lines by the use of ritual.

Every religion makes use of ritual. Even Zen, for all its emphasis on meditation, has no paucity of rituals. There are big ones like initiation and dharma transmission, and everyday ones like prostrating before a statue of the Buddha. Even zazen done in a monastery or Zen center has ritual forms around it.

In religions aimed at social cohesion, ritual can be used as a way of binding people to their "proper" place and role in society. But it is a neutral tool that can also be used for individual liberation. According to religion scholars Steven Heine and Dale Stuart Wright,

> Zen ritual actually does something to practitioners. It shapes them into certain kinds of subjects, who not only think certain thoughts but also perceive the world and understand themselves through the patterns impressed upon them by the repeated action of ritual upon their body and mind.
>
> Ritual establishes a context of experience in

which certain moods dominate and desires, emotions, states of minds, and actions come to the fore. (HEINE, 11)

Much the same can be said about the role of ritual in the Pagan world. It is not (or at least, should not be) a rote repetition of forms, nor a means of wearing down individuality, but rather a tool for change and self-development where external acts can help shape internal thought patterns.

In the ceremonial magic tradition which influenced the development of Paganism, ritual was used as a way to allow the magician to become one with the Divine; (HUTTON,82-83) and this is a fair description of the role of ritual in many Pagan paths today. In these rituals we enact myths, finding the mythic qualities in ourselves. Ritual is "enacted meditation," in the words of Starhawk, one of the contemporary leading figures of the Pagan revival. (STARHAWK, 83)

We can define a magical ritual as a set of actions performed with *intent* to manipulate *mental symbols* in such a way as to create some *desired change* in state of mind. Often the ultimately desired result is a change in the physical universe, but it is understood (at least by sophisticated practitioners) that this is brought about in some fashion by a change of mind.

In a group ritual, consensus about intent has to be developed before the ritual and maintained throughout it. A simple way to bring this about is for whoever is leading or facilitating the work to describe their goal, and explicitly ask the other participants if that goal meets with their approval. In the prosperity ritual described above, this is the motivation behind the question "Is it your intention that this water be sacred?"

Even when performing a solo ritual, we are often of two (or more!) minds about a subject. By clearly stating or expressing our intent, we can bring a unity (however temporary) to our own mind. There are also more subtle ways to develop and indicate a consensus, to draw a group of people, or a single divided mind, together into one intent by setting the circumstances, nature, and participants of the ritual.

With the intent set and agreed upon, it's time to set the stage. Starhawk has noted that ritual "is partly a matter of performance, of theater"; (STARHAWK, 72) and just as a theater has ways of marking off a certain space and time (an elevated stage between curtain rise and fall) as separate from the mundane world, an effective ritual is marked as being outside of ordinary reality.

In the many Pagan traditions influenced by Wicca, ordinary space and time are left behind by casting a "magic circle." According to Margot Adler,

> The circle is the declaration of sacred ground. It is a place set apart, although its material location may be a living room or a backyard. But in the mind the circle, reinforced by the actions of casting it and purifying it, becomes sacred space, a place "between the worlds" where contact with archetypal reality, with the deep places of the mind – with "gods," if you will – becomes possible. It is a place where time disappears, where history is obliterated. It is the contact point between two realities. It is common for Witches to contrast their circle with the circle of the ceremonial magician. The Wiccan circle is not a "protection from demons" but a container of the energy raised. (ADLER, 109)

We don't necessarily need elaborate trappings to take us into this space between the worlds. In the money-washing prosperity ritual, a non-ordinary time and space is invoked just by telling a story of a far-off land and a centuries-old temple. Of course an extraordinary context, such as a festival where people are away from home and encouraged to have extraordinary experiences, helps. But our connection to "ordinary" reality is tenuous enough that a good story, well-told, can always cut across it; that's why we can easily lose ourselves in novels, plays, and films. Ritual works because our brains are story-telling machines, and will readily entrain on a good plot even if the production values are low.

Just as the actors in a stage play have their costumes and props which help them get into character – to put their minds in a certain state – so vestments and ritual tools have their place in magic.

Some prefer to don elaborate regalia to get into character for their rituals, while some use the most unusual outfit of all, the "birthday suit," to break ordinary thinking. Certainly one can do a ritual in ordinary clothing; but dressing up (or undressing up) gives the thing a sense of occasion. It's why groups as diverse as sports teams, armies, and doctors and nurses all have their uniforms. The Catholic priest has his stole, the Buddhist has their kesa. There's no unity on vestments among Pagans, but visit a large gathering and you will see a bewildering variety of dress, each person donning (or doffing) the outfit that best puts them into the magical headspace.

Even a piece of jewelry or ornamentation – something as simple as a coin on a cord worn as necklace – can help. And such an ornament can also be used as a ritual tool.

Tools for manipulating the mental energy of ritual are found in every magical or religious tradition: the wand of ceremonial magicians, the holy water used by Catholic priests, the Wiccan athame, the pipe of the Plains Indian tribes, the *harae gushi* whisk used in Shintō purification rites. Some prefer elaborate ritual tools which are never used for mundane actions, in order to preserve a sense of occasion when the special tools come out; while others, such as "kitchen witches," prefer to use everyday objects and not build a division between the sacred and the mundane. Both camps have valid points, and it's largely a matter of personal inclination. The coin I use in the prosperity ritual is, in Japan, a completely ordinary and mundane coin; but here in the U.S. it has no mundane use and so becomes a purely ritual object.

Once the stage is set and the actors garbed and equipped with their props, it's time for them to deliver their lines, to strut and fret their hour upon the stage. Are those lines set, or made up on the spot? Here again you'll find a spectrum of opinions, from those who improvise as richly as an episode of the comedy show *Whose Line Is It Anyway?* to some who follow scripts as set as any staging of a Shakespeare play.

But whether improvised or scripted, most any play or story has a structure that can be described as rising action, climax, and resolution. Paralleling this, in a ritual we have the steps of raising power, directing that power, and resolving back to ordinary reality.

Anything that takes us out of ordinary consciousness is a way of raising power for a ritual. The Sakai that Gerald Gardner observed danced and sang themselves into a frenzy, and in Pagan traditions, dancing, chanting, and drumming are commonly used. And of course there's the ritual use of sex in some traditions. Anything that sets up some excitement or tension, any behavior that's not mundane, can be used. Since Gardner was an asthmatic who couldn't dance for long enough to trance out, his original Wicca used binding and scourging. But power can be raised by much more subtle means also: the Golden Dawn led initiates around blindfolded, as do the Freemasons.

In the money washing ritual, energy is raised by doing something outside of all social norms – taking money, our culture's highest marker of energy and power, and soaking it in water. Imagine if your friends walked in on you washing money in the kitchen sink! They'd think you'd gone mad.

Any energy-raising practice must keep its aura of oddity around it, its separation from the usual social mandates. When this is lost, it becomes a rote repetition that tends to suppress individuality. This is why we will always need rituals that are new to us, either newly invented ones, ancient ones rediscovered, or ones brought to us from other cultures.

So here you are with this energy, this freedom from social convention. What will you do with it? This is the climax, the focus, the direction of the ritual. With an initiation ritual, we use the energy raised to alter our definition of ourselves to include a new classification. With a healing ritual, we alter the social and psychological circumstances in a favorable manner – illness and healing have large mental and social components. With the money-washing ritual, we use the energy we raise to alter our relationship with money, to wash away both the poverty mindset that believes spirituality is incompatible with prosperity, and the greed that wants to hold on to the energy that must flow to be useful.

Consciousness is thermoplastic: once it is "warmed up" by raising energy, it can be reshaped at the climax of the ritual. But now, we must return to the everyday world. The mind must be cooled in its new mold, allowed to firm up a bit before being placed back into its regular use. And so just as a novel, film, or play does not just cut off after the climactic moment, an effective ritual must allow for a gentle resolution back to practical, "ordinary" consciousness. But since our goal is to emerge from the ritual changed, the resolution should guide us in a new direction as we leave, it should remind us of what has changed.

Pagan rituals often end by ritually closing and dismantling the circle that contained them, and with the refrain "Merry meet, merry part, and merry meet again" – an excellent suggestion for an attitude to hold in the interim. The prosperity ritual draws to a close with concrete suggestions on what to do and where to go next: get the energy moving by spending money.

In this little ritual we can see all the pieces: an environment delineated as separate from ordinary space and time, raising energy by some unusual behavior, an intentional change in our consciousness, and a gentle shift back to ordinary reality.

But these elements are not just found in deliberate magical rituals.

Let's consider a couple going out on a "date night." The date is by definition a special time, and they most likely go somewhere special, somewhere they do not ordinarily go. They dress up for the night. Perhaps flowers are bought – an ancient magical tool dating back to Neanderthal times. They share the intention to develop their romantic connection (at least, if the date is going to go well, they share that intention!), to make a deliberate change in their minds. They act in a non-ordinary manner, behaving in a more romantic fashion, however that may apply to their ideals. With any luck, the date leads to an act of physical and emotional intimacy that draws them closer together. And the transition back to mundane life is gradual – if one partner immediately bolts out of bed and goes about their business, the evening has been a failure.

Ritual magic is not something radically foreign to our lives. We are all magicians.

What Would Buddha Eat?

For the international traveler, food can be both an adventure and a hassle. There are new things to try, but not only can one come to miss comfortable old favorites, it can sometimes be difficult to know just what one is eating. For example, since I can't read enough Japanese to understand food labels, if I hadn't been warned in advance I would never have thought that bread could contain squid ink.

But I've managed to get by, and find some new delights. Like a little food stand in Nara, not far from Tōdai-ji temple and its great bronze Daibutsu statue, where they serve kusamochi daifuku right off the griddle – pastries of rice flour seasoned with mugwort, filled with sweet azuki bean paste. I fell in love with these on my first visit to Japan; I love to grab a few of these kusamochi along with a hot green tea (or, on a warm day, a cold beer), sit on a bench in the park, shoo away the tame deer (considered sacred messengers of the gods, the Nara deer are notorious mooches) and have a wonderful little meal.

There is perhaps nothing so miraculous and yet so commonplace as eating. Several times a day (for those of us fortunate enough to live where food is readily available), we engage in amazing transformational alchemy that turns the food on our plates into our living breathing bodies.

And because of the intimate nature of our relationship with food – "you are what you eat" – we have a tremendous emotional investment in the choice of what things we turn into us.

People will allow their health to deteriorate, they will die of heart disease or diabetes, rather than change what they eat. Many Americans have their bellies ripped open and their digestive tracts surgically modified to "cure" gross obesity, because they find themselves unable to alter their eating habits.

In Mahāyāna Buddhism, one of the fates that can befall the dead who were greedy in life is to be made to roam the world as a "hungry ghost," enormous in appetite but cursed with such small mouths and throats that they cannot swallow. (Offerings of food, a few grains of rice, are left out for these suffering beings at meals in Zen monasteries.) This is a wonderful personification of how powerful our appetite can be – persisting even through death.

I recall my shiatsu sensei, Barbra Esher, once noting that it was easier to get people to change their religion than to change what they eat. This is interesting to ponder – if early Christians had made Gentile converts keep kosher, would anyone have heard of Jesus of Nazareth today? And it sometimes seems that many Westerners are willing to consider Buddhism only so long as they can keep their Big Macs too.

But it's exactly because we have such a charged relationship with our food choices that considering them more deeply is an opportunity for spiritual development. If spirituality concerns our relationship with the Universe, does that relationship manifest in a more intimate way than in how we eat?

Mindfulness requires us to take an honest look at the effect of our choices on our bodies, on the environment, and on the lives and deaths of other sentient beings. All of these considerations recommend a diet based around sustainably-grown plant foods. Many books have been written about the health advantages of a vegetarian or near-vegetarian diet, as well as the environmental devastation caused by modern "factory farming." And surely choosing vegetarian foods is a wonderful way to prevent a tremendous amount of suffering by animals. Rather than repeating those arguments here, I will refer you to the works of John Robbins, especially his books *Diet for a New America* and *The Food Revolution*.

Instead, what I'd like to consider here is the question of how to best move our own stubborn minds towards mindful and compassionate food choices, while avoiding falling into attachments to ideas of spiritually "pure" and "impure" foods.

It's a problem the Buddha faced. He didn't have to worry about sustainable organic farming versus the use of petrochemical fertilizers, or about people gorging themselves to death on Big Macs. But the issue of killing animals for food was one to which he gave considerable thought.

It's clear that his teachings include extending compassion to non-human animals. The precept against taking life forbids killing both humans and other animals, and he spoke of freeing animals destined for the butcher as a great act of kindness. But he did not require his followers to be vegetarians, and explicitly rejected such a requirement when suggested by his cousin (and, later, rival) Devadatta.

In fact, some scholars believe that the Buddha's last meal may have been of wild boar meat, given him by Cunda the smith.

Others hold it was mushrooms, the issue apparently being whether the Pali for something like "pig's delight" should be interpreted as "food pigs like to eat," i.e. mushrooms, or food made from pigs meant to "delight" omnivorous humans.

The Buddhist sutras are contradictory on the issue of vegetarianism, and different schools of Buddhism have taken different attitudes toward it depending on which sutras they believe authoritative. Or, given the way we get attached to our food choices, perhaps they have chosen which sutras they believe authoritative depending on their attitudes toward vegetarianism!

There are some Buddhists who ignore the issue completely. Some (like the Dali Lama and the famous Zen teacher Shunryu Suzuki) praise vegetarianism while continuing to eat meat themselves. And then there are the Japanese Zen temples that have elevated the vegetarian cuisine called *shojin ryori* to a high art.

Hui Neng, the Sixth Patriarch of Zen, supposedly lived with hunters for several years during his exile, but would sabotage their traps and gather vegetables to eat. On the other hands some Vajrayāna Buddhists seem to believe that it's more important to chant mantras or dedicate merit to the souls of slaughtered animals, than to refrain from killing them.

What are we to make of all this? Were the Buddha and his disciples happy to eat animal flesh so long as someone else accumulated the "bad karma" of doing the actual killing? This is how things were once done in Japan, with the *burakumin*, a low caste, getting stuck doing "unclean" work like butchering. Discrimination against the descendants of these people continues today.

Or was the Buddha up to something more subtle?

First we should note that the prohibition against taking the lives of animals is very specific and strong. It applied not just to monks, but to lay followers. If everyone followed the Buddha's teachings, there would be no slaughterhouses, no butchers, no meat to eat. The world he was working toward was clearly a vegetarian one.

Also, we must consider that the early Buddhist monks lived with a very different economic system than we have today. They were forbidden from using money and went begging for their food – essentially, they were trading teaching to the lay community in return for offerings of food, clothing, and medicine. It's a pattern that goes back to the time the Buddha spent under the Bo tree, when local children would bring him food and he would teach them about meditation and mindfulness.

The monks were pretty much expected to accept whatever was offered to them without discrimination, but were expressly forbidden to accept offerings of flesh foods from animals that had been killed specifically to feed them. Even the suspicion that this was so, was enough to put the meat on the forbidden list. It was only when someone had meat that they were going to eat themselves, and decided to offer it instead to a monk or a nun, that he or she could accept. This acceptance wasn't any sort of endorsement, as one of the first things the monk or nun would teach them was the precept against the taking of life.

If the Buddha required his monastic followers to accept only vegetarian food, his message of compassion would be less likely to reach those who did not have vegetarian food to offer. By allowing (but not requiring!) his monks to accept offerings of meat, the Buddha allowed his teaching to spread to many more laypeople.

But there were those in the order who were less enthusiastic about letting laymen into the game. (In the years after the Buddha's death, this was one of the issues that lead to the split between the Theravāda and Mahāyāna schools of Buddhism – would it be a practice centered around monastic practice, or could lay people be full participants too?) When Devadatta proposed that monks be allowed to accept only vegetarian food offerings, it was part of a package of proposals that would have made for greater separation between ordained followers and laypeople.

I believe the Buddha's rejection of these proposals was intended as affirming the importance of being inclusive, not as an endorsement of flesh foods.

So if we look to the principle of mindful compassion toward all sentient beings that the Buddha taught 2,500 years ago, how might we apply it today? If you dropped some money in his begging bowl, what would Buddha buy at the supermarket? Would he be hanging out by the butcher's case looking for a good pork chop, or over in the produce section, thumping melons?

In our economic system, to purchase a product is to reward its maker, to support and endorse the actions taken to produced it. When we buy a shirt or a salad or a steak, we are retroactively hiring everyone who worked to produce it, and we bear responsibility for the actions of our employees.

We cannot avoid responsibility for our choices on the basis that it was someone else's hands that implemented them. If wicked things are done to produce a product – workers exploited, land or water polluted, animals treated cruelly, precious resources wasted – then we must honestly, mindfully, and compassionately consider the consequences, and do our best to find alternatives. It's not enough to refrain from doing harm with our own hands; we must not encourage others to do harm on our behalf.

With all that in mind, I'm pretty sure you'd find old Siddhartha buying broccoli rather than a beef brisket, seeking to give his support to those doing the least harm.

But, rather than telling the butcher to kiss off, the Buddha might well invite that man to come sit down and join him in a meal.

We must keep in mind that the goal is compassion and mindfulness, not attachment to some abstract idea of "purity." We have to be kind to others and to ourselves, to recognize the difficulty of changing fundamental behaviors. The Universe is a complicated place, and we have to maintain mental flexibility to deal with it.

As wonderful as the practices of vegetarianism and veganism are, getting self-righteous about them is not just harmful to our own minds but reduces the opportunity to influence others to choose compassionately.

Brad Warner, a contemporary American Zen teacher, has noted that "The problem of vegetarianism in Zen practice is that it so often becomes a huge mental block…a tremendous way of defining the ego." (Warner, "Better Way") He even mentions Zen masters tricking students into eating meat; I wouldn't call that a good idea, but over the years, I have encountered a few vegetarians and vegans who were so hung up on how they defined themselves by their food choices that they forgot about the compassion and love that motivated the choice in the first place. And I must admit I've fallen into that trap a few times myself.

But even worse than tangling us up in our thought constructions, getting self-righteous about vegetarianism can deprive us of the opportunity to reach out to our fellow humans to work for greater compassion.

In his book *The Food Revolution*, John Robbins – one of the greatest contemporary advocates for veganism and animal rights – tells an amazing story about an encounter he had with the owner of a pig farm.

Robbins was doing undercover research on animal agriculture when he visited a small family farm which he describes as nothing less than "a pig Auschwitz," where pigs were confined for their whole lives in tiny cages stacked three high, so that urine and feces from the upper tiers rained on the pigs lower down.

For some reason, the family that ran the farm invited him to dinner and he accepted. Clearly they weren't going to offer him a vegan meal, but he declined the pork they offered (maintaining his cover by saying his doctor was worried about his cholesterol) and filled his plate with side dishes, and by keeping the discussion on the level of small talk managed to have a reasonably pleasant meal. He wondered at the contrast between their hospitality to him, and the treatment he had witnessed of the pigs.

All was well until, somehow, Robbins's cover was blown. The farmer began a tirade against "you animal rights people," saying he didn't like being accused of mistreating his animals, but that was the way the business worked and he was doing what he had to do in order to feed his family.

But as he talked, the farmer was struck, with an almost physical force, by a long-buried memory. He began to tell Robbins how when he was a young boy, he'd had a pet pig. This man who now ran a hog farm that visited tremendous cruelty on pigs, had once had a pet pig, a sow which he'd treated with the greatest loving kindness. He explained how sometimes in the summer he would sleep in the barn with the pig alongside him, how she would come to him to have her belly rubbed, how the pig would go swimming with him and keep the family dog from bothering him.

And then this man who Robbins had been ready to judge so harshly as the owner of "a pig Auschwitz" went on to tell how his father had made him slaughter and butcher his pet. Robbins tells the story:

> "So I did it," he says, and now his tears begin to flow, making their way down his cheeks. I am touched and humbled. This man, whom I had

> judged to be without human feeling, is weeping in front of me, a stranger. This man, whom I had seen as callous and even heartless, is actually someone who cares, and deeply. How wrong, how profoundly and terribly wrong I had been.
>
> I had judged him, and done so, to be honest, mercilessly. But for the rest of the evening I sat with him, humbled, and grateful for whatever it was in him that had been strong enough to force this long-buried and deeply painful memory to the surface. And glad, too, that I had not stayed stuck in my judgments of him, for if I had, I would not have provided an environment in which his remembering could have occurred.
> (ROBINS, 160-161)

It took several years for all the consequences of that heart-opening conversation to play out. But as a result, a wonderful change occurred. The farmer now runs a small organic vegetable farm. He eats a mostly vegetarian diet, and still keeps a few pigs – for a "Pet-a-pig" program, where he brings school children out and shows them how intelligent and friendly pigs are, and sees to it that each of them gets the chance to give a pig a belly rub. (ROBINS, 153-163)

Had Robbins done what most of us would do when confronted with someone who fundamentally disagrees with our values, had he walked away in disgust from a table where the flesh foods he found repulsive were being served, a tremendous opportunity for furthering the compassionate treatment of all beings would have been lost. But instead, by not staying stuck in judgment, he was able to help one man take a big step toward a more peaceful world.

Compassion and mindfulness should lead us as far down the road toward a vegetarian diet as we can go in our circumstances – maybe in one big jump, maybe in a series of small steps. But they should also remind us of the importance of not being a jerk about it.

Sex [or the lack thereof] and the Single Gaijin

Last Friday, after a day trip to Kyoto, I decided to go out for the evening and biked downtown to Osaka's Shinsaibashi nightlife district. I ended up at Cinquecento, a cocktail bar frequented by gaijin and gaijin-friendly Nihonjin.

A Japanese girl a few stools down decided to introduce herself. Introduce herself rather vigorously, one might say. She was cute, nice to talk to, seemed an outsider in her own country, a hardcore punk rock fan, lonely, and I was happy to talk to her. But I wasn't interested in taking her home, as she quite clearly suggested.

"Do you like Japanese girls?" she asked.

"Sure. I like all kinds of girls – Japanese girls, American girls, whatever." In my life I've changed my taste on many issues over time. I've gone from a hamburger-lover to a vegan, from a Catholic to a Zen Pagan, from a fan of sugary soda to a regular drinker of bitter green tea. But I had it figured out somewhere around age five that I liked girls. It was certainly never a matter of "choice," as some homophobes would have it – I was born heterosexual and seem stuck that way, even if logic suggests we'd all be better off bisexual and thus maximize our chances of a date.

When I said she was cute – which she was, in a punk sort of way – but I didn't think it would be a good idea to take her home, she asked, "So are you gay?" Obviously the only reason a gaijin guy wouldn't want to bed any available Nihonjin girl would be that he preferred guys (presumably Nihonjin guys), right?

"No, no, I'm not gay." (I thought the last question would have covered that.)

"Oh, do you have a girlfriend?"

"Well, I'm sort of dating someone back in America, but it's not an exclusive thing…"

"Well then, we should go back to your place…"

So let us pause to consider why a fellow with a healthy libido and under no pledge of celibacy or sexual exclusivity, might still choose to not jump in bed with a willing and attractive lady.

One of the precepts of Buddhism, the basic ethical guidelines, is to not misuse sexuality. But just what it means to misuse it, is somewhat vague. To best consider that question I've come back to Kyoto to sit in the gardens at Daitokuji, the temple complex where the lusty Zen lunatic Ikkyū Sōjun was once abbot. Ikkyū wore his monk's robes to the brothels, and in his seventies took up with a lover fifty years his junior. He wrote poems like "sin like a madman until you can't do anything else / no room for any more" and "a woman is enlightenment when you're with her and the red thread / of both your passions flare inside you and you see"; (BERG, 64) his philosophy is often called "Red Thread Zen." (BARZAGHI)

There's no question that sex has its hazards on the whole attachment-forming, suffering-causing front. Love and sex cause a lot of misery. We fall for someone, then pine when they don't return our affection. Or we do manage to get a date, and are disappointed when the reality doesn't live up to the fantasy. Or the thing works out and you have a relationship – and suffer when it ends. The best you can hope for is that it ends when one of you dies! And in between are all the opportunities for jealousy, disappointment, fear, and obsession.

What a minefield! What shall we do?

(I write that, look up, and a kimono-ed cutie walks around the corner away from me. Even here in a Zen garden, writing about the problem of it all, my heart jumps.)

Certainly celibacy is one approach. Not having sex does mean that one is unable to use sex harmfully. Assuming that one can keep the vow – not-doing it doesn't take away the desire. As recent revelations about Catholic priests show, celibacy has its pitfalls.

Even if adhered to, it misses an opportunity to use the energy of sexuality. A well-known Zen story tells of a lay woman who supported a monk for many years. One day she sent her lovely young niece to test him. The girl visited the monk in his hut, climbed up on his lap, and said, "How is it now, oh monk?"

The monk replied, "Cold ashes. No fire."

When the girl returned and told her aunt what had transpired, the woman was outraged, called the monk a fraud, and chased him out! He had failed to use the moment to work toward the liberation of all beings.

Does that mean it would have been appropriate for him to

rip off his robe and do the deed with her, right on the floor of his hut? Maybe; I can imagine that Ikkyū just might have. Maybe not, if it would have been just for his own pleasure, without affection or even respect for the girl. But "cold ashes" wasn't right when there was someone bringing energy, heat that could be used to power the liberation of sentient beings.

A story from the Korean Zen tradition about the teacher Won Hyo makes a similar point. As Zen Master Seung Sahn tells the tale, Won Hyo was a seventh century Buddhist teacher, a trusted advisor to the king of Silla. He heard about a very great master, a little old man who would walk around barefoot, ringing a bell and chanting: "De-an [Great Peace], de-an, de-an, de-an don't think, de-an like this, de-an rest mind, de-an, de-an." One day Won Hyo hiked out to the mountains to meet this master. As is usually the case in these stories, the master's unorthodox ways at first puzzled Won Hyo, but after a little while he came to understand that this master was a great bodhisattva, sharing the joy and the suffering of all creatures.

So Won Hyo asked the master to teach him. To his surprise, the master took him to the local red-light district and introduced him to one of the pleasure girls there:

> She led them upstairs, in great happiness, fear, and exhilaration that the famous, handsome monk had come to her. As she prepared meat and wine for her visitors, the Master said to Won Hyo, "For twenty years you've kept company with kings and princes and monks. It's not good for a monk to live in heaven all the time. He must also visit hell and save the people there, who are wallowing in their desires. Hell too is 'like this.' So tonight you will ride this wine straight to hell."
>
> "But I've never broken a single Precept before," Won Hyo said.
>
> "Have a good trip," said the master.
>
> He then turned to the woman and said sternly, "Don't you know that it's a sin to give wine to a monk? Aren't you afraid of going to hell?"

"No," the woman said. "Won Hyo will come and save me."

"A very good answer!" said the Master.

So Won Hyo stayed the night, and broke more than one Precept. The next morning he took off his elegant robes and went dancing through the streets, barefoot and in tatters. "*De-an, de-an, de-an!* The whole universe is like this! What are you?!" (SAHN, DROPPING ASHES, 61-63)

(There is considerable irony in Seung Sahn's use of this story: he was a supposedly celibate Zen monk who was later revealed to have carried on affairs with students. (BOUCHER, 226-227; FORD, 101) Catholic priests aren't the only ones to have trouble with celibacy – though at least the big Buddhist sex scandals have all involved adults. We'll have more on Buddhist sex scandals later.)

We are beings of flesh and blood who are born into this world by sex and desire. Too often, celibacy is an attempt to deny this basic truth about our nature.

We also ought to keep in mind that the celibacy teachings of old wisdom schools were given in an age before reliable birth control. For a man to have regular sexual relations most likely meant having kids, and either taking up the responsibilities of a householder or abandoning his family – definitely not the best karma to go generating. So, teachings about celibacy and marriage should be considered in that light.

Celibacy for clergy was also a tool used in some cultures to control the power of organized religion. A priest with a wife and kids was sometimes tempted to use his power and authority for his family's benefit.

Marriage is the option put forth by most mainstream religions for laypeople, and in many for clergy too. Find one person and agree to exclusive romantic and sexual relations. But marriage doesn't remove jealousy, disappointment, fear, and obsession. The statistics on infidelity and divorce show that.

More than that, marriage as we know it in our culture is based on a lie: that one can make a promise about emotion.

Our feelings, like everything else, are by nature impermanent. We may hold a great romantic love for someone today, but we cannot promise to still love them the same way in five, ten, or twenty years, and we can't promise not to fall in love with someone else along the way. It's no wonder that more and more marriages are ending in divorce now that the law allows it – it's not a failure of people, it's a basic flaw in the model.

That's not to say there are not successful marriages, people who do make it work. Just because we can't promise that romantic love will last, doesn't mean that we can't promise to work at giving it the best chance to do so. It's like cultivating a beautiful but fragile plant: we can promise to water it, to fertilize it, to prune it, to take the greatest care with it. But if we promise that the plant is going to thrive forever, we've made a promise beyond our ability to keep.

Sometimes the seed just isn't hardy, the plant by nature is weak. Perhaps the soil isn't right, or perhaps there is an early frost that catches us unawares. Perhaps there is a blight. At best, the plant may live as long as the gardener. Those who do have successful marriages don't have them forever – just for their lifespan. There is a good reason why the mythologies of most pantheons of immortal gods and goddesses feature many stories of infidelity.

And of course, if marriage is the only allowable solution, one is left with the problem of finding a partner. Under the belief that this is the only possible and allowable model, people turn romantic relationships into auditions for The Big One, rather than seeing each as a worthwhile experience in itself.

Properly understood, marriage can be a fine arrangement for some people. But to put it forth as the only solution is deficient.

So if we don't go down the celibacy route, and if marriage is not an adequate general solution to the issue, how do we deal with sexuality and the misuse thereof? Just screw anyone who's willing? That's jumping into middle of the minefield. You at least need a guideline for spotting the mines.

The advice columnist Dan Savage has suggested that the rule for getting involved with a much younger lover is the same as the rule for campsites: leave them better than you found them. I would suggest that the same rule applies regardless of age – and not just for your lover, but for you as well. If both you and your potential lover aren't going to be improved by your encounter, whether that encounter is for a single hour or a lifetime, it's best to let it go and redirect that energy.

What do we mean by "improved" in a spiritual context?

The thing that most gets in the way of spiritual development is our ego, our sense of ourself as a separate existence, disconnected. So a romantic or sexual experience that improves us is one that improves our connection, helps us feel less separate from the rest of the world.

The Buddha spoke of four aspects of love: loving kindness toward everyone, not just to our intimates (*maitrī*); compassion for the suffering of all beings (*karuṇā*); sympathetic joy, delighting in the happiness of others (*mudita*), a quality similar to the "compersion" often spoken of in discussions of polyamory; and equanimity, accepting calmly both gain and loss, whatever comes (*upekṣā*). If our relationships, sexual or not, help us cultivate these attitudes, then we're on the right track.

Any supportive human relationship can be of help, but a sexual relationship has the potential to be an especially strong aid – or, if misused, an especially strong hindrance. Human beings, like all higher animals, have a tremendous amount of energy tied up with sex. It's evolution in action: if your ancestors didn't have sex, well, then they wouldn't have gotten to be ancestors!

So how can we use that energy for spiritual development?

There are Taoist sexual yoga practices, and schools of "tantric" sex in some forms of Hinduism and Buddhism, having specific techniques that are supposed to help move energy around the body. That's all well and good, but not really the point here. And in Tantric Buddhism, there is often a belief that sex is a negative force but that we live in a "degraded" age in which it's okay to fight fire with fire. I don't think this belief is conducive to the best relationship with sexuality.

Instead, the point should be that sharing this energy, this experience of joy, is a way to develop selflessness, of being in the moment, of letting go of our own selfish desire in order to share.

Does this mean that "casual sex" is a good thing? That, of course, depends of the meaning of "casual."

If we mean "casual" as in unconcerned or irresponsible, that's a bad idea.

But if it means without plan, happening by "chance"? Many of our relationships are started by "chance" encounters, putting aside for the moment the question of what's random and what are forces and influences we don't understand.

Or if we mean casual in the sense of something that occurs from time to time rather than continuously? I think it's perfectly fine to have relationships, romantic or otherwise, that are now and then. A friend or a lover who you only see on occasion – perhaps you live in different cities, even different countries, but why should you not connect with them the best you can?

And casual can also mean natural, unstudied, or effortless – and those sound like fine ways to make love.

But this effortlessness, like the effortless movement of a dancer or martial arts master, or like the brushstrokes of a Zen painter, requires a great deal of groundwork and mindfulness. When it works, a romantic relationship continually calls us back to pay attention to our lover, to ourselves, and to the world around us. There is a danger in thinking that we know our lover thoroughly: we take them for granted and we stop paying attention. But in a healthy relationship we will keep looking and keep being surprised, brought back by our lover into the here and now.

There's a popular song from the late 1970s whose lyrics illustrate this perfectly. Rupert Holmes's "Escape," known to many as "The Piña Colada Song," tells of a man who is "tired of [his] lady," in a worn-out relationship that had lasted too long. He answers a personal ad placed by a woman who promises new adventures, only to find that it is, in fact, his current lover. In the last verse, the narrator says, "I never knew / That you liked Piña Coladas / and getting caught in the rain / And the feel of the ocean / And the taste of champagne." He has re-discovered Bodhidharma's "I don't know."

So the question we face in getting into a relationship is, is going to bed with this person going to hasten – or at least not delay – the day when all sentient beings become enlightened? Is this something that at least has a chance of leaving us both slightly better people? Is getting with them going to get us closer to that ancient heavenly connection in the starry dynamo in the machinery of night? Is this an experience that promotes mindfulness?

I didn't think taking this girl home was going to do that; it just seemed like a tangle with little benefit (past the temporary and obvious). And so I was actually glad (though a little wistful) when she turned her sights on the guy sitting next to me.

Law, Sausages, and Religion

> "Don't follow leaders. Watch your parking meters."
> – Bob Dylan, on the importance of independent thought and attention to practical details in the spiritual quest.*

There is an old aphorism, often attributed to Otto von Bismarck, that those who love sausages or the law should never watch either being made. I've always disagreed with this – if people saw the truth behind the production of these things we'd have many more vegetarian anarchists, which would seem to me a positive development.

And so it is too with religion and spirituality. The hazards of cults, superstitions, delusions, hypocrisy, and manipulation are very real. A peek behind the scenes of both ancient traditions and modern cults of personality around self-help gurus and peddlers of enlightenment-lite is an unpleasant but necessary requirement for spiritual health.

In my years of martial arts training, one of the most important principles of self-defense I've learned is that we have the right to be rude in order to be safe. Criminals who would take advantage of us often rely on our reluctance to offend in order to get us to go along with their plans. The same approach is used by cults and other manipulators: anyone who wants to leave a cult or question an "omniscient" guru is dissuaded by being made to feel as if they are committing a faux pas. Therefore, in this chapter we are going to err on the side of practicing the right to be rude.

In his book *After the Ecstasy, the Laundry*, Jack Kornfield devotes an entire chapter to the "dirty laundry" of spiritual scandals. He notes four common danger areas: power, money, sexuality, and alcohol and drugs. (KORNFIELD, 141-142) As we cast a gimlet eye on some spiritual teachers and schools, we're going to see examples of all four of these, and a fifth as well: dangerous

---

* Or, maybe Bob had some other context in mind. It still serves as good advice for the spiritual seeker.

lack of critical thinking. Neither blind faith nor New-Age muddleheadedness will be given a pass here.

But before we begin, two caveats. First, the goal here is broad illustration; this is not by any means a complete list of misbehaviors. Second, an idea is not responsible for the people who believe in it, or even teach it; the fact that some jerk preaches something doesn't mean that teaching is or is not valid.* In fact, cult leaders will often start off with very reasonable teachings in order to draw the student in. When searching for wisdom we have to look at ideas themselves and not be swayed by either arguments from authority or ad hominem fallacies.

Bastards of Buddhism

When we look critically at Buddhism we can go all the way back to the Buddha and note that he abandoned his wife and son to go off on his spiritual quest! Would we be quick to forgive someone who treated a woman we love this way? Before we accept any "the Buddha said" arguments from authority, then, let's remember: even the Buddha could be a real asshole.

Buddhism, in its modern international and post-colonial form, owes a debt to the work of the Theosophical Society, an organization founded by the fraudulent medium Helena Blavatsky. Other mystics of questionable reputation, such as Aleister Crowley, played important roles in introducing Buddhism (and also Hinduism and Yoga) to the West.

Buddhism was introduced to the U.S. largely through two paths: Zen, and the Tibetan tradition. And since their debut here, both have had their share of problems.

Much of the "Zen boom" of the mid-twentieth century was due to writers with no formal credentials in Zen, such as Alan Watts, the Beat poets, and Eugen Herrigel.† Even D.T. Suzuki is described by many within the Zen establishment as idiosyncratic and untraditional.

Of course, some might argue that to be an advantage – an escape from "square Zen" (to use Alan Watts's phrase), which

---

* I hope you will keep that in mind as you evaluate the ideas put forth in this book.
† As a reminder, your author also has no credentials in Zen.

has plenty of problems of its own. We'll discuss institutional Japanese Zen's problems shortly; on the American side, probably the most famous and illustrative scandal is that around Shunryu Suzuki's hand-picked successor, Richard Baker.

Baker used the resources of his community to live an opulent lifestyle, and sent lifetime members of its Board of Directors off on involuntary "sabbaticals" if they failed to agree with him. (DOWNING, 38-42) He claimed authority over the sex lives of his followers, dictating to them with whom they were or were not allowed to be involved in sexual relationships (DOWNING, 8) – and then was forced to resign after his own exploitative affairs were revealed (DOWNING, 42-49, 302, 305) and senior priests accused him of physical and psychological abuse. (DOWNING, 20) According to one Zen priest, "What Baker transmitted was power and arrogance and an attitude that 'I have it and you don't'." (QUOTED AT FALK, 46-47)

One of Baker's students said, "I give thanks to Dick Baker every day for fucking up so incredibly well that it gave me my life back, because I had given it to him." (QUOTED AT DOWNING, 41)

Supporters say that Baker has mended his ways since this scandal broke in the early 1980s, which may or may not be true; it doesn't alter the danger illustrated by his success in applying Zen to the art of power-tripping.

We haven't had much to say about the Tibetan tradition so far. It became popular in the U.S. later than Zen did, and so has mostly fallen outside our historical discussions.

Tibet, before the Chinese invasion, was certainly never the land of enlightened masters that popular culture has made it out to be; nor was it the oppressive feudal hell that China likes to portray it as. Tibetan Buddhism contains its own unique blend of wisdom and folly. But it does seem that the Tibetan diaspora put some people in teaching positions for which they were not prepared.

Take Chögyam Trungpa, raised since infancy as the reincarnated "Trungpa Tulku" – supposedly a great teacher who can return to each incarnation with his memories and values from all his previous lives. But it seems he must have forgotten some important past-life lessons his most recent time around. In this recent life, he was an alcoholic who became sexually involved with several of his own students. (MULLEN, 55; HORGAN 53) In 1969, driving drunk, he passed out at the wheel, crashed his car, and was seriously injured, leaving him paralyzed on the left side of his body. (DAS, 199; FALK, 112-114)

Trungpa founded the Naropa Institute (later Naropa University) in 1974. According to Bhagavan Das, Naropa at the time was "a huge blowout party, twenty-four hours a day." (DAS, 214) But it doesn't sound like Trungpa hosted good parties, at least not by most people's standards. When a drunken Trungpa didn't like the attitude displayed by poet William Merwin and Merwin's then-girlfriend Dana Naone during a retreat at a remote ski lodge, he had his followers smash down a door to get into their room and drag them out. The couple was then forcibly stripped naked in front of Trungpa. (CLARK, 22-24) As Naone recounted:

> Guards dragged me off and pinned me to the floor...I could see William struggling a few feet away from me. I fought, and called to friends, men and women, whose faces I saw in the crowd, – to call the police. No one did. Only one man, Bill King, broke through to where I was lying at Trungpa's feet, shouting 'Leave her alone' and 'Stop it.' Trungpa rose above me, from his chair, and knocked Bill King down with a punch, swearing at him, and ordering that no one interfere. He was dragged away...Richard Assally was stripping me, while others held me down. Trungpa began punching Assally in the head, and urging him to do it faster. The rest of my clothes were torn off. (QUOTED AT CLARK, 24)

Gary Snyder described the scene around Trungpa as "cultic," with "women bodyguards in black dresses and high heels packing automatics standing in a circle around him while they served sake...It was bizarre." (DOWNING, 251) It's no surprise that Trungpa's students were made to take vows not to discuss his teachings and actions. (FALK, 121)

By 1987, Trungpa had drunk himself to death. His handpicked successor, Thomas Rich (also known as Osel Tendzin), died of AIDS in 1990. Before then, Rich reportedly had unprotected sex with male and female students without telling them of his illness (HORGAN, 53) – supposedly at Trungpa's direction. (PAINE, 104)

According to author and poet Kenneth Rexroth, "Many believe Chögyam Trungpa has unquestionably done more harm to Buddhism in the United States than any man living." (QUOTED AT FALK, 127)

Trungpa was supposedly a "crazy wisdom" teacher. But without the "wisdom" part, what we're left with is just plain crazy – like the cultish abuse of authority, alcoholism, and irresponsible sex.

Zen and the Art of Militarism

The strong association of Japanese Zen with the warrior class dates back to the Hōjō regency, a period that started in 1199. The military dictatorship known to history as the Kamakura shogunate had been established for just a few decades before the Hōjō clan schemed its way into holding power as regents to the shogun. Kamakura was far away from the power centers of established forms of Buddhism in Kyoto, (D.T. SUZUKI, ZEN AND JAPANESE CULTURE, 62) and this gave Zen, only introduced to Japan in 1191, (WATTS, 110) an opportunity to cozy up to the new bosses and increase its power and prestige.

The second Hōjō regent, Tokiyori, devoted himself to the study of Zen and invited Japanese Zen masters from Kyoto and Chinese ones from southern Sung to come to Kamakura. Of course, his example was a strong encouragement to the rest of the military class to adopt at least some semblance of Zen.

Tokiyori's son Tokimune was the ruler who organized the defense of Japan against the Mongolian invasions, one of the greatest feats in Japanese history. He was also a devoted follower of Zen, and with his encouragement Zen became firmly established in Japan – and right from these early days began to fuse with the warrior culture to form *bushidō*, the "Way of the warrior." (D.T. SUZUKI, ZEN AND JAPANESE CULTURE, 64-76) This was especially true of the Rinzai school, so much so that it is sometimes called "warrior Zen." But it also had an impact on the Sōtō tradition started by Dōgen in 1227, even though Sōtō is sometimes referred to contrastingly as "farmer Zen."

To Zen priests, association with the samurai class must have seemed a great opportunity to spread their teaching. And of course the warriors who were defending the nation from the Mongolian hordes of Kublai Khan needed spiritual guidance and comfort as much as anyone – even if, for centuries afterward, they spent much more time in fighting inter-clan power struggles than in defending their country against invasion.

To the samurai, the mindset encouraged by Zen practice was of immense practical use. However, the precept against the taking of life made for a problem. It took some creative thinking to interpret things in such a way that cutting people down with a three-foot-long razor blade for the glory of one's feudal lord could be seen as congruent with the teaching of the Buddha.

But humans have always found ways to justify violence using the language of spirituality. Especially in the decades between the mid-nineteenth century Meiji restoration and World War Two, the Japanese political leadership became masters of this, perverting both Shintō and Zen for imperialist ends.

For example, Soyen Shaku, the teacher who first introduced Zen to the United States, said in a 1905 war memorial address:

> [W]ar is not necessarily horrible, provided that it is fought for a just and honorable cause, that it is fought for the maintenance and realization of noble ideals, that it is fought for the upholding of humanity and civilization. Many material human bodies may be destroyed, many humane hearts be broken, but from a broader point of view these sacrifices are so many phenixes consumed in the sacred fire of spirituality, which will arise from the smouldering ashes reanimated, ennobled, and glorified.
>
> I am by no means trying to cover the horrors and evils of war, for war is certainly hellish. Let us avoid it as much as possible. Let us settle all our international difficulties in a more civilized manner. But if it is unavoidable, let us go into it with heart and soul, with the firm conviction that our spiritual descendants will carry out and accomplish what we have failed personally to achieve. (SHAKU, 211-214)

In a similar vein, Zen master Yamazaki Ekishu described the relationship of Zen to the Emperor as follows:

> In the great concentrated meditative state of Zen, we become united with the emperor. In

each of our actions we live, moment to moment, with the greatest respect [for the emperor]. When we personify [this spirit] in our daily life, we become masters of every situation in accordance with our sacrificial duty. This is living Zen. (QUOTED AT VICTORIA, "JAPANESE CORPORATE," 64)

During World War II, leading Japanese Zen masters claimed that killing Chinese people was an expression of Buddhist compassion meant to rid the victims of their "defilements." (VICTORIA, ZEN WAR, 15) And the abbot of the Hosshin-ji temple, Harada Sogaku, told soldiers, "Forgetting [the difference between] self and others in every situation, you should always become completely one with your work. [When ordered to] march – tramp, tramp; [when ordered to] fire – bang, bang; this is the clear expression of the highest Bodhi-wisdom, the unity of Zen and war." (QUOTED AT VICTORIA, "JAPANESE CORPORATE," 65)

Lest it be thought that all Japanese Buddhists accepted warfare and aggression, we must mention the Sōtō priest Uchiyama Gudo, who opposed the Emperor system itself – and was ousted from the priesthood, imprisoned on trumped-up charges, and executed in 1911. (VICTORIA, "JAPANESE CORPORATE," 63-64) And there was the Youth League for Revitalizing Buddhism (*Shinkō Bukkyō Seinen Dōmei*), a pan-Buddhist reform group which strongly protested institutional Japanese Buddhism and its support for militarism. Sadly this group was persecuted out of existence by the government in the 1930s. (VICTORIA, ZEN WAR, 204-207) But these were exceptions.

Even in the post-war period, Japanese Zen has sometimes retained an aggressive and violent approach. It has not been unknown for monks to be severely beaten – even beaten to death – for disciplinary offenses. (FALK, 39-40)

In the 1970s, Zen training became a mandatory part of orientation for many Japanese companies – certainly not because they wanted enlightened compassionate bodhisattvas on the payroll (bad for the bottom line), but because institutional Japanese Zen is very good at instilling obedience and conformity. In the words of Sōtō Zen priest Daizen Victoria, "Senior monks act much like drill sergeants, and novice monks are their recruits." (VICTORIA, "JAPANESE CORPORATE." 63-64)

Messed-up Magicians and Rascally Witches

We've already traced the history of the ceremonial magic and Pagan movements back through some shady characters. There's the Theosophical Society, founded by fraudulent medium Helena Blavatsky; SRIA and its highly questionable claims of connections to the Rosicrucians; and MacGregor Mathers's convenient claims of authorization from Blavatsky's "Secret Chiefs" to create the Rosy Cross.*

Then we have Aleister Crowley's personality problems (to put it mildly), and the psychotic break around his "Aiwass" experience, which led him to believe that he was anointed by the secret Masters of the Universe to be "the Prophet chosen to proclaim the Law which will determine the destinies of this planet for an epoch." (CROWLEY, CONFESSIONS, CH 66, 615)

And there's Gerald Gardner, a man with what one of his own students called a "devious creative attitude to factual truth," (LAMOND, 10) who plagiarized wildly, (HUTTON, 227-238) misrepresented his relationship with witchcraft (HUTTON, 206-207) and made bogus claims of academic qualifications. (HUTTON, 207, 218-219)

With a heritage like this, it would be remarkable if the Pagan movement hadn't seen its share of misbehavior.

However, since Pagans tend to operate in small groups and have little patience with the "guru" notion – perhaps because we have such shining examples of human flaws and foibles in our history – the damage has been limited. Small groups have meant that even the most abusive leaders have had limited opportunities to victimize others with power-tripping behavior. And since few Pagan organizations own much property, financial hanky-panky is also self-limiting. This may change in years to come, but for now Paganism's outsider status seems to be protective against some sorts of scandals.

But there's one area of human behavior that can stir up trouble even in the smallest groups: sex. And when sex is used for ritual or magical purposes, we get to combine the volatility of sexual taboos with that of religious dogma – an explosive combination best viewed from a distance.

---

* See the earlier chapter, "The Tapestry of Zen Pagan History, Part I."

Paganism comes from a heritage that views sex positively, from the sexuality of Whitman's poetry to the sexual revolution of the 1960s counter-culture. And not just vanilla sex: Gardner's original Wicca had people tying up and whipping each other (GARDNER, 7-9, 49) (however lightly (HUTTON, 235)) and engaging in Dominance/submission behavior (GARDNER, 31) in a sexually charged atmosphere, to raise ritual energy.

But sexual license plus hierarchy – such as the levels of initiation found in Wicca and other traditions – can make a ripe ground for abuse. Among "big name" Pagans, few have stirred as much controversy on this front as Gavin and Yvonne Frost.

In their book *The Witch's Bible* the Frosts discuss the use of sexual intercourse as an entry-level initiation rite. That in itself should raise eyebrows, as a power differential between a candidate and a member operating with the backing of a full coven raises serious sexual ethics issues. Their claim that this is part of the "old path" of Wiccan tradition (FROST, 61) is of course, a load of hooey – no Wiccan rite has a claim on ancient provenance.

But what has stirred such controversy that some Pagans have threatened to burn the Frosts in effigy is that before describing the initiation they say, "When a child develops to a stage where the physical attributes of reproduction are present, he can become a full member of the coven...It is hoped by Wicca that the first full sexual experience will take place in the pleasant surroundings of the coven and that the spiritual as well as the physical aspects of the experience will lead the child to a complete life," and they discuss the surgical destruction of the physical attributes of male and female virginity before such initiation. (FROST, 65-67)

A later edition adds a disclaimer: "No formal initiation into a group that practices the great rite should be done before the candidate attains the age of eighteen." (FROST, 61) And there is absolutely no evidence, nor even credible suggestions, that the Frosts have engaged in child abuse. Still, the power differential issue, the fact that material suggesting sexual relations with minors was originally included at all, and the fact that it has not been removed but only had a disclaimer added, has caused a firestorm. Even their defenders can only claim the Frosts included the material for the sake of controversy, while detractors describe the Frosts as dangerous charlatans.

Ian Corrigan, a noted leader in the Pagan community – and a man who even says he considers the Frosts "friends on some level" (CORRIGAN, E-MAIL) – says of *The Witch's Bible*,

> When this book came out in the early 70s, it was considered abject nonsense by the few folks who had any actual knowledge of Wicca in those days. The Frosts came out of nowhere, appropriating the term 'Wicca' for their own version of what religious witchcraft might be. Their synthesis bore almost no resemblance to the traditions of Wicca, either in ritual or theology, and certainly not in the grotesque suggestions about the sexual upbringing of children. (CORRIGAN, "UNFORTUNATE MISTAKE")

While the provocation provided by the Frosts was extreme, there is a definite tension within the Pagan community about sexual freedom. Part of this is legitimate concern about issues of power, consent, and maturity, but more than that, there is also an almost prudish counter-tendency starting to arise.

Many Wiccan covens have either reduced the use of binding and scourging from active means of consciousness alteration to mere symbolic references, or have dropped them all together. Many Pagans have no idea of the key role that these practices played in the historically important tradition of Gardnerian Wicca, and will harshly criticize those who do choose to use them.

According to religion scholar Jo Pearson,

> Wiccans have at times been desperate to shake off the tabloid sensationalism that has dogged them since the 1960s, and to avoid implication in satanic ritual abuse scares....Wicca felt it had to present a 'clean' image which, while retaining a view of sex as sacred, played down the role of sex magic and emphasized 'spirituality' rather than sexuality. The now very evident commercialization and commodification of Wicca has come about largely because of this desire on the part of Wiccans...to present Wicca as an acceptable religion for the post/modern world. (PEARSON, 32)

This trend is not limited to Wiccans but is part of a broader current in Paganism. I know one fairly large non-sectarian Pagan organization, known for putting on festivals of several hundred people, that underwent a split over what would and would not be taught and practiced in the "sacred sexuality" track of workshops and events at their festivals. The more "prudish" faction (for lack of a better term) went off and formed their own organization, whose charter disallows the use of scourging at their events, equating it with animal sacrifice as a violent practice.

Or, there's the supposed "sanctuary of Earth religion" which claims to find inspiration in Wicca, but who has banned people being skyclad on their land. A group that claims to derive its spiritual inspiration from nature, yet takes offense at the natural state in which human beings arrive on Earth!

This sort of prudery and objection to practices such as binding, scourging, and nudity in Pagan groups can only be described as ahistorical. That doesn't mean that knowledgeable and honest Pagans have to do these things, or like them; just that they must accept the use of them by others as a legitimate means of raising ritual energy.

But the desire to set taboos around what other adults do with their own bodies penetrates even into the supposedly sexually free Pagan community. And in the long term, this judgmentalism, this desire to dilute the power of sexuality to the point that it loses the power to offend, much less transform, may be more of a threat to its integrity than the danger of sex scandals.

Silly Shamans and Goofy Gurus

Our look behind the scenes would not be complete without a quick look at some of the big names in New Age-iness.

• Andrew Cohen is an American guru, and the publisher of *EnlightenNext* (originally *What Is Enlightenment?*) magazine. According to his own magazine, Cohen is "an inspiring phenomenon...Powerless to limit his unceasing investigation, he has looked at the 'jewel of enlightenment' from every angle and given birth to a teaching that is vast and subtle, yet incomparably direct and revolutionary in its impact." ("ANDREW COHEN: FOUNDER...") (Modest, too, isn't he?)

He became a spiritual "teacher" (to use the word loosely) after an entire two and a half weeks of training under his guru,

H. W. L. Poonja. (Tarlo, 54, 114) He has claimed, "[V]ery few people like me exist in the world. I can destroy a person's karma....If you trust me, I have the power to completely destroy your past," (quoted at Tarlo, 92) and "Anyone who loves me...is guaranteed enlightenment." (quoted at Tarlo, 64)

"You know...sometimes I feel like a god," (quoted at Tarlo, 109) Cohen once said. Certainly feeling a union with the divine is all well and good; but we should remember the words of *Star Trek*'s Captain Kirk: "Above all else, a god needs compassion!" ("Where No Man Has Gone Before") So how did this "god" treat the mere mortals around him? When one of his followers told him that her parents were pressuring her to leave, he told her, "You're a hypocrite, a liar, and a prostitute." (quoted at Tarlo, 87) He controlled his followers' romantic and sexual relationships, (Tarlo, 210; Braak, 141, 166-167, 173) convinced them to throw their secular books into the Ganges, (Tarlo, 68) and had them throw away or burn their own writings. (Tarlo, 77, 233-239) He had one woman perform two thousand prostrations every day – a task that took ten hours a day, so that she had to quit her job to obey his demands. (Tarlo, 281) He told one of his long-time students, "I don't give a damn about your personal evolution anymore. I just want to be able to use you for my community." (quoted at Braak, 185)

Brad Warner, a Sōtō Zen monk and author of several popular books about Zen, says of Cohen's writings that he

> says just enough interesting stuff to make me believe that at one point in his life he had a fleeting glimpse of something profoundly true. But, like so many others, he was unwilling to follow through on what he discovered. When the Universe showed him that perfection is a fantasy...he took that to mean that fantasies are perfection....He wants so badly to believe in the ideal of the Perfectly Enlightened Being that nothing, not even Reality itself, can get in the way of his vision. (Warner, Review)

But perhaps the most damning evaluation of Cohen comes from his own mother – his Jewish mother, (Tarlo, 7) no less – who says, "It just seems to me that [Andrew] is as duped by his own propaganda as were all those other brother-gurus in the marketplace who promised deliverance from suffering – from

Hitler to David Koresh." (TARLO, 291)

- Ken Wilber is "perhaps the most comprehensive philosophical thinker of our times," "the most cogent and penetrating voice in the recent emergence of a uniquely American wisdom" – at least, in the completely unbiased opinion of his publisher. ("KEN WILBER: WELCOME")

On the other hand, Robert Anton Wilson named Wilber as an example of the sort of writer whose work is "an ocean of semantic mush":

> Any sentence from such writers could easily be inserted into a political speech; just change "God" or "True Self" to "the government" or "the chief executive," and the general tapioca-like fog will remain the same – vapid, rhetorical, hollow, but vaguely "inspirational" if you don't think about it. (WILSON, "INTRODUCTION," IX-X)

Wilber's claim to mystical fame rests partly on his boast that he experienced, and sustained for several years, an extraordinary state of consciousness:

> I slept not at all during those eleven days; or rather, I was conscious for eleven days and nights, even as the body and mind went through waking, dreaming, and sleeping: I was unmoved in the midst of changes; there was no I to be moved; there was only unwavering empty consciousness... (WILBER, ONE TASTE, 69)

But this is not some sort of spiritual breakthrough; staying conscious for eleven days through dreaming and sleeping is a sleep disorder. This is "Zen sickness" to the highest power. Rather than setting him free, his experience has made him reliant on people who recognize his "enlightenment."

One such person is Andrew Cohen. Wilber and Cohen have a nice mutual admiration society going. Cohen's magazine often features Wilber's work, and Cohen has said that Wilber's "unparalleled scholarship and experience has provided an invaluable theoretical context in which to understand some of my own deepest insights and discoveries about the evolution of consciousness." (Cohen, Editorial)

For his part, Wilber often fawns over Cohen, such as in a piece on "Integral Transformative Practice" published in 2000 in *What is Enlightenment?*:

> But Andrew is quite right to blow the whistle on this, and I support him wholeheartedly in that. Andrew has always been a strong voice reminding us of absolute Freedom and Emptiness....
>
> Andrew points out that the "new" approaches to spirituality...are often nothing more than new forms of boomeritis. And again, I could not agree more....
>
> Needless to say Andrew is not impressed. Me neither....
>
> Andrew's concern, again, is that all this fussing around with the relative vehicles can detract from the radical, absolute, nondual Truth – and again I agree with him. (Wilber, "Integral," 38, 126, 127)

I can almost imagine Wilber sighing and batting his eyelashes all through this. Get a room, guys.

Wilber's claims of special understanding aren't restricted to spiritual insights – he claims to have "read at least a Ph.D. level in 23 disciplines" and to have "an idiot savant level of pattern recognition." (Quoted at Sunfellow) Apparently this is what prepared him to offer a "theory of everything" in his book *A Brief History of Everything*. (Wilber, Brief History, xxi)

As philosophy, Wilber's theory is mostly mush, too soft to be either useful or disproven. But as science, it's just wrong. Wilber claims to explain the evolution of life from matter, and mind from life, but he gets basic evolutionary biology wrong – he's a proponent of his own version of "Intelligent Design," as David Lane, a professor of philosophy, sociology, and religious studies, explains:

> Wilber has misrepresented the fundamentals of natural selection. Moreover, his presentation of

how evolution is viewed today is so skewed that Wilber has more in common with creationists than evolutionists, even though he is claiming to present the evolutionists' current view. (LANE)

Wilber's case is interesting, because his earlier work is not bad. His 1979 book *No Boundaries*, for example, is a fairly sensible look at the psychological problem of alienation. Since in that work he mostly sticks to the psychology of subjective experience, it has only a minimal number of whoppers.* But it seems that somewhere along the way, Wilber lost his bearings and started believing his own hype.

• Daniel Pinchbeck is perhaps the guy most responsible for popularizing the idea that some great transformation is going to occur in 2012.† He didn't originate it – I recall discussions of the idea on-line in USENET forums in the early 1990s – but he has done much to spread the meme. In his bestselling book *2012: The Return of Quetzalcoatl* (which he modestly offers to us as "a gift handed backward through space-time, from beyond the barrier of a new realm" (PINCHBECK, 2012, 15)), he claims to have received "transmissions" from the Mayan deity Quetzalcoatl telling him about this momentous event. An excerpt from these transmissions:

> The writer of this work [i.e., Pinchbeck] is the vehicle of my arrival – my return – to this realm. He certainly did not expect this to be the case. What began as a quest to understand prophecy has become the fulfillment of prophecy. The vehicle of my arrival has been brought to an awareness of his situation in sometimes painful increments and stages of resistance – and this book follows the evolution of his learning process, as an aid to the reader's understanding.

---

* Perhaps only a few more than this book.
† I posted an early version of this section on my blog, and Pinchbeck responded. You can see the exchange at http://unreasonable.org/node/3267 and judge for yourself.

> The vehicle of my arrival had to learn to follow synchronicities, embrace paradoxes, and solve puzzles. He had to enter into a new way of thinking about time and space and consciousness.
>
> Almost apologetically, the vehicle notes that his birthday fell in June 1966 – 6/66 – "count the number of the Beast: for it is the number of the man; and his number is Six hundred threescore and six."
>
> The Beast prophesied is the "feathered serpent," Quetzalcoatl. (PINCHBECK, 2012, 370)

Because these "revelations" came after many years of heavy experimentation with substances like psilocybin mushrooms, LSD, ayahuasca, iboga, and DPT, (GRIGORIADIS, 90, 114) Pinchbeck is sometimes described as a modern-day Timothy Leary or Terence McKenna. But a modern-day Aleister Crowley seems a better comparison – complete with voices "channeled" from "higher powers" which name him as their special agent on Earth, identification with "the Beast," and a wonderful degree of apophenia. (But without Crowley's wit, discipline, or insight.[*])

The "transmissions and coincidences" phenomenon was also experienced by Robert Anton Wilson, who in 1973 entered what he calls a "belief system" in which he was "receiving telepathic messages from entities residing on a planet around the double star Sirius," while at the same time encountering "implausible coincidences" which led him to discover links between Sirius and the Illuminati, (WILSON, COSMIC, 8) an eighteenth-century Masonic group much beloved by conspiracy theorists.

Wilson, though, skipped the megalomania and the Beast, and later came to understand that the "telepathic messages" theory was only one possible explanation of his experience.

---

[*] See the earlier chapter "It's All in Your Mind." And notice how 2012 manifests the Law of Fives – using the usual rule of numerological reduction, 2 + 0 + 1 + 2 = 5

(Though some of the alternatives he proposes are equally far out.) Pinchbeck pays lip service to the idea that there might be other explanations besides his being a chosen messenger of a god, but it's clear that he believes himself to be special – "I'm generally a humble person, but I do feel I'm surfing the edge of consciousness on this planet," he says (GRIGORIADIS, 114) – and that Quetzalcoatl is "not just my dream," but everyone's. (GRIGORIADIS, 116)

Crowley and Wilson didn't have blogs. But Pinchbeck has "Reality Sandwich," into which you can peer to get a look into his thought processes, befuddled as they may be.

For example, on December 9, 2009, a strange light was seen in the skies over Norway. Something quickly traced out a brilliant spiral in the sky, mystifying observers and sparking furious speculation on web forums as to its nature. The explanation turned out to be a Russian missile that misfired during testing. (MURPHY)

According to Pinchbeck's blog, though, "this seems extremely unlikely – in the category of explanations that includes the theory that the most complex and virtuosic crop circles were the products of board and rope, or that Building 7 of the World Trade Center fell as a result of the Twin Towers collapse." (PINCHBECK, "THOUGHTS") Now, crop circles are in fact created with boards and rope, in combination with good planning and simple surveying techniques (and you can learn how to do it yourself by searching the web*), and conspiracy theories about the World Trade Center buildings falling because of some sort of controlled demolition have been so thoroughly debunked that it takes either a confusion perhaps arising out of post-traumatic shock, or a deliberate dedication to ignorance, to hold on to them. But Pinchbeck gets wilder, continuing:

> The magnificent spiral spectacle...seems to be a kind of focusing event for human consciousness...It is possible that such an apparition is somehow co-created or imprinted by the collective field of the human psyche....

---

* See, for example, www.circlemakers.org, or search for "crop circles" on www.csicop.org

> The Norway spiral has resonance with the Hopi prophecies of the Blue Star Kachina, which appears at the end of the Fourth World – if not that signifying event itself, perhaps a foreshadowing or retro-causal echo of it. The spiral seems like a message, invitation, or indication that the earth and its inhabitants are on the threshold of a deep transformation.
> (PINCHBECK, "THOUGHTS")

I especially like the "retro-causal echo" of the Blue Star Kachina theory. It takes a very special mind to think that an echo of the end of the world traveling back in time is a more plausible explanation for a light in the sky than a misfired rocket.

In Pinchbeck's opinion, "the rational, empirical worldview...has reached its expiration date." (ANASTAS) But the fact that he can make statements like the Blue Star Kachina retro-causal echo thing and still be taken seriously demonstrates that many people haven't even opened the wrapper on rationality.

And perhaps this is the big difference between the "industrial strength shamanism" we've been discussing, and the plastic shamanism of Pinchbeck and his ilk: where plastic shamans will put aside rationality and become more and more attached to the fantastic, an industrial strength shaman knows the importance of grounding and sees rational thinking as a valuable reality tunnel for getting practical things done.

Pinchbeck seems so ridiculous that I can almost imagine that he is playing a giant practical joke: that when nothing especially momentous happens in December 2012, he will pull off the mask and say, "Gotcha! Boy, I can't believe people took that stuff seriously!"

That might be pretty funny, if it wasn't for what happened to Dan Carpenter.

Carpenter was a member of Pinchbeck's psychedelic circle, from the early days before Pinchbeck went cuckoo for Quetzalcoatl. He was a frequent poster on Pinchbeck's online discussion board, and went to New York to meet Pinchbeck in person. (GRIGORIADIS, 114) He was close enough to Pinchbeck that Pinchbeck wrote an encouraging forward to Carpenter's book, *A Psychonaut's Guide to the Invisible Landscape*; (PINCHBECK, "FOREWARD") the book describes thirteen trips Carpenter took on DXM powder, the anesthetic in cough syrup.

These trips took him into a powerful experience of apophenia, a headspace where every little coincidence and event was fraught with meaning and portent, and left him with the impression everything was "somehow a program....[t]here is no free will – only the sense there is." (QUOTED AT GRIGORIADIS, 116)

And so, following the program – the program he had found while engaging in a behavior pattern that Pinchbeck encouraged – Daniel Carpenter hanged himself. Sadly, this is the danger when psychedelic visions are prized to the exclusion of "the rational, empirical worldview."

To be clear: I am by no means opposed to the responsible use of psychedelic or entheogenic substances. Far from it. They are powerful tools of transformation, and used properly might – just might – help us find new ways of thinking that can help us get the planet out of the mess it's in.

But when someone starts taking their own feedback-saturated perceptions as seriously as Pinchbeck does, it's time to point out that drug-induced hallucinations are a piss-poor guide to objective reality.

There are a lot of very fine people who like Pinchbeck's work. I've even attended several great discussions put on by the Baltimore "spore" of "Evolver," a social network that developed out of Pinchbeck's blog. But Pinchbeck himself is in need of a good solid grounding, and a class in remedial critical thinking.

• James Arthur Ray used to be a sales manager for AT&T. (O'CONNOR) He seems to have gotten more ego gratification once he became a self-help guru, gaining the confidence to play a "game" in which he wore white robes, played God, and ordered people to commit mock suicide. (DOUGHERTY, "FOR SOME")

He certainly found his new gig more lucrative. With the fame generated by his book *Harmonic Wealth: The Secret of Attracting the Life You Want,* and appearances in the film *The Secret* and on *The Oprah Winfrey Show,* he built his company James Ray International into a $9.4 million concern by 2008.

In October 2009, more than 50 people paid $9,695 each for a "spiritual warrior" retreat with him, (DOUGHERTY, "FOR SOME") scheduled to last for five days. ("ANGEL VALLEY SEDONA")

That seems pretty lucrative, but Ray had ways to squeeze some more profit out of the deal. A "vision quest" exercise sent participants out into the desert for 36 hours without food or water. They had sleeping bags – but Ray also offered to sell them

"Peruvian ponchos" for an extra $250. (Dougherty, "For Some")

(For comparison, the 2009 edition of the six-day Starwood Festival mentioned at the start of this book cost $235.)

The day after the "vision quest," participants were packed into a bogus "sweat lodge ceremony" – bogus, because no genuine sweat would ever try to pack in fifty people. The proper size is usually 8 to 12, small enough to allow for adequate supervision and care. Nor is a genuine sweat lodge covered in plastic. (Dougherty and Roth) Nor is a proper sweat lodge done after a 36-hour ordeal in the desert.

If this had been all that happened during this retreat, it would be stupid and tragic enough that a charlatan plastic shaman had managed to defraud so many people. But this time, it got much, much worse: while Ray sat outside in the shade, three people died and about twenty were injured from the heat and neglect of an improperly managed sweat. (Dougherty, "New Details") In June 2011, Ray was convicted of negligent homicide in those deaths. (Lacey, "New Age Guru")

Why Are There So Many Losers in Spirituality?

I recently came across a marvelous article by martial arts writer Dave Lowry, "Why Are There So Many Losers in the Martial Arts?" (Lowry) Lowry is a man who loves the martial arts as devoutly as anyone, but here he writes:

> And you can bet before your tour [of martial arts schools] is finished, you'll have come across a dozen more of the oddest assortment of ego and megalomaniacs, pathological liars, pathetically inept impostors; people who run the gamut of the strange all the way from the seriously mentally ill to the merely insufferably pompous. And it is to these misguided souls that students are going every day in hopes of finding some embodiment of the ideals of the martial arts, only to be met with greed, deceit, and a gross kind of hypocrisy that rots the spirit with the worst corrosion, leaving stains of bitterness and disillusionment.

He describes how the martial arts can serve as ego gratification for people who would otherwise be "just another face in the crowd":

> When Joe goes to his dojo, he takes off his work clothes and exchanges them for a uniform with a scarlet jacket and bright blue pants. He ties on a red and gold belt and if that isn't enough a sign of his status, the letters "Sensei" stitched across his breast should make it clear. Outside these walls, Joe might be just another ordinary person, but in the dojo, he's Master Shlomotol. His students bow when he enters the room, and address him respectfully. To his wife, kids, boss, and co-workers, Joe's pretty average. In his dojo though, he is Sensei Somebody with a capital S.

And he notes how, as practitioners like this don't have other accomplishments to distract them, they often become the ones who devote the most energy to their arts and end up propagating those arts to the next generation.

I've seen enough of the martial arts world to know that Lowry is regrettably on target. Why is this relevant to our discussion? Because the same phenomenon can be found in spiritual communities.

We've seen the dangers in the abuse of power, money, sex, and drugs, but simple ego is a more common and everyday threat. Someone with an otherwise undistinguished life who can lay claim to be a Wiccan "High Priestess," or an "Adeptus Major" in one of the Golden Dawn traditions, or a "Dharma Teacher" running a Buddhist meditation group – or a church deacon, or a "Reverend" at some storefront church, or a lector at the synagogue, the phenomenon is non-denominational – can get a tremendous ego boost from their position.

Of course reputable Wiccans, ceremonialists, Buddhists, etcetera, will say that such ego-seekers don't represent their true traditions. But they are out there, and all too often end up being the people representing their traditions to students and seekers.

So what can be done?

Respect and support good teachers in every way you can. You can spot good teachers by looking at how they live their lives – they "walk their talk," and that walk takes them in a positive direction. They're not perfect and they know it, but they're using the methods that they recommend to others in order to improve themselves.

But if you find perfect enlightened gurus who are doing the work of God or the Ascended Masters or whatever, or people whose entire ego revolves around their positions in a religious or spiritual organization – run!

And always remember the last words of the Buddha: "Be a lamp unto yourself, make of yourself a light." (KORNFIELD, 156)

Life and Death in the Stream

Today I took a little hike up into the woods uphill from the Tekishin Zen center, where I'm spending a few days. I sat zazen by the stream for a while, watching the water eddy around the rocks.

I've written about the precepts, about the Noble Truths, about magic and mysticism, but I haven't much touched on the big one, the thing that makes so many people turn to religion for comfort: death.

The most popular way to deal with death, of course, is to deny it, to believe in a survival of the self in some sort of afterlife. In our culture this usually entails believing "I'm going to Heaven when I die!" – never mind that, as Mark Twain pointed out in his satirical story *Letters from Earth*, the popular notion of Heaven sounds like an awful, dreary place.

An alternative dodge, long popular in the East and gaining in the West, is to say, "I will be reincarnated when I die." Many people think that the Buddha taught reincarnation – indeed, the emphasis on reincarnation seems to be one of the big draws of Tibetan Buddhism for some Westerners, at least on the pop-culture level – but the truth is a little more complex. Teaching in a culture where the idea was widely accepted, the Buddha certainly used parables about reincarnation. The tales of the "past lives" of the Buddha most likely either arose from this practice, or were added by later devotees who applied their notions of transmigration of souls to the story of their favorite holy man.

But as for the Buddha's own opinion on the topic, when pressed by one of his monks he compared asking about the afterlife or other metaphysical issues to a man who has been shot with a poisoned arrow but insists that his physician tell him all about the clan and caste and appearance of the shooter, the construction of the arrow, and so on, before removing it. (WARREN, 121-122) The Buddha tells us that the trouble we stir up – the cause-and-effect of karma – will keep going after we die, but as for the rest, the lessons about the origin and end of suffering apply regardless of whether we continue to persist in some form after our death.

Of course, the Buddha's injunction has not stopped various Buddhist schools from laying down all sorts of teachings about reincarnation and other metaphysical topics.

The idea of reincarnation came into Paganism partly through these Buddhists. We can track it back through Gardner, who picked it up in while living in Ceylon and who wanted to be reborn in a witch coven; (LAMOND, 17) and Crowley, who believed himself to be the reincarnation of Eliphas Levi; (CROWLEY, "THE FORMULA") back through the Theosophists, who picked it up both from Buddhist and Hindu sources in the East and from some Western mystery traditions, such as the Pythagorean. (In addition to being the ancient Greek mathematician who came up with the famous theorem about right triangles, and one of the first to propound a theory of harmony in music, Pythagoras was also a mystic.)

Reincarnation is sometimes argued as being "natural," the way of the seasons. Plants die in the fall and return in the spring, after all, and so many Pagans are prepared to project this on to our lives as individuals. As one popular chant written by Ian Corrigan goes, "Hoof and horn, hoof and horn / All that dies shall be re-born / Corn and grain, corn and grain / all that falls shall rise again." (ÁR NDRAÍOCHT FÉIN, "HOOF AND HORN")

But when the corn falls, are the stalks that rise again the next spring the same plants?

Let's go back to the stream. Sit near some rocks in its flow. Perhaps you'll see a spot where whirlpools form for a bit, a knot of water that takes on a perceptible form for a few seconds due to certain conditions, then melts away as those conditions change.

But then, a little later, in the same spot, another whirlpool forms.

Is it the same whirlpool?

The question as phrased does not admit of an accurate answer. It depends on how we define and conceive sameness. "Same" is a construction of our minds.

Indeed, as the water flows downstream, and the molecules pass through the whirlpool, we might ask if the whirlpool is the same from moment to moment.

Consider the puzzle of Theseus' ship – during the voyage, every single plank and nail and bit of rigging is replaced. Is it the

"same" ship that pulls into the final harbor as that which set out?*
To say that it is or it isn't is to make a judgment about the use of
words, not about the facts of the situation.

Now consider – is it the "same" Tom Swiss that writes this,
as the infant that fell into this world decades ago? Every atom has
been replaced over the years, every cell is different.

The Buddha taught that the idea of a distinct, persistent
"self" is an illusion, just as the idea is of a whirlpool separate
from the stream, or a ship separate from the boards and other
parts that make it up. Saying it's the "same" whirlpool, or ship, or
person, is just an idea.

If the person I think I am is only a mental construction, if
"I" am a character in the story my brain is telling, then how can
this fictional thing be reincarnated or reborn?

Better, and more hopeful – how can it die? This is the up
side of the "no self" teaching of anātman! If there is nothing to be
reborn, it's because there is nothing to die in the first place. One
story about the Zen master Bankei says that he was very scared of
death as a child. When he had his great enlightenment, he
realized that "he" could never die, because "he" had never been
born. (SMULLYAN, 180-181)

If our usual idea of "self" is wrong, then what am I?

Psychologically, we're conglomerations of mental energy.
We are made of thoughts and ideas and beliefs that have each
been part of many other people.

Timothy Leary used to speak of himself as the
reincarnation of everyone whose works had made a strong
impression on his brain, from Socrates to Crowley (WILSON, COSMIC, 116)
– a neurological, not a metaphysical, phenomenon. But if we take
it one step further and see that each of those people was a
"reincarnation" of everyone who affected them, and so on, we see
a web that makes us all the reincarnations of everyone; and that

---

* A real-life example of the Theseus's ship puzzle is provided by *Constellation*,
a sailing ship that's now a museum in Baltimore's Inner Harbor. There was a
frigate called *Constellation* launched in 1797; in 1853, it went into the Gosport
Navy Yard in Norfolk to be broken down. In 1854, a corvette called
Constellation came out of that shipyard. Naval historians have spilled much
ink over the subject of whether or not it was the "same" ship that sailed in the
year before, or an entirely new vessel.

we will be reincarnated in those whose lives we have touched.

I once met a man who told me that he had been Jesus in a past life; if I'd been a little quicker-minded and brave enough, I should have told him, "me too."

If we look more deeply, beyond the verbal/psychological levels to the emotional, biological, chemical, physical, and energetic, we see that we are interconnected with not just our fellow humans, but with all life on Earth. Indeed if we look deep enough we can see that "interconnected" is the wrong word, as it implies distinct units; that to draw a line around a piece of this life and call it "me" is arbitrary.

In his commentary on the Heart Sutra, Thich Nhat Hanh talks about how he saw this while contemplating the relationship between a leaf and a tree:

> I asked the leaf whether it was scared because it was autumn and the other leaves were falling. The leaf told me, "No. During the whole spring and summer I was very alive. I worked hard and helped nourish the tree, and much of me is in the tree. Please do not say that I am just this form, because the form of leaf is only tiny part of me. I am the whole tree, and when I go back to the soil, I will continue to nourish the tree. That's why I do not worry. As I leave this branch and float to the ground, I will wave to the tree and tell her, 'I will see you again very soon.'"...
>
> You have to see life. You should not say, life of the leaf, you should only speak of life in the leaf and life in the tree. My life is just Life, and you can see it in me and in the tree. (HAHN, HEART OF UNDERSTANDING, 26)

Knowing that in our true essence we are one with all life, we can let go of much of our fear. The more we adopt the point of view that "I am the whole tree," the less we need stories of how this leaf will live on in Leaf Heaven, or how its leaf soul will transmigrate to a bud in the spring, in order to find peace with the fact of death.

But now we face a problem not encountered by the

Buddha: we know that the biosphere is not immortal. In fact, it is rather sick at the moment, and it is possible that we humans will destroy the ecology of Earth as we know it.

Now, just as we can see that the whirlpool is one with the stream, and the leaf is one with the tree, and we are one with the biosphere, so we can – with another mental jump – see that the biosphere of planet Earth is one with the entire Universe. And with that understanding, knowing we are one with the stars and the galaxies, even the end of the Earth will not destroy our peace.

And even if the human race is not responsible, someday life on this pale blue dot will end. Maybe a big rock from the sky will get us; or maybe we'll last until the sun grows old and swells to swallow the planet. And in the big picture, with the right understanding, we can be okay with that.

But it would be a damn shame, aesthetically speaking, if we did it to ourselves, if we wrecked the planet. Even the most equanimous spiritual masters like the Buddha, unperturbed by death, know that how each of us gets there can be beautiful or disharmonious, and the same can be said for the life of the planet. The fact that it will eventually end, does not mean that destroying it is not an ugly thing to do. It's the difference between having your sand castle kicked down by a bully, and leaving it for the wind and tide to claim.

And so we come back around to the aesthetic question, to the matter of beauty as applied to life – that is, the mystic sense. To have a beautiful life, to perceive beauty in the relationship between our life experience and the broader world, we need to see both our life and the world as sacred. But so long as we remain "hungry ghosts" seeking to devour the world with consumption, not knowing that what we want can never be found in the accumulation of things, we will never know tranquility or beauty.

We can't live forever, and neither can the Earth. But we can and should strive for beauty – for sacredness – in both our own lives, and in the life of the Earth.

* * *

It's now January 2010, a few years after the trip to Japan that started this book. As I have been concluding work on the first draft in the past few months, death has come and paid me a visit, taking the two dogs who were my close companions for over twelve years.

People are much more forthcoming with questions and advice when you lose a dog than when you lose a parent or a spouse or a child. And so friends have been asking me "Will you get another dog?" (Compare the questions "Will you marry again?" or "Will you have another child?", which we often wonder about but seldom ask the bereaved spouse or parent.) Many have suggested that I do so; some even to the point of implying that grief is something to avoid, that I should fill the void as soon as possible.

Another advisor, though, pointed out that taking another dog into my life will just have me back in this same place of grief some years down the road. And this is true – but it is also true for any relationship. Every connection we make eventually ends with us saying good-bye, from one side of the grave or the other.

The only way to avoid that grief would be to never love – an even greater tragedy. I am reminded of an aphorism attributed to author John A. Shedd: "A ship in harbor is safe, but that is not what ships are built for." Just so, a heart that never loves is safe from the pangs of grief; but that's not what hearts are for.

And so the death of a loved one (two-footed or four-footed) is a reminder of the grief that is common to us all, a call to tenderness, a call to open the heart and let the whole Cosmos in.

As I knew that my second dog, Piccolo, was in failing health and likely to pass on soon, I wrote this prose poem:

> The snow is gone. Where did it go to? There were billions of snowflakes, in my backyard, each perfectly detailed, dazzling faceted. Now they have gone, and my yard is mud.
>
> Did they go to snowflake heaven? Did they reincarnate as packed powder on some ski slope?
>
> Each snowflake was a nexus of conditions, of water and temperatures and altitudes of clouds. Each snowflake was a mass of Arctic air, plus an ocean breeze, plus a low pressure system. Each snowflake contained the cycle of seasons, the tilt of the Earth's axis, the deep ocean currents that make the climate, the Milankovitch cycles that make the Ice Ages. And more: the formation of

the Earth itself, the Sun, the element of oxygen born in a dying star, the hydrogen that condensed out of the Big Bang, the whole universe in each snowflake.

And then those elements move apart, no longer overlap and the snowflake cannot be seen. But it is not gone, because the seasons, the Earth, the Sun, the Universe, remain.

And what is true for a snowflake is no less true for a dog or a human. We are the snow that appears when conditions are just so, and then melts and goes into the soil, and is taken up by trees and grasses, and rises to become the cloud skittering across the sky, and then falls to become the stream and the ocean and the puddle, part of other sets of conditions, each glorious and beautiful. We melt into the world, and our oneness with it – which never went away – is again revealed.

And this oneness is also revealed when we open our hearts, remove the boundaries, and let death remind us of our own tender Buddha nature.

Zen Paganism [Reprise]

In the course of our discussion, we've been around the world and through thousands of years of history. We've considered meditation and magic, sex and death, monks and madmen. But what does it all mean? What's the point of this label that several people have independently discovered, "Zen Pagan"?

It's easy enough to put a little Buddha statue next to the athame on your personal altar, or to add zazen to your daily routine while still being a Wiccan or a Druid – or an Episcopalian or a Reform Jew or whatever your preference may be. And if you want to do that and call yourself a Zen Pagan, or Zen Christian, or Zen Jew, fine; no one has a monopoly on these words.

But if that's as far as it goes, then I think that something important is missing.

There are many people who have adopted labels like "Buddhist" or "Pagan" but have merely painted new faces onto their old, usually Christian, ideas: a Kwan Yin mask for the Virgin Mary, the generic Goddess of the Romantics for Jehovah, the Shakyamuni Buddha instead of Jesus…and most especially, the Summerlands or the Pure Land instead of Heaven.

The religions that have been inflicted upon us for centuries have declared that this life is nothing but a preparation or a test for some eternal, non-physical life to come (either immediately after this life, or after a long series of incarnations). It's certainly a useful idea for maintaining hierarchical power structures: if you're getting the short end of the stick now, hey, relax, no need to work for equality or anything crazy like that. Keep quiet and you'll get your Eternal Reward in the Great Beyond.

But the problem goes deeper than just that. In putting forth the existence of some more important supernatural realm, these religions have denigrated the physical world, calling it "mere matter" – as if there were anything "mere" about atoms forged in the heart of exploding supernovas, slowly organizing into complex forms, pulling on and being pulled by every other particle in the Universe through the mystery of gravity; as if the stuff that makes you and me and whales and diamonds and the rings of Saturn and the Orion nebula is deficient, worthy of contempt.

In the Platonic tradition that has affected so much of

Western thought, even outside of religion, the actual world is seen as an inferior shadow of the world of ideals. And many Hindus and Buddhists fall into the error of trying to renounce the real physical world rather than understanding renunciation as being about rejecting social constructs.

Our culture is often accused of "materialism", but as Alan Watts noted, this is far from accurate:

> A materialist is one who loves material, a person devoted to the enjoyment of the physical and immediate present. By this definition, most Americans are abstractionists. They *hate* material, and convert it as swiftly as possible into mountains of junk and clouds of poisonous gas. As a people, our ideal is to have a future, and so long as this is so we shall never have a present. But only those who have a present, and can relate to it materially and immediately, have any use for making plans for the future, for when their plans mature they will enjoy the results. (WATTS, DOES IT, 29)

Why the bias against the material world, against physical reality? Largely because it changes: it cycles around, it is subject to birth and decay. And rather than accept that it is our impossible desire for changelessness that is at fault, mainstream religions – as well as many "New Age" beliefs, and some of the more "woo-woo" strands of Paganism – have held the Universe guilty for not being what we think we want, and have looked to some metaphysical realm for transcendence.

In contrast, the naturalistic strand of Paganism tells us that this world and everything in it is a wonder; in Whitman's words, "each part and tag of me is a miracle...the scent of these arm-pits is aroma finer than prayer" (WHITMAN, COMPLETE POETRY, 51) and "a leaf of grass is no less than the journey-work of the stars, / And the pismire [ant] is equally perfect, and a grain of sand, and the egg of the wren." (WHITMAN, COMPLETE POETRY 57)

And on the Zen side, a famous koan tells us that the Buddha-nature is present even in the lowliest objects. The story goes that Master Yun-men was just coming out of the outhouse when a student asked him, "What is the Buddha?" At that moment the master chanced to see the paddle used to spread the outhouse manure into compost piles, and so he answered, "Dry shit on a stick!" (SŌSAN, 134)

Zen Paganism is all about this world, here, now.

And I mean now! Here! Wherever you are, reading an electronic copy of this on your computer screen, or sitting with a dead trees version in the library, or outside under a tree, or inside on the toilet. The dust on your keyboard, the ant crawling on your foot, the annoying guy talking too loud, the shit stain in the toilet bowl, that funny smell, the ache in your knee, the ache in your heart, this is IT, the dance of atoms, the net of jewels. There's nothing to wait for. The universe has a billion billion billion tellers, no lines, no waiting, instant service. Enlightenment? "You're soaking in it," as an old TV commercial for dish soap said.

To quote no less square a source than Dale Carnegie, "One of the most tragic things I know about human nature is that all of us tend to put off living. We are all dreaming of some magical rose garden over the horizon – instead of enjoying the roses that are blooming outside our windows today." (CARNEGIE, 10)

(But apparently Dale couldn't understand that concept in the biggest picture, for he also wrote that "If religion [more or less meaning Christianity, to him] isn't true, then life is meaningless. It is a tragic farce." (CARNEGIE, 165) Poor Dale didn't see that the question of whether there might be some magical rose garden in heaven, shouldn't affect his enjoyment of the roses here and now.)

An old *Calvin and Hobbes* cartoon by Bill Watterson puts it well. Calvin asks, "What if there's no afterlife? Suppose this is all we get?" Hobbes looks around for a moment, and then replies, "Oh, what the heck. I'll take it anyway." (WATTERSON, 202)

Like many of the big truths, that's easy to say, but hard to put into practice. To truly "take it anyway," we must be in love with this world as it is. Not with our ideas or desires about it, or with fantasies that others have given us about how it should be, but in love with the actual world that presents itself to us every day.

And love is not easy! Love means that we can be hurt, and that we will have to do the hard work of learning to listen, and to pay attention, and to not take our lover – the world as it is – for granted.

In a lot of ways, it's a real pain in the ass. But the goal is not a trivial one, and is worth the effort.

If I were to phrase it as a manifesto, I might say that to be a Zen Pagan is to attempt to build a spirituality suitable for the next phase of human development. We seek to go beyond the shamanism of our tribal childhood, when we looked at the world with wonder and ignorance, and were largely powerless victims of circumstance; and beyond the priestly religions of our adolescence in city-states and nation-states, when we organized our societies around political hierarchies and our mythology around celestial ones, and learned how to take from the land, and take more, until we turned grasslands and forests to deserts and wastelands.

We will not forget these stages of our development, and will build upon the lessons we learned in them. But now we seek something suitable for a humanity that's mature – or at least something that will help us to grow up, make us ready for an adult relationship with the world. We seek a spirituality with democracy and equality, not monarchy or other primitive primate hierarchies at its heart; one capable of being in the here-and-now rather than looking to speculative metaphysics; one without superstition, that can learn from, and give ethical direction to, science and technology; one that seeks to protect and nurture the ecology of the planet, knowing that we are part of it, physically and spiritually.

To accomplish this will take all the disciplines we've talked about: meditation, and ritual, and mindfulness, and critical thinking, and ethical behavior – and a robust sense of humor.

So let's close, then, with a list of some concrete suggestions on how to cultivate a more mature and loving relationship with the Universe, a few Zen Pagan aphorisms:

1. Slow down. Pay attention. Question everything. Start now.

2. Remember that just as an infinite number of curves can be drawn through any finite set of points, an infinite number of stories can be told about a finite set of happenings. What sort of stories are you telling yourself?

3. Cultivating compassion expands the self and thus, in the long run, reduces our suffering. Don't make choices that cause, or encourage others to cause, death or suffering to sentient beings – including non-human ones, including annoying ones, and including yourself. We're all in this together. Try to apply this understanding to the way you choose your food, your clothing, your job, your toys, your tools, your household and business

supplies, your lovers, your companions.

4. Every once in a while, hug a tree. Walk barefoot on the grass. See if you can still pull off a cartwheel.

5. Sex and drugs are power tools of consciousness changing; like a chainsaw, they can be dangerous to yourself and others if used recklessly. Treat them with respect. Use more subtle tools if they are more appropriate. On the other hand, for some jobs a chainsaw is just the right tool.

6. Being dragged around in chains of desire is unlikely to result in lasting satisfaction. So is being dragged around in chains of mortification. Yes, playing with chains, of whatever sort, can be fun for a while, but don't forget your safeword – remember that it's a game.

7. Chasing truth outside yourself is like chasing the end of a rainbow. The rainbow that you see is a product of your position; as you move forward, you see a different rainbow at every step.

8. We all have our moments of clouds that hide the moon. Even wise men get the blues. Take a breath and remember that the world is as it is, whether you like it or not, and that it's necessary to accept reality regardless of your opinions or judgments. But, your opinions or judgments or feelings are also part of reality. Being okay with not being okay with things, is an important part of accepting that the world is as it is.

Appendix

Seton, Zen, and the Nature of Consensus Reality

In the course of my researches for this book, I came across an interesting example of how questionable claims can enter the historical record and become a part of our "reality."

John Michael Greer and Gordon Cooper's article "The Red God: Woodcraft and the Origins of Wicca" discusses the evidence for the influence of Ernest Thompson Seton's Woodcraft movement on the development of Gardnerian Wicca. Given my interest in both Buddhism and Paganism, I was absolutely floored to see Greer and Cooper claim that Seton had studied Zen during his time in London. (J. GREER, 53) Cross-checking this claim, I also found it in H. Allen Anderson's biography of Seton, *The Chief: Ernest Thompson Seton and the Changing West.* (ANDERSON, 20)

This would be an amazing Zen Pagan connection! And the timing would have been remarkable: Seton arrived in London in 1879, the same year that *The Light of Asia* was published and that Blavatsky and Olcott arrived in Ceylon. It would have been a fine bit of timing if he had encountered a Buddhist teacher, especially a Zen teacher, at such an early date.

I had to investigate this.

I was able to contact Mr. Greer by e-mail, and he told me that their source for this claim was John Henry Wadland's dissertation on Seton, *Ernest Thompson Seton: Man in Nature and the Progressive Era.* I found that this was also the source referenced by Anderson.

Thanks to interlibrary loan, I was able to track down a copy of this rare book. Wadland does indeed make this claim. (WADLAND, 70) But his reference for it is Seton's autobiography, and requires an overreaching interpretation of a brief mention of Buddhism found there:

> It was during this period, nearly two years, that I discovered the dangers of meat diet, and salutary calm of food that was "the grass"; and I

> knew now why the saints of old and the Buddhists of today abstain from meat, eat nothing but the herbs and fruits of the field.
> (SETON, TRAIL, 146)

Nowhere else in his autobiography does Seton mention the words "Buddhist," "Buddhists," or "Buddhism," and he does not mention "Zen" at all.*

From this passage we can only conclude that by the time of its writing (the autobiography was published in 1940), Seton had heard that (some) Buddhists were vegetarians, and felt comfortable making a positive mention of Buddhism. And Wadland has here conflated Zen with the entirety of Buddhism.

An encounter with Buddhists during his London sojourn would be very unlikely given the dates, although it cannot be completely ruled out. (If anything, it would have most likely been with the Theravada school.) If he had an encounter with Buddhism at all in those years, it's most likely only that he read *The Light of Asia*, and perhaps discussed it with others.

It seems much more likely that he learned a bit about Buddhism much later, perhaps through his first wife's Theosophy.

But, the extraordinary nature of a claim that Seton could have studied Zen in London around 1880 would only be noticed by someone who was interested in both Seton's history and the history of Buddhism in the West – a narrow intersection.

Now this claim that Seton studied Zen has appeared in several places, including a highly regarded biography of Seton, and has thus become part of the official record, of "consensual reality": an interesting illustration of the way that historical facts are sometimes born.

---

* Based on results of a Google Books search within the text of Seton's *Trail of an Artist-Naturalist*.

Smokey the Bear Sutra
by Gary Snyder

Once in the Jurassic about 150 million years ago, the Great Sun Buddha in this corner of the Infinite Void gave a Discourse to all the assembled elements and energies: to the standing beings, the walking beings, the flying beings, and the sitting beings — even grasses, to the number of thirteen billions, each one born from a seed, assembled there: a Discourse concerning Enlightenment on the planet Earth.

"In some future time, there will be a continent called America. It will have great centers of power called such as Pyramid Lake, Walden Pond, Mt. Rainier, Big Sur, Everglades, and so forth; and powerful nerves and channels such as Columbia River, Mississippi River, and Grand Canyon. The human race in that era will get into troubles all over its head, and practically wreck everything in spite of its own strong intelligent Buddha-nature."

"The twisting strata of the great mountains and the pulsings of volcanoes are my love burning deep in the earth. My obstinate compassion is schist and basalt and granite, to be mountains, to bring down the rain. In that future American Era I shall enter a new form; to cure the world of loveless knowledge that seeks with blind hunger: and mindless rage eating food that will not fill it."

And he showed himself in his true form of

SMOKEY THE BEAR

A handsome smokey-colored brown bear standing on his hind legs, showing that he is aroused and watchful.

Bearing in his right paw the Shovel that digs to the truth beneath appearances; cuts the roots of useless attachments, and flings damp sand on the fires of greed and war;

His left paw in the Mudra of Comradely Display — indicating that all creatures have the full right to live to their limits and that deer, rabbits, chipmunks, snakes, dandelions, and lizards all grow in the realm of the Dharma;

Wearing the blue work overalls symbolic of slaves and

laborers, the countless men oppressed by a civilization that claims to save but often destroys;

Wearing the broad-brimmed hat of the West, symbolic of the forces that guard the Wilderness, which is the Natural State of the Dharma and the True Path of man on earth—all true paths lead through mountains—

With a halo of smoke and flame behind, the forest fires of the kali-yuga, fires caused by the stupidity of those who think things can be gained and lost whereas in truth all is contained vast and free in the Blue Sky and Green Earth of One Mind;

Round-bellied to show his kind nature and that the great earth has food enough for everyone who loves her and trusts her;

Trampling underfoot wasteful freeways and needless suburbs; smashing the worms of capitalism and totalitarianism;

Indicating the Task: his followers, becoming free of cars, houses, canned foods, universities, and shoes; master the Three Mysteries of their own Body, Speech, and Mind; and fearlessly chop down the rotten trees and prune out the sick limbs of this country America and then burn the leftover trash.

Wrathful but Calm. Austere but Comic. Smokey the Bear will Illuminate those who would help him; but for those who would hinder or slander him,

HE WILL PUT THEM OUT.

Thus his great Mantra:

> Namah samanta vajranam chanda maharoshana
> Sphataya hum traka ham nam
>
> "I DEDICATE MYSELF TO THE UNIVERSAL DIAMOND.
> BE THIS RAGING FURY DESTROYED"

And he will protect those who love woods and rivers, Gods and animals, hobos and madmen, prisoners and sick people, musicians, playful women, and hopeful children.

And if anyone is threatened by advertising, air pollution, television, or the police, they should chant SMOKEY THE BEAR'S WAR SPELL:

> DROWN THEIR BUTTS
> CRUSH THEIR BUTTS

DROWN THEIR BUTTS
CRUSH THEIR BUTTS

And SMOKEY THE BEAR will surely appear to put the enemy out with his vajra-shovel.

Now those who recite this Sutra and then try to put it in practice will accumulate merit as countless as the sands of Arizona and Nevada.

Will help save the planet Earth from total oil slick.

Will enter the age of harmony of man and nature.

Will win the tender love and caresses of men, women, and beasts.

Will always have ripe blackberries to eat and a sunny spot under a pine tree to sit at.

AND IN THE END WILL WIN HIGHEST PERFECT ENLIGHTENMENT.

Thus have we heard.

(may be reproduced free forever) (SNYDER, 25-28)

* * *

I've always thought that "Smokey the Bear Sutra" was an excellent exemplar of Zen Paganism with a twist of Discordian ridiculousness, even if (to my knowledge) Gary Snyder never used either of those labels. Snyder composed the poem in February 1969 to hand out at a Sierra Club Wilderness conference. The mantra that it mentions is that of Fudō Myōō, a wrathful, snaggle-toothed deity known in Sanskrit as Ācala, usually portrayed carrying a sword and a lariat and surrounded by flames.

According to Snyder,

> The Circumpolar B____r cult, we are told, is the surviving religious complex (stretching from Suomi to Utah via Siberia) of what may be the oldest religion on earth. Evidence in certain Austrian caves indicates that our Neanderthal ancestors were practicing a devotional ritual to the Big Fellow about seventy thousand years ago. In the light of meditation once it came to me that the Old One was no other than that Auspicious Being described in Buddhist texts as having taught in the unimaginably distant past, the one called 'The Ancient Buddha.'

During my years in Japan I had kept an eye out for traces of ancient B___r worship in folk religion and within Buddhism, and it came to me that Fudo Myoō...whose name means the "Immovable Wisdom King," was possibly one of these traces. I cannot provide an academic proof for this assertion; it's an intuition based on Fudo's usual habitat: deep mountains. (SNYDER, 29-30)

Enlightenment of a Seeker
by Camden Benares

This piece by Camden Benares appears in the Principia Discordia *under the title "A Zen Story," and also in Benares's* Zen Without Zen Masters *under the title "Enlightenment of a Seeker." It may be the first American Zen story.*

A serious young man found the conflicts of mid 20th Century America confusing. He went to many people seeking a way of resolving within himself the discords that troubled him, but he remained troubled.

One night in a coffee house, a self-ordained Zen Master said to him, "go to the dilapidated mansion you will find at this address which I have written down for you. Do not speak to those who live there; you must remain silent until the moon rises tomorrow night. Go to the large room on the right of the main hallway, sit in the lotus position on top of the rubble in the northeast corner, face the corner, and meditate."

He did just as the Zen Master instructed. His meditation was frequently interrupted by worries. He worried whether or not the rest of the plumbing fixtures would fall from the second floor bathroom to join the pipes and other trash he was sitting on. He worried how would he know when the moon rose on the next night. He worried about what the people who walked through the room said about him.

His worrying and meditation were disturbed when, as if in a test of his faith, ordure fell from the second floor onto him. At that time two people walked into the room. The first asked the second who the man was sitting there was. The second replied "Some say he is a holy man. Others say he is a shithead."

Hearing this, the man was enlightened.

The Magick of Large Fire Circles by Tom Swiss

The fire circle, where celebrants drum and dance around a bonfire late into the night, is the heart of large Pagan gatherings. This piece was composed for inclusion in the program of the Free Spirit Gathering, and gives a bit of an idea of what such circles are like on the mundane level. (If you would like to use it for your gathering, please feel free, just maintain attribution.) For a deeper explanation of the elemental magic of fire circles, though, there is no better text than Billy Bardo's "Fire Circle Rap," which follows.

Fire. Drumming. Dancing. All are older than history, older than modern *Homo sapiens*. Putting them together is probably one of our oldest magickal activities.

You may have held fire circles in your own coven, circle, or grove. However, the large circles held at gatherings – bringing together scores, even hundreds, of people of many different paths and traditions – require a bit of extra thought and consideration for everything to go smoothly. Please consider the following guidelines for participating in large fire circles.

The Fire Circle Triangle: Physically, fire requires a triangle of elements – oxygen, fuel, and heat – to burn. Fire circles also rely on three elements: fire tenders, drummers, and dancers.

Fire tenders start the fire and keep it fed, and are responsible for fire safety. They often have to maneuver through the circle carrying heavy bits of wood. Give them the right of way and much love, for without them the circle is cold.

Drummers (and chanters, and other makers of joyful noise) take the heat and light of the fire and turn it into sound that reaches our hearts. Do not block them from the fire's warmth, and give them space and much love, for without them the circle is silent.

Dancers take the energy of the fire and the drums and transmute it into motion that moves our spirits. Do not crowd them into the fire, or block their path around it. Give them space in which to move and much love, for without them the circle is still.

Fire and flesh don't mix: You may have done rituals that involved leaping over fire. THIS FIRE IS NOT SIZED FOR SUCH

LEAPING. Don't do it. Leave a safe distance around the fire at all times. Keep your spirit in the fire, but your flesh out of it.

Respect the space, and those people in it: Please do not throw trash in the fire. (Small offerings to the fire, however – a sprinkle of herbs, a small paper with a prayer written on it, and so on – are generally ok.)

It shouldn't have to be said, but it does: don't leave your trash around the fire. If you carry it down to the fire, either carry it back with you or put it in a trash can. Your Mother thanks you.

Respect other people's way of respecting the space. Gatherings are a time of diversity; you might do things differently in fire circles held by your group, but festival circles belong to no one tradition.

You may dance. You may drum. You may chant. You may do whatever magick you are moved to do. You may watch. You may socialize. You may party.

For all acts of love and pleasure are Her rituals; and Gatherings are a time of unity and sharing. Therefore let us come together around the fire in love and trust and celebration. Blessed Be!

(May be reproduced free forever.)

The "Fire Circle Rap"
by William "Billy Bardo" Thorpe

"Doktor" Billy Bardo (a.k.a. William J. "Billy Joe" Thorpe), one of the foremost bards of the Pagan community, has been described as "a master metalsmith, channeler of arcane weirdness, artist, musician, preacher, husband, and father. He is also an accomplished bullshit artist and has been endorsed by countless questionable authorities." (BARDO BROTHERS) His "Fire Circle Rap" (THORPE) is the best explanation I've ever encountered of the elemental magic of fire circles, and a fine example of the blend of humor and wisdom that marks the best Pagan teachings.

So imagine the scene: a blazing bonfire, somewhere around four in the morning, with a group of exhausted and ecstatic dancers and drummers tranced out around it. During a pause in the drumming, a wild-looking fellow steps into the firelight and starts to speak…

Brothers and Sisters and Folk of the Tribe,
Can I have your attention a minute?!

For you Alphas and Elders, this stuff is old hat,
But there are some that are just jumpin' in it.

They've got the primal call, but not the protocol
That changes Fire to Fire and Place to Place.

Now I don't claim to know it all, but my knowledge isn't small,
And I speak for the common good and face to face.

Egocentric exhibitionist? What can I say?
But don't forsake this gift by explaining it away,

'Cause I'm not doing this for pay; I'm not looking for a lay;
I've got esoteric knowledge here; I'm giving it away!

It's cheaper than a workshop and not scheduled for all day,
And if you trust in my intentions and attend to what I say,

If you just listen for a minute you'll find the magic in it,
That can help your work and really help your play

Still if you're thinking I'm a bore or you've heard it all before,
Some truth could be the kernel of that thought.

But if it's just redundant lore, then what'cha waitin' for?
Weave a wonder of your own or wander off and don't get caught!

'Cause it just makes sense; don't get tense!
Cut a gate or jump the fence!
'Cause I don't want to give or take offense!
I just want a moment in the light.

It's only time; I'll make it rhyme.
You could even get a cosmic sign.
And when I've done my job we'll return to the throb of the Drums,
And everything will be all right.

So settle back and listen; let me tell you of my mission,
'Cause my mind it was trapped and I freed it!

This is not an intermission; it's an open invitation.
And it's a way to give permission to those that think they need it,

'Cause learning Wicca 101 or introduction to the Drum,
It don't reveal what we do here after dark.
To the Fire Light we come; it's a tribal thing say some,
Where intention is the glue and play is the spark…

So some are asking what's the point? What's the deal with this thing?
It's a bunch of crazy drummers and some dancers in a ring.

And every now and then someone will try to chant or sing.
I mean, come on and tell me what's the point?

What's real?!?

I mean I wanna get down, but I don't know the deal!
I'm groping for guidance, and it's gettin' surreal!
I don't know how to act; I'm not sure how to feel!
C'mon share in the mystery! I need some history!
Make it consistery, 'cuz we need to know, bro!

Where are these know-it-alls? Share in those protocols!
If this thing's gonna go at all, we need to know!

As old as human memory and deep within the myth collective,
Gathering around a Fire is like a Pagan prime directive.

A kind of tribal retrospective.
As a path to the past it is most effective,
'Cuz Fire was first and most likely will be last.

And we who would recall the primal patterns of the past,
Open up our souls to possibilities so vast,
Call the ancient powers and the sacred circles cast,

We all know it takes investment to be more than just half-assed.

So leave behind your preconceptions and get this simple truth at last:
It's as much about surrender as it is about control.

Sound droll?
Well to make the soul whole is just part of the goal.
Drum roll!

You gotta rise with the energy, go with the flow;
'Cuz the moment's always changin' on ya dont'cha know
That the moment isn't still; the circle isn't static.
Sometimes it's perfect skill, and sometimes it gets erratic!

Sometimes you get your fill by reaching points ecstatic,
And intrusion on that can seem rude.

But no one means to intrude on your solitude,
As you chance to enhance the trance of your dance, dude.
Cut some slack, don't cop an attitude,
And don't look at that sister askance!

Because where perchance is the great romance
In trying to control every circumstance?
Don't lose your pants if by mischance
Your own agenda don't advance,
Or someone else's scene seems like a hindrance.

Why Buddha Touched the Earth

Just wait with a little bit of tolerance,
And the moment will return to the sweet balance.

And those who seek the chance
To lose themselves in trance
To the rhythm of the drum
And the writhing of the dance,

To transcend beyond the ego,
To become the vast expanse,

We all know there are no limits
To the gifts that spirit grants.

So this is not an Open Mic or a Bardic Circle, true!
But don't concern yourself with what you may or may not do!
It's not just about this trancing and the ego to eschew.

We're also here to celebrate the best of us in you!

I mean to listen to each other that's an ego lesson too.
And there'll be time and space for everything before this night is through.

This is a marathon of magic, it's a dark to dawn to-do,
And there'll be time and space for everything before this night is through!

Fire is one of the five primal powers,
Transformative tool of the southern watchtowers;
And it's not wise to work with this stuff for hours
Without protecting yourself from the heat.

So I entreat:
Don't just run around like slow-roasting meat.
Don't burn out too fast and become obsolete.
If you just pound the beat you defeat the sweet
Healing power of the circle and the rhythm of the drum beat.

And if you're gonna work the Fire till 3 or 4 or more,
Pay attention to those other four.
These are primal powers not just metaphor.

Tom Swiss

They're real!
Get 'em back in your body and feel!

As around and around and around and around
Around and 'round the circle you go.
Around and 'round and around and around and
Around and 'round the circle you go.

Around and 'round, around and 'round
Around and 'round and around and around
Around around and around and around
C'mon you picked it up you got to put it back down.
Put it back where you found it put it back in the ground.
You picked it up, you got to put it down.
Put it back back back in the ground.
Put it back where you found it put it back in the ground.

I'll say it again, though I said it before,
That grounding isn't just a metaphor.

As around and around in the dust and the smoke,
You breathe the air and gasp and choke.
After hours and hours of breathing ash,
You'd think you're under the master's lash!

But you ain't no slave! That's not a yoke!
You gotta breathe! that's not a joke!

Everybody, breathe…

Don't forget to breathe!
Anywhere but the Fire, mon frere, is where!

And if doing the distance is your destination,
Never underestimate dehydration!
Your body is a temple; pour a deep libation,
'Cuz Goddess knows your bones could use the lubrication.

I mean, not to drink water, that's an act insane!
You got no brain; you deserve the pain
Of a predawn crash and a sharp migraine!

Why Buddha Touched the Earth

I ain't sayin' that'cha oughta, it's watta, ya gotta!

And eye to eye and heart to heart,
Every single one of us a vital part!
You can't complete this journey unless you start,
And we are starting fresh right now and right here!

So connect the eyes and connect the hearts,
'Cuz the soul is greater than the sum of the parts.
That's what puts the magic in the magic arts:
The sharing of magic and the shedding of fear.

Magic is energy; energy moves; energy is moving us all in a circle.

If you get with the synergy go with the groove,
When you dance to the trance you are answering her call.

Magic is energy energy moves; energy is moving us all in a circle.

I don't want to run this show; I just wanted you to know
These thoughts I had throughout the living year.
Like if magic is an art, worked with will and from heart,
Listen to your inspiration and not your fear.

If magic is an art worked with will and from heart,
Listen to your inspiration and not your fear.

© 2001, William J. Thorpe
Used by kind permission of the author.
www.bardobrothers.com

Glossary

alchemy: the art of transformation. Often associated with the quest to turn lead into gold, or for the "Philosopher's Stone," or for physical immortality, but there is also an "internal" aspect of spiritual growth and transformation. There are traditions of alchemy in both the West (such as the Hermetic tradition) and in the East (Taoist alchemy).

anātman: (Sanskrit) the Buddhist doctrine of "no self"; the idea of śūnyatā (q.v.) applied to the individual human being. Sometimes used in a more general sense to apply to all objects.

apophenia: the erroneous perception of connections in random data – finding meaning in coincidences, for example.

arhat: (Sanskrit) a person who has purified themselves of all attachments. Taken as an ideal in Theravāda Buddhism; in Mahāyāna, an arhat is seen as not completely enlightened, still needing to progress on to become a bodhisattva.

Ásatrú: a modern religion based on a reconstruction of ancient Norse practice. Since it does not arise from Greco-Roman roots, many of its adherents prefer to be referred to as "Heathen" rather than as "Pagan," but for our purposes we can consider it part of, or at least closely allied to, Paganism.

Beat Generation: an American literary and spiritual movement of the 1950s. Prominent Beat writers included Allen Ginsberg, Jack Kerouac, and Gary Snyder. (Some critics consider Snyder and other West Coast writers to constitute a "San Francisco Renaissance" movement separate from the East Coast Beats, but for our purposes we'll consider Beat in the broadest sense.)

bhikkhu: (Pali) a Buddhist monk.

bhikkhuni: (Pali) a Buddhist nun.

Blavatsky, H.P.: (1831–1891) One of the co-founders of the Theosophical Society, and probably the driving force behind it during her lifetime. Madame Blavatsky claimed to have the supernatural powers of a Spiritualist "medium," but was later exposed as a fraud.

Bodhidharma: the "First Patriarch" and founder of Zen; lived somewhere around 500 CE.

bodhisattva: (Sanskrit) the ideal state in Mahāyāna Buddhism, an enlightened being of infinite compassion.

bosatsu: (Japanese) a bodhisattva (q.v.).

Buddha: (Sanskrit) "awakened one." The historical Buddha was Siddhartha Gautama, who was born 567 BCE, according to one estimate. Some Buddhist sects believe in other, more supernatural Buddhas.

Buddha nature: the enlightened mind present in all beings, but obscured in most of us most of the time.

bushidō: (Japanese) literally, the "warrior way"; the philosophy of the samurai, combining Zen with the Japanese versions of feudalism and chivalry.

Cabala: also Qabbala, Kabbalah. The esoteric, mystical, and magical teachings of (some forms of) Judaism.

Ceylon: the island nation now known as Sri Lanka. A stronghold of Theravāda Buddhism since the second century.

Crowley, Aleister: (1875–1947) British occultist and ceremonial magician, and one of the first Westerners to write about Yoga and Buddhism.

Chuang Tzu: Taoist storyteller and poet who lived around 300 BCE; after Lao Tzu, the most influential figure in Taoism.

Daruma: (Japanese) Bodhidharma. Also, a figurine associated with him, symbolizing determination.

dharma: (Sanskrit) the teachings of the Buddha (usually *Dharma*). Sometimes translated as "law," but this should be understood more in the sense of a law of nature than of the state. More generally, ethical duty. Also, an unrelated meaning, a phenomenon of human existence

Discordianism: originally a spoof religion established in the 1950s based around Eris, the Greek goddess of chaos. Discordianism has developed to fill a sort of "sacred clown" role within the Pagan movement.

Druid: originally, the learned priestly class of the ancient Celts. Modern Druidism is a Neopagan movement that looks to ancient Celtic spirituality for inspiration.

gaijin: (Japanese) a non-Japanese person. Considered a somewhat blunt term in some contexts (versus the more polite *gaikokujin*), but widely used by gaijin in self-reference.

Gardner, Gerald: (1884–1964) British civil servant, writer, amateur anthropologist, and occultist generally regarded as the founder of Wicca.

Hermeticism: the Western alchemical tradition, following writings attributed to Hermes Trismegistus – "thrice-great Hermes," the syncretic combination of the Greek god Hermes with the Egyptian deity Thoth.

Hīnayāna: (Sanskrit) the "lesser vehicle"; a term used by Mahāyāna Buddhists to denigrate other schools such as Theravāda. Many sources from the mid-twentieth century use it as a synonym for Theravāda, but this usage is now generally considered inaccurate.
Hui Neng: Sixth Patriarch of Zen. Brought the "sudden awakening" doctrine to prominence.
Kamakura: a small city outside of Tokyo, Kamakura was the effective capital of Japan during the "Kamakura period" from 1185 to 1333, when shoguns first ruled the nation. It was during this period that Zen was introduced and popularized. Kamakura is home to several historically important shrines and temples.
Lao Tzu: author of the *Tao Te Ching*, the primary text of Taoism. Supposedly lived around 600 BCE. Quite likely, a wholly mythological character.
Mahāyāna: (Sanskrit) the "greater vehicle"; the branch of Buddhism found in China, Japan, Korea, Vietnam, and Tibet. In each of these cultures Mahāyāna has mixed with the indigenous religion. It takes as its ideal the bodhisattva, a being of limitless compassion.
magick: some practitioners of ritual or ceremonial magic – "the art of changing consciousness at will," in one definition – use this spelling to distinguish their practice from stage magic.
mandala: (Sanskrit) a geometric pattern with mystical symbolism. Originally referring to the patterns used in Hinduism and Buddhism, it is also used in a wider sense for any such pattern. According to Joseph Campbell, the development of mandalas (in the wider sense of the word) in art was associated with the patterns of cultivated fields in Neolithic societies.
mantra: (Sanskrit) a sound or phrase believed to have supernatural power or mystical symbolism. Often chanted.
mudra: (Sanskrit) a hand gesture with mystical symbolism
Neopagan: "new Pagan": a Pagan (q.v.) in the modern sense.
Nihongo: (Japanese) the Japanese language.
Nihonjin: (Japanese) a Japanese person.
Nirvana: (Sanskrit; properly, Nirvanā) literally, "blowing out"; in Buddhism, the state of inner peace that arises when attachments are released.
Pagan: up until the 1800s, a pejorative term for non-Christian persons and ideas. Since then, and especially since the 1960s, Pagan has come to refer to pantheistic or polytheistic spirituality or religion centered around nature, including Wicca, Druidism,

and many eclectic and individual paths.

Pali: the language of the Theravāda Buddhist canon. Where Sanskrit was the language of classical literature and religion in ancient India, Pali (also spelled Pāli) is related to Sanskrit but was more of a vernacular, a language of the common people. (Some Buddhist terms have become more widely known in English under their Pali names (e.g., "bhikkhu", "dukkha"), some under the Sanskrit equivalents ("sūtra", "Nirvana"). I have tried to use the more widely-known term in each case.)

pantheism: literally, "all [is] god." Religious viewpoints which see the entire Universe as divine, and deny any creator or other divinity standing outside and apart.

pareidolia: the misclassification or misinterpretation of sensory perceptions; for example, the purported dirty words in the Kingsmen's recording of "Louie Louie".

polytheism: literally, "many gods." Religious viewpoints which believe in many gods and/or goddesses: Hinduism, the ancient Greek religion, etcetera.

Rosicrucians: also known as the Fraternity of the Rosy Cross, a supposed hidden society of adepts founded in the fourteenth century, possessed of secret knowledge and dedicated to religion and healing. First written about in a series of pamphlets published between 1614 and 1616. Many groups have claimed connections with the Rosicrucians; but the existence of the original group, much less these connections, remains unproven.
(HUTTON, 69-70)

Rinzai: one of the two main branches of Zen, Rinzai is known for rigorous training centered around *kōan* practice, where the student must give a reply to some story or question meant to confound the rational mind.

sangha: (Sanskrit) Buddhist community.

satori: (Japanese) in Zen, enlightenment, seeing into one's own true nature. A sudden, intuitive, transformative insight.

shaman: "medicine man" (or woman); a person with access to special states of consciousness from which they can gain power and knowledge that they use for the benefit of their community, often in healing rituals. In traditional shamanic cultures, the position of shaman is socially sanctioned – the tribe decides who is and is not a shaman.

Shintō: (Japanese) literally the "way of the Gods/spirits"; the native, nature-centered religion of Japan, with roots going back thousands of years.

shogun: (Japanese, properly, shōgun) *literally a military rank equivalent to "general," the term "shogun" usually refers to the military leaders who effectively ruled Japan for several centuries.*
Sinhalese: the ethnicity of the majority of the population of Sri Lanka/Ceylon.
Snyder, Gary: (born 1930) American poet, essayist, environmental activist, and student of Asian culture, including Zen. Often considered part of the Beat movement. A slightly fictionalized version of Snyder appears as the character Japhy Ryder in Jack Kerouac's novel *The Dharma Bums*.
Sōtō: one of the two main branches of Zen, Sōtō focuses on "just sitting" meditation, and stresses that enlightenment is not a state to be achieved but is the practice of meditation itself.
Spiritualism: a nineteenth century religious/spiritual movement centered around belief in an afterlife in a "spirit world," and around seances performed by mediums who could supposedly contact the souls of the departed.
stūpa: (Sanskrit) a burial mound used as a place of worship; the forerunner of the pagoda.
sutra: (Sanskrit, properly sūtra) a holy text; in Buddhism, one recording the Buddha's teachings. (In Pali, this is called a sutta.) With a handful of exceptions, only texts attributed to the Buddha are referred to as sūtras.
śūnyatā: (Sanskrit) "emptiness"; the Buddhist teaching that nothing has an independent, unchanging existence, that nothing has a separate "self." The concept of anātman (q.v.) applied to all things.
Suzuki, D.T.: (1870-1966) Japanese author and translator who was an important popularizer of Zen in Europe and America.
Suzuki, Shunryu: (1904-1971) Japanese Zen master of the Sōtō school. Founder of the San Francisco Zen Center and author of *Zen Mind, Beginner's Mind*, a popular book about Zen philosophy. No relation to D.T. Suzuki.
Taoism: a Chinese philosophy of great antiquity, centered around the *Tao*, or the way of the natural world.
Theosophy: a world religion founded in the nineteenth century by H.P. Blavatsky and her associates. Theosophy took inspiration from Christianity, Hinduism, Buddhism, Cabala, and the Hermetic tradition.
Theravāda: (Pali) Literally, "way of the elders"; the "Southern" branch of Buddhism, which is more focused on monastic practice, and has less of a focus on deities and supernaturalism than is

found in Mahāyāna Buddhism.

Transcendentalism: a nineteenth century American literary and spiritual movement. Included Ralph Waldo Emerson, Henry David Thoreau, and (in the categorization of many scholars) Walt Whitman. An entry in Emerson's journal from October 6, 1836: "Transcendentalism means, says our accomplished Mrs. B., with a wave of her hand, *a little beyond."* (PERRY, 105)

Wicca: possibly derived from roots meaning "wise" or "to shape." First applied to witchcraft by Gerald Gardner in his 1954 book *Witchcraft Today,* the word now refers to a set of religious traditions derived from or inspired (directly or indirectly) by Gardner's work.

Witch: in Pagan usage, a Wiccan or other practitioner of "low magic." Generally considered to be a gender-neutral term.

zazen: (Japanese) seated meditation.

Zen: (Japanese) a form of Buddhism stressing meditation practice and direct insight.

A Partial Time-line of the Pagan and Buddhist Revivals

This time-line includes some incidents and dates of questionable veracity, as some of the persons featured were "charming charlatans" (to use the phrase Gardner – with considerable irony – applied to Crowley (HUTTON, 206)) or had unique and unusual relationships with consensual reality, or may indeed have been wholly mythological; and some of the organizations described are "secret societies" which delight in obfuscation.

Because the history of the Pagan and Buddhist revivals can only be understood with reference to broader historical trends, some events that are not directly relevant have been included for context.

- c. 10,000-300 BCE Jōmon period in Japan. This hunter-gatherer culture may be the first in the world to make pottery. Originally nomadic, they eventually establish semi-permanent settlements and are of the very earliest Neolithic cultures. (VARLEY, 2) According to some scholars the roots of Shintō can be found here. (SHIMAZONO, 281)
- c. 7000-3500 BCE The Neolithic Revolution and the birth of civilization. Human beings begin to settle into agricultural villages, and then into cities. (T. GREER, 12-15) The complexities of civilization require that humans become specialists, each a fraction of a larger whole; (CAMPBELL, 142-144) the myths and ceremonies that develop are often concerned with suppressing individuality and maintaining the social order. (CAMPBELL, 163)
"The beginnings of civilization and the appearance of temples are simultaneous in history. The two things belong together. The beginning of cities is the temple stage of history." – *The Outline of History*, H. G. Wells. (WELLS, 167)
- c. 604 BCE According to legend, the birth of Lao Tzu, author of the *Tao Te Ching*, the fundamental work of Taoism. (SMITH, 96)
- c. 567 BCE Birth of Siddhartha Gautama. (FIELDS, 4) (Large uncertainty exists about the year of his birth.)
- c. 460 BCE The Golden Age of Athens. (T. GREER, 52) Greek religion gives order to the lives of citizens, but there is no

authoritative dogma, and no special priestly class – instead there are rites and festivals rooted in customs and in the work of early poets such as Homer. Unlike Egyptian and Mesopotamian societies before them, the Greeks understand themselves as individuals deserving substantial personal freedom. (T. GREER, 56)

323 BCE Alexander the Great dies. In the wake of his empire, which had stretched to the borders of India, a Greco-Buddhist culture forms in Gandhara. Influenced by Greek artistic traditions, this is the culture that eventually produces the first sculptures of the Buddha. (FIELDS, 14-16) Some of these sculptures also feature the Alexandrian trinity of Serapis (a Hellenized version of Osiris), Isis, and Horus. From this comes a link between Isis and the Buddhist goddess Hariti, which may have influenced the development of the Chinese Buddhist deity Kuan Yin (known in Japan as Kannon). (WELLS, 320)

272 BCE The reign of King Asoka begins in India. (MCCLELLAND, 473) Asoka eventually converts to Buddhism and sends missionaries across the ocean to Sri Lanka (which remains a stronghold of Theravādan Buddhism today) and as far west as Egypt and Greece. (FIELDS, 10, 15)

c. 100 BCE Mithraism, an offshoot of Zoroastrianism, is carried westward from Asia Minor throughout the Roman Empire. Some of its elements appear to have been influential on the later formation of Christianity: Mithra's birth was celebrated on December 25th, he was known as "Lord," Sunday was his day of worship, worship rituals included baptism in water and the sharing of a meal of bread and wine, followers spoke of being "born again," and Mithra was believed to have ascended into the heavens but would return to guide his followers to their reward in paradise. (T. GREER, 129)

c. 30 CE After a mystical experience triggered by a water purification ritual, a Jewish rabbi, Yeshua ben Yoseph, starts preaching and stirs up a lot of trouble in Galilee.

c. 64 Buddhism first reaches China. (WELLS, 323)

c. 200-284 Rome is wracked by plagues (T. GREER, 119-120,145) and attacked by Germanic tribes. (WELLS, 407) Things get so bad that Emperor Diocletian moves his capital to Nicomedia, beginning the split of the Empire into East and West. (T. GREER, 121)

313 After centuries of persecution, the religion that was formed by Yeshua's followers, Christianity, is legalized in Rome. (SMITH, 346)

380 Christianity becomes the official religion of the Roman Empire. The newly dominant Christians are only too happy to pay back the persecution endured by their ancestors: idols of the old Roman gods are smashed and their worshipers attacked. By the century's end, Pagans (original sense), as well as Christians who don't toe the party line, are being put to death. (SMITH, 346; T. GREER, 144)

410 The Visigoths sack Rome, the beginning of the end for the Roman Empire. As the Empire dissolves, the Christian Church stands as a preserving and moderating influence. By the end of the fifth century, the Western Empire has been carved into several Germanic kingdoms, and the Middle Ages have begun. (T. GREER, 124, 159)

520 According to legend, Bodhidharma arrives in China and starts the teachings that will develop into Zen. (WATTS, 89) (The legend is most likely a load of hooey, but it's still a good story.)

577 Buddhism comes to Japan from Korea. (BAYS, 90)

622 Muhammad the Prophet leaves Mecca and begins his preaching career. (GREER, 167)

675 In China, Hui Neng becomes the Sixth Patriarch of Zen. (WATTS, 95) (This also is based on highly questionable legends.) It is about this time that Zen starts to take on its characteristic form.

732 Islamic Saracens have control of Spain and are sending raiding parties into France. There, Charles Martel becomes a hero defending the abbey of St. Martin in Tours. Looking to bolster his homeland's defenses, he promotes the use of cavalry forces (*chevaliers*, the forerunners of knights and the origin of our word chivalry), and seizes land from the Church and grants it to noble warriors in return for an agreement to provide fighting men. This eventually develops into the feudal system, where control of property is granted to fief holders in exchange for military service. (T. GREER, 175-176, 186)

771 Charlemagne (Martel's grandson) becomes sole king of the Franks. (WELLS, 512) During his 46 year reign, he forcibly spreads Christianity, including conquering and converting the Saxons and pushing back the Muslims. He also uses

the Church as an arm of his government. (T. GREER, 177-179)

800 Charlemagne is crowned Emperor of the Romans by Pope Leo III. (T. GREER, 181)

c. 814 After Charlemagne's death, his Empire falls apart, but leaves behind an ideal of unity. (T. GREER, 182)

962 Otto the Great is crowned Emperor of the Holy Roman Empire. His Empire covers only Germany and Italy, but keeps alive the ideal of Charlemagne. (T. GREER, 185)

1185 In Japan, Minamoto Yoritomo establishes military rule – the shogunate – in Kamakura. (HORNER, 70)

1191 Eisai brings Zen (of the Rinzai school) to Japan. (WATTS, 110)

1199 The Hōjō regency comes to power in Kamakura: far enough away from the power centers of established forms of Buddhism in Kyoto that the newcomer Zen sect has an opportunity to cozy up to the new rulers. (D.T. SUZUKI, ZEN AND JAPANESE CULTURE, 62)

1227 Dōgen founds the Sōtō school of Zen in Japan. (WATTS, 110)

c. 1300 A period of cooling climate begins in Europe. Farmlands are flooded by rain and the growing season is shortened. The medieval pattern of civilization begins to break up. (T. GREER, 245-246)

> One of the changes that marks the end of the medieval period is the start of land enclosure: peasants are denied access to common pasture and woodland, and instead those lands are rented out to paying tenants. (T. GREER P 446-447)

1348 The "Black Death" strikes. During the fourteenth century, it kills an estimated twenty-five million people, a quarter of the European population. (T. GREER, 246-247)

1378 During the "Great Schism" of 1378 to 1417, a group of Italian cardinals and a group of French ones each declare their own pope. The moral authority of the papacy and the Church is greatly weakened. (T. GREER, 313)

1398 A date claimed for the founding of the Rosicrucian Society. (REGARDIE, 64)

c. 1400 In Europe craft guilds begin to lose control of industry, and the domestic system of production develops. Goods are produced in piecework fashion by semi-skilled workers rather than by skilled craftsmen. (T. GREER, 248)

> The social and ceremonial functions of medieval craft guilds (T. GREER, 198) probably began to take on more importance around this time; this is when we see evidence (the Cooke and the Regius Manuscripts) that the mason's

guild was using the "Old Charges" in initiations and at gatherings. (STEVENSON, 22) These are recitations which describe the legendary history of the mason's guild (emphasis on legendary) and the obligations ("charges") laid upon members.

1492 Looking for a route to India, Columbus makes one of the luckiest blunders in history. (Lucky, that is, for him and for Spain, not so much for the Native Americans.)

1498 Succeeding where Columbus failed, Portuguese explorer Vasco da Gama sails to India, opening Asia to European exploration, trade, and exploitation. (T. GREER, 254)

c. 1500 Serfdom has disappeared in England and is mostly gone from Western Europe. The feudal lord demanding labor and produce from serfs has transformed into a capitalist landlord demanding rent payments from tenants – and with the right to evict them. (T. GREER, 251)

1501 Failing to convert the Sinhalese from Buddhism to Christianity, the Portuguese set about killing them and destroying Buddhist books and temples. Buddhism in Ceylon is nearly wiped out. (FIELDS, 22)

1517 Martin Luther writes his "Ninety-five Theses" – the start of the Protestant Reformation. (T. GREER, 316)

1534 Henry VIII gets the Act of Supremacy passed by Parliament, breaking the Church of England away from the Pope. The resulting religious and political turmoil lasts until Elizabeth I takes the throne in 1558. (T. GREER, 328-330)

1542 Portuguese explorers reach Japan. (WELLS, OUTLINE VOL II, 810)

1585 Through a great and wonderful confusion, the Buddha is accidentally canonized as "Saint Barlaam." (FIELDS, 19)

c. 1600 The first modern Masonic lodges are established around Edinburgh and St. Andrews, Scotland. These are the first to be "Masonic" rather than merely "masonic": they admit non-masons, initiate members through a series of degrees, and are more concerned with ethics and lore than with stoneworking. (HUTTON, 53) Masonry is evolving into a fraternal organization with ritual aspects. Emphasis on fraternal – women are excluded. It is non-denominational – which causes much consternation among clergy – but definitely theist, and the religious imagery is strictly patriarchal. (HUTTON, 65) (Co-Masonry, a 19th century movement to include women, has still had little effect on the broader Masonic tradition.)

1614-1616 Pamphlets are published claiming the existence of the "Rosicrucians," a hidden society of adepts possessing secret knowledge and dedicated to religion and healing. (HUTTON, 69-70) In years to come many groups will claim a connection to this legend, but the various "Rosicrucian" organizations do not necessarily have any connection to each other or to this original group (if it existed at all).

1638 In response to conflicts between Spanish, Portugese, Dutch, and English missionaries, and their involvement in local feudal struggles, Japan expels almost all foreigners. (WELLS, 810)

1642 The English Civil War begins. (T. GREER, 394)

1648 In England, George Fox, the primary founder of the Society of Friends (Quakers), starts preaching that all people are enlightened by the divine light of Christ. (WAGSTAFF, 7)

1649 The English Civil War ends when Oliver Cromwell and the "Rump" Parliament have Charles I executed, and declare the (short-lived) Commonwealth of England. (T. GREER, 395-396)

1687 The publication of Newton's *Principia* – a date often cited as the start of the Enlightenment period. (T. GREER, 373)

1688 A Jesuit translation of the teachings of Confucius is published. (FIELDS, 32, 386)

1696 Earliest surviving records of highly ritualized and esoteric Masonic initiation rituals. (HUTTON, 53)

c. 1700 Thomas Newcomen develops his steam engine (T. GREER, 448), one of the first stirrings of the Industrial Revolution.

1735 Carl Linnaeus publishes his *Systema Naturae*: a landmark in the field of natural history, and a huge influence on the development of the genre of nature writing. "Nature writers are the children of Linnaeus." – Robert Finch and John Elder (FINCH, 19)

1739 John Wesley, founder of Methodism, begins preaching (KAGAN, 696-670) his notion of "inward, present salvation, as attainable by faith alone" (WATSON, 129) in Western England.

c. 1750 Abroad, Britain has built an empire that rings the globe, (T. GREER, 447) bringing foreign influences home. Domestically, the process of land enclosure accelerates, with the aim of increased agricultural production. (T. GREER, 446) Between 1761 and 1792, almost 500,000 acres was enclosed (KAGAN, 530) – 780 square miles, more than 11 times the area of Washington D.C. Eventually 21% of England's land, almost 7 million acres, was enclosed. (SURRY COUNTY COUNCIL)

People displaced by these agricultural changes begin to shift into the cities. In rural areas, the result is "the death of tradition itself." (T. GREER, 454)

1755 Johann J. Winckelmann publishes *Thoughts on the Imitation of Greek Art in Painting and Sculpture*, in which he lauds not just the art but the culture and lifestyle of the ancient Greeks, including their acceptance of nudity. (WINCKELMANN) Along with his 1764 *History of Ancient Art*, it "constituted one of the major turning points in the history of Western taste. Almost single-handedly Winckelmann made the Greek experience alive and vitally interesting to intellectual and creative writers throughout Germany and the rest of Europe even though he never visited Greece himself," according to Frank Turner. (FRANK TURNER, 39-40)

1756 The Greco-Roman pantheon is in fashion in the art world. *The Conoisseur* magazine: "While infidelity has expunged the Christian theology from our creed, taste has introduced the heathen mythology into our gardens. If a pond is dug, Neptune, at the command of taste, emerges from the basin, and presides in the middle; or if a vista is cut through a grove, it must be terminated by a Flora, or an Apollo." (QUOTED AT HUTTON, 12)

1757 With victory in the Battle of Plassey, the British East India Company becomes the de facto ruler of India.
As one English schoolbook from the late 19th century put it, "Hitherto the East India Company had been only merchants and traders; henceforth we shall find them conquerors and sovereigns." (BERARD, 330)

1760 Jean-Jacques Rousseau, the "father of Romanticism," is at his creative height. In the words of historian Thomas Greer: "[Rousseau's] religion consisted of a simple faith in God and immortality. All that needs to be known about the Deity and his commandments...can be found in one's heart and in the study of *nature*." (T. GREER, 423) [emphasis in original]

1773 With the Regulating Act, the British government asserts some control over the East India Company's rule of India. The Act also establishes a Supreme Court to protect the interests of natives. (ROBINSON, 112, 182; FIELDS, 38)

1775 Tea exported from India to Boston under the terms of the Regulating Act is dumped into the harbor in an act of protest that comes to be known as the "Boston Tea Party".

(ROBINSON, 124)

c. 1775 Richard Arkwright builds the first water-powered textile spinning mill at Cromford, in Derbyshire. It employs about 500 people at thousands of spindles. (T. GREER, 447, FITTON, 224) Children as young as seven are employed and shifts are twelve hours long. A night shift keeps the machines going 24 hours a day. (FITTON, 225-226)

1776 Order of the Illuminati formed in Bavaria. (WILSON, COSMIC, 4) Conspiracy theorists have been nuts about them ever since.

In North America, the intellectuals and landlords of the British Colonies decide they no longer need a king, and – with the help of the French – start a war to break away from Britain.

1782 Even as exploitation of India continues, some European intellectuals are fascinated with its ancient culture, building a mythical image of the Orient. Pierre de Sonnerat publishes *Voyage aux Indes Orientales* in which he claims that India gave wisdom, law, and religion to every other culture, including Egypt and Greece. William Macintosh publishes a travel narrative, *Travels in Europe, Asia, and Africa*: "All history points to India as the mother of science and art. This country was anciently so renowned for knowledge and wisdom, that the philosophers of Greece did not disdain to travel thither for their improvement." (WILLSON, 25)

1785 Sir William Jones, who arrived in India the previous year to take a position on the Supreme Court, founds the Asiatick Society. (FIELDS, 41-42) Charles Wilkins publishes a translation of the Bhagavad Gītā, the first Sanskrit work to be directly translated in a European language. (WILLSON, 46)

1788 The first volume of *Asiatck Researches* (the Society's journal) contains a report by William Chambers which discusses Buddhism in Ceylon. (The volume also contains a story of a Tibetan expedition, but somehow this does not mention Buddhism). (FIELDS 44-50) This may be the first significant writing about Buddhism in English.

Johann von Schiller's poem "The Gods of Greece" is published. (HUTTON, 22)

1789 The French Revolution – the end of the Enlightenment, according to some historians. (T. GREER, 373)

Gilbert White's *A Natural History of Selborne*, a seminal

work of nature writing admired by Darwin and Thoreau, is published. (FINCH, 19-20)

1796 A group of physicians investigating conditions in textile factories in Manchester find that the lack of fresh air and active exercise is "generally injurious to the constitutions" of workers, that they are "peculiarly disposed to be affected by the contagion of fever," that the crowded conditions help disease to spread, and that child workers are being developmentally impaired and "generally debarred from all opportunities of education, and from moral or religious instruction." (MALTBY, 121)

c. 1795 Christian mystic Karl von Eckartshausen writes *The Cloud Upon the Sanctuary*, in which he speaks of a "society of the Elect," an ancient and invisible "community of light," the "true school of God's spirit." It has three degrees of development: 1) moral and acting through inspirations, 2) rational intellect and interior illumination, and 3) metaphysical visions. (VON ECKARTSHAUSEN, 25) Its notion of a hidden society of masters, and possibly its three degree system, have a strong impact on later occultists. (The degree system might also have emerged out of the apprentice – journeyman – master system of medieval guilds).

1805 the first American publication of a Sanskrit work in translation: the drama *Sacontala*, translated by Sir William Jones and published in *The Monthly Anthology and Boston Review*. The editor of the *Review* is William Emerson, father of Ralph Waldo Emerson. (FIELDS, 55)

1811 Shelly publishes *The Necessity of Atheism* and is expelled from Oxford. (SHELLEY, WORKS, 300)

1818 Keats writes *Endymion*, an epic poem which and tells of a mortal's love for Diana, the goddess of the moon. (HUTTON, 32) It contains a powerful invocation to Pan, (KEATS, BOOK I) and at one point has the Greek goddess Diana assume the form of a woman of India, in which guise she tells a pantheon-mixing tale in which "Great Brahma from his mystic heaven groans, / And all his priesthood moans; / Before young Bacchus' eye-wink turning pale." (KEATS, BOOK IV)

1819 William Hazlitt writes: "Perhaps the genius of our [English] poetry has more of Pan than of Apollo; 'but Pan is a God, Apollo is no more!'" (HAZLITT, 569)

1821 Shelly mentions in a letter to Thomas Jefferson Hogg how he "raised a small turf altar to the mountain-walking Pan" (HUTTON, 25)

1822 Emerson remarks in a letter to his Aunt Mary, "I am curious to read your Hindoo mythologies." (FIELDS, 56)

1830 The "age of railways" opens with the first locomotive run on the Liverpool and Manchester line. (T. GREER, 448)

1833 American abolitionists begin agitating for the end of slavery. (WELLS, 792)

1836 In *Anacalypsis: An Attempt to Draw Aside the Veil of the Saitic Isis*, Godfrey Higgins puts forth the modern myth of Atlantis: an ancient civilization that passed its spirituality and philosophy on to India, the ancient Hebrews, Egyptians, and Druids. (HUTTON, 18) He is perhaps the first to put forth the notion of a common ancient high religion of which modern practices are decayed remnants – an idea that turned out to have much staying power in occult, and later in "New Age," circles.

1837 James Prinsep translates the script of the Pillars of Ashoka and discovers that India was once home to a great Buddhist civilization. (FIELDS, 46) That this discovery comes so late may partly explain the confusion exhibited by early writers between Hinduism and Buddhism.

Emerson delivers his address "The American Scholar" to the Cambridge Phi Beta Kappa Society. It is a declaration of America's literary and intellectual independence: "[T]his confidence in the unsearched might of man belongs, by all motives, by all prophecy, by all preparation, to the American Scholar. We have listened too long to the courtly muses of Europe....We will walk on our own feet; we will work with our own hands; we will speak our own minds....A nation of men will for the first time exist, because each believes himself inspired by the Divine Soul which also inspires all men." (EMERSON, "AMERICAN SCHOLAR")

1839 Conflicts between China and Britain over the smuggling of Indian opium heat up into a shooting war. is The amount of opium being consumed in Britain is largely ignored: "For not all opium from India ended up in China: three hundred chests a year [at 170 pounds per chest – possibly a high estimate – 51,000 pounds] were diverted to England....[I]n England's grim and grimy industrial cities...workers on payday lined up outside the chemist's (pharmacy) for the inexpensive palliative to their industrial hell." (HANES, 82)

1842 Emerson presents his lecture "The Transcendentalist" at the Masonic Temple in Boston. In it he claims Buddhists for the Transcendentalists: "The Buddhist who thanks no man, who says, 'do not flatter your benefactors,' but who, in his conviction that every good deed can by no possibility escape its reward, will not deceive the benefactor by pretending that he has done more than he should, is a Transcendentalist." (EMERSON, "TRANSCENDENTALIST")

Yet in the same year, perhaps caught up in a misunderstanding of "annihilation" for "Nirvana," he expresses a negative opinion of Buddhism: "The trick of every man's conversation we soon learn. In one, this remorseless Buddhism lies all around threatening with death and night. We make a little fire in our cabin but we dare not go abroad one furlong into the murderous cold. Every thought, every enterprise, every sentiment, has its ruin in this horrid Infinite which circles us and awaits our dropping into it. If killing all Buddhists would do the least good, we would have a slaughter of the Innocents directly." (EMERSON, JOURNALS WITH ANNOTATIONS, 318) Showing that when he wrote "A foolish consistency is the hobgoblin of little minds," (EMERSON, "SELF-RELIANCE") he meant it.

The Treaty of Nanking ends the First Opium War. Its terms, which include China ceding Hong Kong to Britain, are humiliating to China. (HANES, 154-155) It's the beginning of the end for the Qing Dynasty and Imperial China.

1844 Thoreau publishes "The Preaching of Buddha" in *The Dial*. ("PREACHING OF BUDDHA," 391) It is the first publication of the Lotus Sutra in English. (FIELDS, 61) (Or of any sutra in English.)

1848 Spiritualism begins in the U.S., with the Fox sisters' manifestations of spirit-rapping, slate-writing, and other phenomena. (FIELDS, 83-84)

1849 German classicist Edward Gerhard proposes that behind the numerous goddesses of ancient Greece is one prehistoric "Mother Earth" goddess. (HUTTON, 35)

Thoreau writes in a letter to H.G.O. Blake: "Depend on it that, rude and careless as I am, I would fain practice the yoga faithfully. To some extent, and at rare intervals, even I am a yogi." (FIELDS, 64)

Thoreau publishes *A Week on the Concord and Merrimack Rivers* (written several years earlier), in which he writes of his love for the Buddha and also says, "In my Pantheon, Pan still reigns in his pristine glory, with his ruddy face, his flowing beard, and his shaggy body, his pipe and his crook, his nymph Echo, and his chosen daughter Iambe; for the great god Pan is not dead, as was rumoured. No god ever dies. Perhaps of all the gods of New England and of ancient Greece, I am most constant at his shrine." (THOREAU, A WEEK, XIV, 56)

1851 Half of the population of Britain is living in urban areas, a rapid and tremendous break from the past. (WALLER, 1; T. GREER, 454)

1854 Perry's "black ships" steam into Tokyo Bay, and start to pry Japan open to American trade and exploitation. (FIELDS, 77)

1855 The first edition of Walt Whitman's *Leaves of Grass* is published. Whitman later says it is "avowedly the song of Sex and Amativeness, and even Animality – though meanings that do not usually go along with those words are behind all." (WHITMAN, COMPLETE POETRY, 669) He cites "the ancient Hindoo poems" as being among the works he read that lead up to his work. (WHITMAN, COMPLETE POETRY, 665)

1857 The Sepoy Mutiny in India. Indians rebel against the British East India Company's rule. There are several motives, but one is a reaction to the presence of Christian missionaries: some native soldiers believe that the British intend to trick them into sinning against Hindu taboos by giving them rifle cartridges containing cow fat, and then after such a serious fall from grace convert them to Christianity. (BERARD, 440-442)

1858 Helena Petrova Blavatsky encounters Spiritualism while in Paris. (HUTTON, 18)

In the wake of the Sepoy Mutiny, the British Crown liquidates the East India Company and assumes direct rule of India. (BERARD, 447)

1859 September 17: San Francisco businessman Joshua A. Norton, in an act that will later inspire legions of Discordians, proclaims himself Emperor of the United States. Norton will later be recognized as an Illuminated Being, granted the 33rd degree, and given a full Masonic funeral by the Ancient and Accepted Freemasons. (GORIGHTLY, 147)

British naturalist Charles Darwin, in an act that will infuriate legions of religious fundamentalists for at least a century and a half, publishes his book *The Origin of Species*.

(APPLEMAN, 5)

1860 Due to immigration from the Gold Rush, 10% of the population of California is now Chinese. (FIELDS, 70-71)
The first Japanese envoy to the U.S. arrives in San Francisco. His party is observed in New York by Walt Whitman months later. (FIELDS, 77)
Eliphas Zahed Levi (Alphonse Louis Constant) publishes his *Historie de la magie*. (HUTTON, 70, 424)
Ernest Thompson Seton born.

1861 With the attack by secessionist terrorists on Fort Sumter, the American Civil War begins. (WELLS, 794)

1865 American Civil War ends. (WELLS, 795) In the wake of the war, Spiritualism takes a central place in the U.S.; it comforts many with its "evidence" of life after death. Many new Christian sects also rise, but most quickly fade. (FIELDS, 83-84)
In England, the "Societas Rosicruciana in Anglia" is founded by high-ranking Freemasons, including Kenneth H.R. Mackenzie and Robert Wentworth Little. Its purpose is to study Cabala and the Hermetic tradition. Mackenzie claimed to have been initiated into the German "Order of the Gold and Rosy Cross", and he and Little claimed to have discovered encrypted papers describing old Masonic rituals for initiation and the like, which form the basis for the Society's rituals. The group does not practice any ritual magic, but is strictly theoretical. (HUTTON, 72, 73) William Wynn Westcott, William R. Woodman, and Samuel Liddel (who later used the name, and became better known as, MacGregor Mathers) are also members. (REGARDIE, 73, 75; HUTTON, 74)

1866 Swinburne's *Poems and Ballads* is published. His work is a conscious imitation of Shelly; it portrays Christianity as sad and morbid, and praises the old gods. It is later influential on Aleister Crowley, Dion Fortune, and Gerald Gardner. (HUTTON, 25-26)

1868 Meiji restoration in Japan: the end of the rule of the shoguns and the transfer of power to the Emperor. The first ordinary Japanese citizens are allowed to travel abroad – some go to Hawaii to work as laborers. (FIELDS, 77) The Meiji government makes a perverted form of Shintō the state religion and tries to repress Buddhism with the slogan "Haibutsu Kishaku" – "Expel the Buddha; Destroy the Teachings," though it soon reverts to a more neutral position. (FIELDS, 80)

c. 1870 Italy and Germany become unified nations, and the balance of power within Europe stabilizes. As nationalism turns to imperialism, a scramble for overseas colonies heats up. (T. GREER, 481)

A tremendous wave of emigration to the New World begins: 26 million Europeans leave between 1870 and 1914. (T. GREER, 454)

One estimate claims 11 million people are following Spiritualism. (FIELDS, 84)

1874 Colonel Henry Steel Olcott and Madame Helena Petrova Blavatsky meet while pursing their interests in Spiritualism. (FIELDS, 84-86)

1875 Theosophical Society founded (HUTTON, 18). Blavatsky and Olcott later claim that the Society was founded on the suggestion of hidden Indian and Tibetan "Adepts" with extraordinary abilities. (FIELDS, 89-92)

Aleister Crowley born. (HUTTON, 171)

1877 Blavatsky publishes *Isis Unveiled*. It follows many of the themes (as well as the title!) of Higgins' 1836 *Anacalypsis*, but she does not credit him, instead claiming that her information came from the "Masters of the Hidden Brotherhood," the same immortals who had taught religion to the Atlanteans. (HUTTON, 19)

1878 Bronson Alcott helps get Edwin Arnold's *The Light of Asia*, an account of the life of the Buddha, published. (FIELDS, 67-68; BICKNELL, 17)

With the Theosophical Society starting to break up in the U.S., Olcott and Blavatsky decide to follow up contacts in India and Ceylon, where Vedanta and Buddhism are rising with anti-colonial and nationalist movements. They leave the Society in the hands of – believe it or not – Abner Doubleday, and head for the East.* (FIELDS, 92-94.)

Robert W. Little dies, and is succeeded as head of the Societas Rosicruciana by William R. Woodman. (REGARDIE, 75)

1879 Blavatsky and Olcott arrive in India, then go to Ceylon.

---

* It is too bad that Doubleday's involvement in the invention of baseball seems to be a myth, else this fact could inspire wonderful occult conspiracy theories about our national pastime as a Theosophical plot.

Among those who join their orbit are writer A.P. Sinnett (FIELDS, 95) and young David Hewavitarne, who would later take the Buddhist name Anagarika Dharmapala. (FIELDS, 98) Ernest Thompson Seton goes to London.

1880 May 25: in a ceremony in Ceylon, Blavatsky and Olcott are the first Americans to formally become Buddhists. (FIELDS, 97-98)

1881 A.P. Sinnett's *The Occult World* is published, and introduces occult ideas to a wide audience. (HUTTON, 73)

1882 Even as intellectual and academic interest in Eastern thought builds, prejudice builds even faster; Congress passes the Chinese Exclusion Act. (FIELDS, 70-71)

Deciding that the Sinhalese are largely ignorant of their own religion, Olcott, together with Sumangala (Sinhalese high priest of Sripida and Galle, Principal of Vidyadaya College), develops a "Buddhist Catechism" to help educate the people about their religion. (FIELDS, 101) It is later translated and published in Japan and India. (FIELDS, 106)

1883 A.P. Sinnett's *Esoteric Buddhism* published. (FIELDS, 95)

Anna Kingsford becomes president of the London Lodge of the Theosophical Society. (PERT, 108) (A fascinating figure, Kingsford was one of the first English women to obtain a degree in medicine, (PERT, 79) an anti-vivisection campaigner, (PERT, 91) and an activist for women's rights (PERT, 20) and vegetarianism. (PERT, 79))

As the Theosophical Society takes up an Eastern bent, Kingsford reacts by encouraging more research into the Gnostic texts and Hermetic traditions. (HUTTON, 19)

1884 Olcott goes to London and gets the British government to agree to increased religious and cultural freedom for the Sinhalese. (FIELDS, 101)

Blavatsky's displays of paranormal abilities are investigated by the Society for Psychical Research, and are declared a fraud. (HUTTON, 74)

Kingsford, with Edward Maitland, founds the Hermetic Society in Britain. Its emphasis is more on the Western tradition, "Greek mysteries and the Hermetic Gnosis" and cabala and the mystical side of Christianity. (PERT, 127-132) William Wynn Westcott and Samuel Liddel Mathers are prominent members. (HUTTON, 74)

Gerald Gardner born. (HUTTON, 205)

1885 Amidst allegations of fraud in her occult and spiritualist demonstrations, Blavatsky resigns as corresponding secretary of the Theosophical Society. (FIELDS, 103-105)

1887 Japanese Rinzai Zen monk Soyen Shaku comes to Ceylon to study how Theravāda Buddhists practice as bhikkhus. Probably the first Japanese monk to visit and study with a Theravāda school. (FIELDS, 109)

William Wynn Westcott, William R. Woodman, Alphonsus F.A. Woodward, and MacGregor Mathers, start to organize the Hermetic Order of the Golden Dawn. They claim authorization of a Rosicrucian Adept from Nuremberg named Anna Sprengel. (REGARDIE, 70) Mathers would later claim that Westcott's contact with Sprengel was forged. (REGARDIE, 84) The Order is open to both men and women, and teaches members to regard Theosophy as a companion tradition, originating from "the same stock of Magi – the Scientific priests of a remote antiquity." (HUTTON, 76)

1888 Anna Kingsford dies on February 22. (PERT, 167) The Golden Dawn is officially chartered a week later, March 1. (HUTTON, 75) At the invitation of a committee of Japanese Buddhists, Olcott and Dharmapala visit Japan, carrying a letter from Sumangala to the committee. This may have been the first official communication between Mahāyāna and Theravāda branches of Buddhism in centuries. Olcott gives 75 lectures in 3 months to 187,000 people, and returns to Ceylon with three Japanese priests who intend to study Pali and Theravāda Buddhism. (FIELDS, 107-108) One of these priests is Kozen Gunaratna. (FIELDS, 115-117)

1889 Olcott, working with Sumangala, designs a Buddhist flag as a symbol to help unite the world's Buddhists together. (FIELDS, 106)

1890 Olcott organizes a meeting of Buddhist representatives from Ceylon, Burma, and Japan, and gets them to sign on to a declaration of Fourteen Buddhist Beliefs that they hold in common. (FIELDS, 113-114)

c. 1890 Edwin Arnold writes an article in the *London Daily Telegraph* decrying the neglect of Bodh-Gaya, the site of Buddha's enlightenment. He meets with Sumangala and makes plans to petition the British government in India to purchase the site and give control of it to Buddhists. (FIELDS, 115)

Around this time, up to 20% of American men belong to a

Masonic-style secret society. (HUTTON, 64)

1891 Shaku becomes master of Engakuji temple. (FIELDS, 109)
Dharmapala and the Japanese priest Kozen Gunaratna go to Bodh-Gaya. The Bodh-Gaya Maha Bodhi Society, dedicated to returning Bodh-Gaya to Buddhist ownership, is founded, with Sumangala as president, Olcott as director, and Dharmapala as secretary. They organize an International Buddhist Conference in Bodh-Gaya, with attendees from Chittagong (in present-day Bangladesh), Ceylon, China, and Japan. (FIELDS, 115-117)

1892 William Sharp founds *The Pagan Review*. While it aims at ushering in a new age of sexual liberation and equality, its first and only issue contains only "risibly bad" stories written by Sharp under various pen names, (HUTTON, 28) but it is still notable for its use of the term "Pagan" in the title.

Shaku is invited to the World Parliament of Religions. His letter of acceptance, and his address, are translated into English by his student D.T. Suzuki. (FIELDS, 109)

The first issue of the *Maha Bodhi Journal* is published, with Dharmapala as editor; the issue features contributions from him and Olcott. Dharmapala is invited to the World Parliament of Religions. (FIELDS, 118)

Blavatsky dies. (HUTTON, 76)

Mathers claims that he had been contacted by the same "Secret Chiefs" behind the Theosophical society, and authorized by them to set up an inner order within the Golden Dawn, called the "Rosy Cross" or "Rosicrucian Order" (with no proven link to any previous Rosicrucian organization). It goes beyond the Golden Dawn's training and allows its members to engage in magical rituals meant to invoke and work with deities and spirits. (HUTTON, 76; REGARDIE 81-82)

1893 Kenneth Grahme publishes a collection of his essays entitled *Pagan Papers*, including "The Rural Pan": "Yes: to-day the iron horse has searched the country through — east and west, north and south — bringing with it Commercialism, whose god is Jerry, and who studs the hills with stucco and garrotes the streams with the girder. Bringing, too, into every nook and corner fashion and chatter, the tailor-made gown and the eyeglass. Happily a great part is still spared — how great these others fortunately do not know — in which the rural Pan and his following may hide their heads for yet a little longer, until the growing tyranny has invaded the last common, spinney, and sheep-down, and driven the kindly god, the well-wisher to man — whither?" (HUTTON, 28; GRAHME, PAGAN, 70)

The World Parliament of Religions is held in Chicago, chaired by Dr. John Henry Barrows. Barrows sees India and the Far East as a "new field for [Christian] evangelization." While most delegates and attendees are Christian, there are also Hindus, Parsis, Sikhs, Jains, a Confucian, and Zen, Jodo Shinshu, Nichiren, Tendai, and Esoteric Buddhists, representing Japan, India, China, Siam, and Ceylon. Japanese delegates lament that the West has heard little of Mahāyāna Buddhism. Dharmapala gives several talks and proves a favorite with Americans. The Parliament seems to do more to introduce Buddhism and Hinduism to the West than to introduce Christianity to the heathen Orient.

At the Parliament, Dr. Paul Carus, editor for Open Court Press, befriends both Dharmapala and Shaku. He helps found an American branch of the Maha Bodhi Society. Also he proposes that Shaku help him translate and edit Open Court's new series of works on Asia; Shaku suggests instead that Carus invite his student, D.T. Suzuki.

September 26: shortly after the Parliament, Dharmapala gives a lecture under the auspices of the Theosophical Society of Chicago. Afterward, he conducts a brief refuge ceremony for Charles T. Strauss of New York, the first time a person formally becomes a Buddhist in America. (FIELDS, 119-129)

1897 D.T. Suzuki arrives in the U.S., living with Carus and works, helping to translate Asian texts. He starts work on his own first book, *Outlines of Mahayana Buddhism*. (FIELDS, 138-139)

Westcott, pressured by harm to his career caused by rumors of his occult activities, resigns from the Golden Dawn, leaving Mathers in full charge.

1898 Inspired by von Eckartshausen's book *The Cloud on the Sanctuary* to search for the hidden "society of the Elect," (REGARDIE, 108) Aleister Crowley is initiated into the Hermetic Order of the Golden Dawn. His sponsor is George Cecil Jones. (REGARDIE, 37)

Around this time Allan Bennett (who would later take the Buddhist name Ananda Metteyya) lives with Crowley for about 18 months, mentoring him in Cabala, Tarot, and other aspects of magic. (REGARDIE, 40-42, 112)

1899 "I am Pan and the Earth is mine," writes Maurice Hewlett in *Pan and the Young Shepard*. (HUTTON, 45)

Crowley is admitted to the inner order within the Golden Dawn, the Rosicrucian Order. (REGARDIE, 162)

Charles Godfrey Leland publishes *Aradia, or the Gospel of the Witches*, which was purportedly presented to him by a descendant of a Witch family. Elements from this work have come forward to modern Wicca. (ADLER, 57)

1900 Gerald Gardner moves to Ceylon, where he remains until 1908. (PEARSON, 65)

Alan Bennett goes to Ceylon. (HARRIS, 8) (Or maybe this was in 1898 (OLDMEADOW, 89) or 1899 (CROW, 1).)

Ernest Thompson Seton, a naturalist of mystical inclinations, deals with a group of juvenile delinquents by taking them on a camping trip, engaging them in athletic games and teaching woodcraft and (his interpretation of) Native American culture. (HUTTON, 162; SETON TRAIL, 367-385)

1901 Early in the year Crowley is introduced to raja yoga by Oscar Eckenstein. (REGARDIE, 211) Later in the year, Crowley goes to Ceylon and studies yoga, Vedanta, and Buddhism with Bennett. (REGARDIE, 229) He writes an essay on *Science and Buddhism* and attempts but abandons a versified version of the *Dhammapada* ("The Sayings of the Buddha"). (REGARDIE, 249-251)

1902 After an article by Seton in *The Ladies' Home Journal*, bands of "Seton Indians" are formed all over the nation. The movement's stated intentions include wildlife conservation and the preservation and promotion of "the culture of the Redman". (HUTTON, 162-163; SETON TRAIL, 374-376)

c. 1903 The Reverend Mazzinanda, who claimed to have studied with the Dalai Lama, establishes a Buddhist church in Sacramento – perhaps the first in the U.S. (FIELDS, 143)

1904 In April, Crowley "channels" (in a convoluted fashion) a "being" named Aiwass, and under "his" direction writes *The Book of the Law*. Crowley first claims that Aiwass was one of the "Secret Chiefs"; later, he identifies him as his "Holy Guardian Angel" (a reference to Abramelinean magical practices). He later regards this as the single most important event of his life. (REGARDIE, 462-463)

The O.T.O. – Ordo Templi Orientis, Order of Oriental

Templars – is formed in Germany. It is an offspring of Freemasonry that is influenced by the writings of Eliphas Levi, Indian tantra and yoga, and the myth of the Knights Templar. (HUTTON, 222)

1905 After a badly failed attempt to climb Kanchenjunga (the third highest mountain on Earth), a frustrated and hostile Crowley writes in a private letter, "[T]o hell with Christianity, Rationalism, Buddhism, all the lumber of the centuries. I bring you a positive and primaeval fact, Magic by name; and with this I will build me a new Heaven and a new Earth. I want none of your faint approval or faint dispraise; I want blasphemy, murder, rape, revolution, anything, bad or good, but strong." (REGARDIE, 287)

Soyen Shaku returns to the U.S., to stay at the home of Mr. and Mrs. Alexander Russell of San Francisco, and teach them and their family and friends about Zen. Shaku is briefly reunited there with former student Nyogen Senzaki. (FIELDS, 168)

1906 Kipling's story collection *Puck of Pook's Hill* includes the piece "A Tree Song," with a stanza that has become famous in the modern Pagan movement:

Oh, do not tell the Priest our plight,
    or he would call it a sin;
But – we have been out in the woods all night,
    A-conjuring Summer in!
And we bring you news by word of mouth -
    Good news for cattle and corn -
Now is the Sun come up from the South,
    With Oak and Ash and Thorn! (KIPLING; HUTTON, 153)

Seton meets Robert Baden-Powell, and the Boy Scout movement is born. (HUTTON, 163)

1908 In a chapter of Kenneth Grahame's *The Wind in The Willows* titled "The Piper at the Gates of Dawn," Pan appears as an awe-inspiring but kindly demigod who protects the forest animals. (GRAHAME, 144)

Gerald Gardner moves to Borneo. (PEARSON, 65) During his years here he witnesses the shamanic healing rituals of the Dyaks. (LAMOND, 8)

1909 Crowley and Jones found the "A∴A∴," whose full name is often believed to be the Astrum Argentinum, or Silver Star. (Others have claimed that name does not stand for anything.) Ceremonial initiations are eliminated from this order, which focuses on personal magical work using much of the same framework as the Golden Dawn. (REGARDIE, 359)

Gerald Gardner is initiated as a Freemason. (LAMOND, 9)

1910 Seton's woodcraft movement has approximately 200,000 members in the U.S. (J. GREER, 50)

1912 Crowley is approached by the O.T.O., and becomes leader of its English branch. (HUTTON, 223)

Seton founds the Red Lodge. (SETON, RED LODGE)

1914 The era of imperialism explodes into the First World War. (T. GREER, 487, 493)

1915 Disappointed with the militarism and jingoism in Scouting under Baden-Powell, Seton resigns. This influences several in the British scouting movement to do the same. (HUTTON, 163)

1916 Ernest Westlake founds the Order of Woodcraft Chivalry, with Seton as honorary Grand Chieftain. (HUTTON, 163)

1917 J.R.R. Tolkien starts work on his tales of Middle Earth. (TOLKIEN, 17)

1918 WWI ends. 9,400,000 soldiers (KAGAN, 920) and 30,000,000 civilians (T. GREER, 495) are dead from war, famine, and disease. European political, social, artistic, and spiritual systems are all set into flux.

1919 Prescribed heroin for bronchial spasms, Crowley becomes an addict. (REGARDIE, 114)

1920 John Hargrave leaves Scouting to start another Woodcraft group in Britain, the Kibbo Kift Kindred. He intends to give boys a senses of kinship with nature, and pulls elements from sources including Freemasonry and Native American, African, Polynesian, and Inuit culture. Members of the Kibbo Kift eventually include H.G. Wells, Havelock Ellis, and Maurice Hewlett. (HUTTON, 163-164)

1921 Margaret Murray's *The Witch Cult in Western Europe* is published. It contributes greatly to the myth of Witchcraft as the survival of a universal, organized pre-Christian religion in Europe, but its scholarship is questionable. (ADLER, 47)

1924 D.H. Lawrence in an essay "Pan in America": "The Pan relationship, which the world of man once had with all the world, was better than anything man has now." (HUTTON, 160)

1925 Dharmapala buys a London house and turns it into a Buddhist monastery. (FIELDS, 135)

1927 D.T. Suzuki publishes the first series of his *Zen Essays*, which builds him a strong reputation in England. (FIELDS, 186)

1928 Senzaki establishes what may be the first Zen Center in the U.S. in San Francisco. (BENARES, HANDFUL, 36)

1929 D.H. Lawrence publishes the story "The Man Who Died" (also published as "The Escaped Cock"), in which Jesus survives his crucifixion, abandons his old life, and is healed in a sacred sexual ritual by a priestess of Isis, with Jesus taking the role of Osiris. (HUTTON, 160) (Not likely to be assigned reading in your local high school anytime soon, more's the pity.)

1932 The first version of Goddard's *A Buddhist Bible* is published. (GODDARD, VII)

1938 Gardner moves to the New Forest district of Hampshire, and joins the Rosicrucian Theatre at Christchurch, a group with Masonic and Theosophic ties. (HUTTON, 205, 213; ADLER, 61)

The Church of Aphrodite, the first self-conscious modern pagan religion, established in West Hempstead, Long Island, by Gleb Botkin. (HUTTON, 340; ADLER, 233)

T.H. White's *The Sword in the Stone* is published. In White's formulation of the Arthurian myth, the young King is tutored by Merlyn, who's favorite exclamation is the suggestive "by-our-lady!"; and Merlyn teaches Arthur largely by transforming him into various animals (at one point invoking Neptune to transform the boy into a fish), (WHITE, 36, 46, 64, 132) a method with more than a little resemblance to shamanic journeying.

Kerry Thornley – Discordian Society co-founder, Marine Corps buddy to Lee Harvey Oswald, Zenarchist, paranoid schizophrenic, and possible pawn in a conspiracy to assassinate JFK – is born. (GORIGHTLY, 24)

1939 Gardner's claimed initiation into the New Forest coven of witches. (HUTTON, 206) Theories about the actual identity of this group range from an actual surviving old religion (HUTTON, 206), to the Order of Woodcraft Chivalry (HUTTON, 216) or some group splintered off of it, to a complete fabrication.

Gregory Hill born. ("MALACLYPSE THE YOUNGER")

WWII begins. (T. GREER, 522)

1941 Alan Watts' paper "The Problem of Faith and Works in Buddhism," which ponders an old Christian conundrum from a Buddhist point of view, is published in the *Columbia Review of Religion*. (FIELDS, 190)

1942 Following the Japanese attack on the U.S. naval base at Pearl Harbor, FDR signs Executive Order 9066, ordering Americans of Japanese ancestry on the West Coast to report to concentration camps. 110,000 people are forced into the camps. Senzaki holds small zazen sessions at the Heart Mountain camp in Wyoming. (FIELDS, 193)

1943 April 19: "Bicycle Day": Albert Hoffman takes the first deliberate LSD "trip". (STEVENS, 4)

May 5: Years before the close of World War II, the decision to drop the first atomic bombs on Japan rather than Germany is made. The scientists of the Manhattan project are not informed. (BYERS; BROAD)

1944 Jack Kerouac, Allan Ginsberg, and William Burroughs first meet each other in New York City. (PROTHERO, 11)

1945 WWII ends and the Atomic Age begins as tens of thousands of people in Hiroshima and Nagasaki are incinerated. The problem of finding ways to live together peacefully suddenly becomes much more urgent.

1946 Gardner joins the Circle of the Universal Bond, a.k.a. the Ancient Druid Order, a group best known for their public ceremonies at Stonehenge each summer. By December he is a member of its governing council. (HUTTON, 224) Any historical continuity between this group and actual ancient Druids is unproven.

1947 Crowley and Gardner meet for the first time. (HUTTON, 217) By this time Crowley is more or less regarded as head of the O.T.O. (HUTTON, 222) and initiates Gardner into that organization. (HUTTON, 206) (Gardner put their meeting in the previous year in his account, but Hutton makes a strong case that Gardner's recollection was off, citing Crowley's diary.)

Crowley dies. (HUTTON, 171) Some in the O.T.O. assume that Gardner will assume leadership of the O.T.O. in Europe. (HUTTON, 222)

1948 Gardner abandons plans to revive the O.T.O. From this point, it seems he directs his energy more toward witchcraft and "low magic". (HUTTON, 222)

1949 Gardner publishes *High Magic's Aid*, a novel containing disguised descriptions of (what he claimed was) the surviving form of witchcraft. He portrays it as equal in status to the "high magic" of the ritual magicians, while being more closely linked to natural forces and to the common people. (HUTTON, 206, 224)

1950 Chinese army enters Tibet. (FIELDS, 275)

1951 Witchcraft and Vagrancy Acts repealed in Britain. (HUTTON, 206)

1954 Gardner publishes *Witchcraft Today*, in which he poses as an independent anthropologist reporting on the discovery of a surviving pre-Christian religious system, rather than writing as a practitioner. (HUTTON, 206)

Aldous Huxley publishes *The Doors of Perception*, recommending the use of mescaline as "an experience of inestimable value to everyone and especially to the intellectual." (STEVENS, 49)

1955 In the fall, Alan Ginsberg takes peyote and has a vision of Moloch, the ancient god whose worship involved the sacrifice of children. He identifies Moloch with American culture, and writes the poem *Howl*. (STEVENS, 113)

October 13: a poetry reading is held at the Six Gallery in San Francisco. First public reading of Ginsberg's *Howl*. Announcements for the event promise "free satori". A landmark in American poetry. Often cited as the start of the Beat movement, but really more of a coming-out party. (TONKINSON, 10) Other readers include Gary Snyder and Philip Whalen; Kerouac is also there (FIELDS, 212)

c. 1957 Gregory Hill, Kerry Thornley, and Bob Newport develop Discordianism. (Hail Eris!) (GORIGHTLY, 57)

1958 A break-out year for Buddhism in the United States. A special "Zen" edition of *Chicago Review* features work by Snyder, Watts ("Beat Zen, Square Zen"), Kerouac, D.T. Suzuki, Ruth Fuller Sasaki, Senzaki, Philip Walen, and others. (FIELDS, 220)

Kerouac's *The Dharma Bums* is published. On the day of its publication, he, Ginsberg, and Peter Orlovsky visit D.T. Suzuki. (FIELDS, 223)

1959 Tendzin Gyatso, Fourteenth Dalai Lama, flees Tibet. (FIELDS, 273) The Tibetan diaspora does much to expose the world to Tibetan Buddhism.

Shunryu Suzuki arrives in San Francisco. (FIELDS, 226) He is perhaps the first to popularize the Sōtō school of Zen in the West.

1960 In Mexico, Timothy Leary takes psilocybin "magic mushrooms" for the first time. (STEVENS, 122)

1962 Gary Snyder and Allen Ginsberg visit India, and meet with the Dali Lama. (FIELDS, 294)

1963 The Reformed Druids of North America (RDNA) is formed at Carleton College in Minnesota. RDNA starts as a satirical protest against a requirement that students attend a certain number of religious services, but persists long after the requirement is lifted in 1964 and goes on to have a definite impact on the Neopagan movement. (ADLER, 321-324)

1964 Gerald Gardner dies. (HUTTON, 205)

Rosemary and Ray Buckland found a Gardnerian coven in the U.S. (ADLER, 118)

1965 The first edition of the *Principia Discordia*, consisting of only 5 copies, is published by Gregory Hill (under the name Malaclypse the Younger). (GORIGHTLY, 61)

(This first edition was long thought lost, but in 1978, due to co-author Kerry Thornley's testimony regarding the JFK assassination, a copy was placed in the House of Representatives Select Committee on Assassinations's JFK collection as document 010857. A scan has been made available on-line at http://appendix.23ae.com.)

1966 D.T. Suzuki dies. (FIELDS, 265)

Thornley joins Kerista, "a sexually swinging psychedelic tribe". He writes in the group's newspaper, *Kerista Swinger*:

"...[L]et us look at the jobs of the far less intellectual, but far more constructively functional religions of old. These were the 'pagan' religions – the religions that survive to this day in England and the United States as 'witchcraft.'

"Kerista is a religion and the mood of Kerista is one of holiness. Do not, however, look for a profusion of rituals, dogmas, doctrines, and scriptures. Kerista is too sacred for that. It is more akin to the religions of the East and, also, the so-called pagan religions of the pre-Christian West. Its fount of being is the religious experience and that action or word or thought which is not infused with ecstasy is not Kerista. And Kerista, like those religions of olden times, is life-affirming." (ADLER, 294; GORIGHTLY, 73)

In *Drawing Down the Moon*, Margot Adler credits this as the first usage, at least in the U.S., of "Pagan" to describe past and present nature religions – not just to the Witchcraft revival, but to the broader movement. (ADLER, 294) (Thornley said his influence on the movement had been exaggerated. (GORIGHTLY, 227))

1967 The first Human "Be-In" occurs in San Francisco. Gary

Snyder reads his poems, Alan Ginsberg chants the Heart Sutra. Shunryu Suzuki makes an appearance. Timothy Leary and Richard Alpert speak. (FIELDS, 249)

Tim Zell (later Oberon Zell-Ravenheart) picks up Thornley's use of the word "Pagan". (ADLER, 293-295)

1968 WITCH – the Women's International Terrorist Conspiracy from Hell – is founded. It is a surrealist political group that taps into the mythology of witchcraft and the "Burning Times": "Witches have always been women who dared to be: groovy, courageous, aggressive, intelligent, nonconformist, explorative, curious, independent, sexually liberated, revolutionary. (This possibly explains why nine million of them have been burned.)" (ADLER, 179)

The Church of All Worlds – a group inspired in part by Robert Heinlein's science fiction novel *Stranger in a Strange Land* – is founded by Zell and others, and publicizes the use of "Pagan" in its newsletter *Green Egg*. (ADLER, 289-295)

The Dog Question

Ringo in the Snow

For those wondering: yes, I did adopt another dog.

> *the puppy that knows not*
> *that autumn has come*
> *is a Buddha – Issa*
>
> (And I think the same goes for winter.)

Bibliography

I've made wide use of on-line versions of books (including limited previews on Google Books) and newspaper and magazine articles. Since URLs can be unstable, where possible I've also given a traditional "dead trees" citation for these sources.

Adler, Margot. *Drawing Down the Moon*. New York: Penguin/Arkana, 1997.
> The best general orientation to Paganism. Highly recommended.

Aitken, Robert. *The Morning Star: New and Selected Zen Writings*. Washington: Shoemaker & Hoard, 2003.
<http://books.google.com/books?id=h5bf3QQrQb8C>

Aitken, Robert. Foreward. *A Buddhist Bible*. Dwight Goddard, ed. Boston: Beacon, 1994.

Almon, Bert. *Gary Snyder*. Boise: Boise State University, 1979. Number 37 in *Boise State University Western Writers Series*.
<http://scholarworks.boisestate.edu/cgi/viewcontent.cgi?article=1004&context=wws>

Anastas, Benjamin. "The Final Days." *New York Times Magazine*. 1 Jul. 2007
<http://www.nytimes.com/2007/07/01/magazine/01world-t.html>

"Angel Valley Sedona" <http://www.angelvalley.org/> as of Jan 6 2010.
> None of the news coverage I saw of James Arthur Ray's deadly "spiritual warrior" retreat mentioned how long the retreat was intended to be, but the calendar on the retreat center's website showed that this was intended to be a five day event.

Anderson, H. Allen. *The Chief: Ernest Thompson Seton and the Changing West*. College Station: Texas A&M University Press, 1986.

"andrew cohen: founder of *What is Enlightenment?* magazine." *What Is Enlightenment?* Fall/Winter 2000: 8

Appleman, Philip. Introduction. *The Origin of Species*. By Charles Darwin. New York: Norton, 1975.

Ár nDraíocht Féin: A Druid Fellowship, Inc. "Hoof and Horn."

<http://www.adf.org/rituals/chants/nature-spirits/hoof-and-horn.html> as of 17 Feb. 2010.
Bardo Brothers. "Bardo Brothers | Details." <http://www.bardobrothers.com/main.php> as of 2 Aug. 2010.
Barzaghi, Subhana. "Red Thread Zen - The Tao of Love, Passion, and Sex." *Mind Moon Circle: The Journal of the Sydney Zen Center*, 1994(?) <http://www.sacred-texts.com/bud/zen/red-thrd.txt>
Batchelor, Stephen. *The Awakening of the West*. Berkeley: Parallax, 1994.
<http://books.google.com/books?id=xzzZKe6J_OkC>
Bays, Jan. *Jizo Bodhisattva*. Boston: Tuttle, 2002.
> A wonderful book about Zen Buddhist practice with Jizo, the Bodhisattva of the Earth.

Beal, Samuel. *The Romantic Legend of Sakya Buddha*. London: Trubner, 1875.
<http://books.google.com/books?id=TDAiAAAAMAAJ>
Beatles. *The Beatles Anthology*. San Francisco: Chronicle Books, 2000.
<http://books.google.com/books?id=HWuQu8EMDKcC>
Beck, Charlotte. *Everyday Zen*. Ed. Steve Smith. New York: HarperSanFrancisco, 1989.
Benares, Camden. *A Handful of Zen*. Tempe: New Falcon, 1996.
Benares, Camden. *Zen Without Zen Masters*. Tempe: New Falcon, 1993.
> These two books by Camden Benares books are Discordian classics. Somewhat rare but highly recommended.

Berard, Augusta Blanche. *School History of England*. New York: A.S. Barnes, 1874.
<http://books.google.com/books?id=AsEZAAAAYAAJ>
Berg, Stephen. *Crow with No Mouth: Ikkyu*. Port Townsend: Copper Canyon, 2000.
Bicknell, Kent. *Educational Ventures Influenced by the Transcendentalists: Amos Bronson Alcott, Ralph Waldo Emerson, and Henry David Thoreau: Parallel Perspectives of the 19th & 21st Centuries*. Transcript of a Presentation by Kent Bicknell at "Conversations in a Changing World", The Sant Bani School, October 5th, 2007
<http://www.santbani.org/kent/Transcendental_Ed_klb.

pdf>

Blavatsky, H.P. "The Theosophical Society: Its Origin, Plan and Aims." *Collected Writings (Volume I, 1874-1878)*. Ed. Boris de Zirkoff. Wheaton, IL: Theosophical Publishing House, 1950. 375-378
<http://www.katinkahesselink.net/blavatsky/articles/v1/>
> The specific pages referenced are at http://www.katinkahesselink.net/blavatsky/articles/v1/y1878_024.htm

Blunt, Wilfrid and William Thomas Stearn. *Linnaeus: The Compleat Naturalist*. Princeton: Princeton University Press, 2001.
<http://books.google.com/books?id=m6lsDLevuJ4C>

Boucher, Sandy. *Turning the Wheel*. Boston: Beacon, 1993.
<http://books.google.com/books?id=ht4QqV_HIh8C>

Braak, Andre van der. *Enlightenment Blues*. Rhinebeck: Monkfish, 2003.

Braude, Ann. *Radical Spirits: Spiritualism and Women's Rights in Nineteenth-century America*, 2nd ed. Bloomington: Indiana University Press, 2001.
<http://books.google.com/books?id=iGP2t8lxsToC>

Broad, William J. "Wartime Atomic Strategy Is Reassessed." *New York Times* 18 Apr. 1995, New York ed.: A12.
<http://www.nytimes.com/1995/04/18/us/wartime-atomic-strategy-is-reassessed.html>

Brunton, Paul. "A Pioneer Western Buddhist." *Ceylon Daily News, Vesak Number* May, 1941.
<http://www.bps.lk/other_library/pioneerwesternbuddhist.pdf>

Byers, Nina. "Physicists and the 1945 Decision to Drop the Bomb." *CERN Courier* 1 Nov 2002.
<http://cerncourier.com/cws/article/cern/28739>

Byron, George Gordon (Lord). *The Works of Lord Byron Complete in One Volume*, 3rd ed. H.L. Broenner, 1837.
<http://books.google.com/books?id=jxc3AAAAIAAJ>

Campbell, Joseph. *The Flight of the Wild Gander*. Chicago: Henry Regnery, 1972.
> Campbell's essay "The Symbol Without Meaning" featured in this volume is essential reading about the nature of religion.

Carus, Paul. *The History of the Devil and the Idea of Evil: From the*

Earliest Times to the Present Day. Open Court, 1900.
<http://www.sacred-texts.com/evil/hod/index.htm>
The cited tale of Mara and the Buddha is at http://www.sacred-texts.com/evil/hod/hod10.htm

Carnegie, Dale. *How to Stop Worrying and Start Living*. New York: Pocket, 2004. <http://books.google.com/books?id=yCKmKv99NoIC>

Chesterton, G. K. *The Man Who Was Thursday: a Nightmare*. London: Penguin, 2007.

Clark, Tom. *The Great Naropa Poetry Wars*. Cadmus Editions: Santa Barbara, 1980.

Cleary, Thomas.. *Vitality, Energy, Spirit : A Taoist Sourcebook*. Boston: Shambhala, 1991.

Cohen, Andrew. Editorial. *What Is Enlightenment?* June-August 2006. <http://www.enlightennext.org/magazine/j33/editorial.asp> as of 3 Jan. 2010.

Corrigan, Ian. "An Unfortunate Mistake." Amazon.com review of *The Good Witch's Bible*, 4 Jul. 2007. <http://www.amazon.com/review/RQKF0KE0CUSAH>

Corrigan, Ian. E-mail to the author. 2 Jan. 2010.

Crow, John L. "The Bhikkhu and the Magus: Exploring Allan Bennett's Influence on Aleister Crowley." Unpublished work presented at the 2008 International Conference of CESNUR, the Center for Studies on New Religions. <http://www.cesnur.org/2008/london_crow.pdf>

Crowley, Aleister. "Berashith: An Essay in Ontology." *The Works of Aleister Crowley (Vol II)*. Foyers: Society for the Propagation of Religious Truth, 1906. <http://lilytears.com/spirituality/thelema/qabalah/berashith.htm>

Crowley, Aleister. *The Confessions of Aleister Crowley*. Ed. John Symonds and Kenneth Grant. <http://www.hermetic.com/crowley/confess/>

Crowley, Aleister. "The Formula of the Holy Graal, of Abrahadabra, and of Certain Other Words; with Some Remarks on the Magical Memory." *Liber ABA (Magick)* Part III. <http://hermetic.com/crowley/book-4/chap7.html>

Das, Bhagavan. *It's Here Now (Are You?)*. New York: Broadway, 1997.

Deford, Miriam Allen. "A Poet's Science." *The Open Court* Vol 35 No 9, Sep. Ed. Carus, Paul (1921): 549-551. <http://books.google.com/books?id=zL8NAQAAIAAJ>

Dougherty, John. "For Some Seeking Rebirth, Sweat Lodge Was End.". *New York Times* 22 Oct. 2009, New York ed.: A1. <http://www.nytimes.com/2009/10/22/us/22sweat.html>

Dougherty, John. "New Details About Deaths in Sweat Lodge Are Revealed." *New York Times* 30 Dec. 2009, New York ed.: A18. <http://www.nytimes.com/2009/12/30/us/30sweatlodge.html>

Dougherty, John and Gregory Roth. "Questions About 'Sweat Lodge' Rite Where 2 Died." *New York Times* 10 Oct. 2009. <http://www.nytimes.com/2009/10/11/us/11lodge.html>

Douglass, Frederick. *The Narrative of the Life of Frederick Douglass.* Project Gutenberg, January 2006 [Ebook #23]. <http://www.gutenberg.org/files/23/23-h/23-h.htm>

Downing, Michael. *Shoes Outside the Door: Desire, Devotion, and Excess at San Francisco Zen Center.* Washington, D.C.: Counterpoint, 2002. <http://books.google.com/books?id=9cck8nzxny0C>

Dumoulin, Heinrich. "Early Chinese Zen Reexamined." *Japanese Journal of Religious Studies* 1993 20.1: 31-53. <http://www.nanzan-u.ac.jp/SHUBUNKEN/publications/jjrs/pdf/387.pdf>

Ekai. *The Gateless Gate*. Trans. Nyogen Senzaki and Paul Reps. Forgotten Books, 2007. <http://books.google.com/books?id=8590Wf9gtCoC>

Ellis, Jonathan. "Pop Will Shit Itself with Grant Morrison: Grant Morrison Is..., an interview by Jonathan Ellis." PopImage. <http://www.popimage.com/profile/morrison/012501_grant6.html>

Emerson, Ralph Waldo. *Journals of Ralph Waldo Emerson with Annotations 1841-1844.* Ed. Edward Waldo Emerson and Waldo Emerson Forbes. Boston: Houghton Mifflin Company, 1911. Vol. VI of *Journals of Ralph Waldo Emerson.* <http://books.google.com/books?id=3cXjZ99GpqgC>

Emerson, Ralph Waldo. "Self Reliance." *Essays: First Series*. 1841. Jone Johnson Lewis. <http://www.emersoncentral.com/selfreliance.htm>

Emerson, Ralph Waldo. "The American Scholar." *Nature; Addresses and Lectures*. 1849. Jone Johnson Lewis.
<http://www.emersoncentral.com/amscholar.htm>

Emerson, Ralph Waldo. "The Poet". *Essays: Second Series*. 1844. Jone Johnson Lewis.
<http://www.emersoncentral.com/poet.htm>

Emerson, Ralph Waldo. "The Transcendentalist." *Nature; Addresses and Lectures*. 1849. Jone Johnson Lewis.
<http://www.emersoncentral.com/transcendentalist.htm>

Falk, Geoffrey. *Stripping the Gurus*. Toronto: Million Monkeys, 2009.
<http://www.strippingthegurus.com/ebook/Stripping_the_Gurus.pdf>

> I don't agree with all of Falk's opinions and interpretations, but Stripping the Gurus is worth a look, chock-full of cautionary tales about the misbehavior of spiritual leaders.

Fairbanks, Arthur. *A Handbook of Greek Religion*. New York: American Book Company, 1910.
<http://books.google.com/books?id=HWzXAAAAMAAJ>

Fields, Rick. *How the Swans Came to the Lake*. Boulder: Shambhala, 1992.

> A well-written narrative of the introduction of Buddhism to the West. Uncritical, but still highly recommended.

Finch, Robert and John Elder. *The Norton Book of Nature Writing*. New York: W.W. Norton, 1990.
<http://books.google.com/books?id=NmOA7xXGO1kC>

Fischer, Norman. "The Highest Meaning of the Holy Truths: Commentary on Blue Cliff Record." 1 Aug. 1997.
<http://www.everydayzen.org/index.php?Itemid=27&option=com_teaching&topic=Zen+Koans&sort=title&studyguide=true&task=viewTeaching&id=text-131-90>

Fitton, R.S. and Alfred P. Wadsworth. *Strutts and the Arkwrights, 1758-1830: A Study of the Early Factory System*. Manchester University Press ND, 1973.
<http://books.google.com/books?id=qGS7AAAAIAAJ>

Ford, James. *Zen Master Who?*. London: Wisdom Publications, 2006. <http://books.google.com/books?id=-

kut6gcyTNEC>

Frost, Gavin and Yvonne Frost. *The Good Witch's Bible.* 7th ed. Hinton, WV: Godolphin, 2000.

> For a book that has stirred such controversy, copies are very hard to locate – interlibrary loan came up blank, telling me that no library in the country holds a copy for lending. And I was only able to locate one copy from a used bookseller. Fortunately the famously controversial sections have been posted on the web, so you can read and judge for yourself:
>
> Forward To Chapter IV:
> http://www.freewebs.com/controversialstudy/WB/ForwardToChapterIV.htm
>
> Chapter IV:
> http://www.freewebs.com/controversialstudy/WB/ChapterIV.htm

Gaiman, Neil. "A Midsummer Night's Dream." *The Sandman: Dream Country.* New York: DC Comics, 1991.

Gardner, Gerald. *The Gardnerian Book of Shadows.* Forgotten Books, 2008. <http://books.google.com/books?id=9x_T20ESuakC>

Getty, Alice. *The Gods of Northern Buddhism: Their History, Iconography, and Progressive Evolution Through the Northern Buddhist Countries.* London: Oxford University Press, 1914. <http://www.archive.org/details/northernbuddhism00gettuoft>

Giles, Lionel. *Taoist Teachings: Translated from the Book of Lieh-Tzü.* 1912. <http://www.sacred-texts.com/tao/tt/>

Ginsberg, Allen. *Howl, and Other Poems.* San Francisco: City Lights, 1956. <http://books.google.com/books?id=xbeUMn6pi2UC>

Goddard, Dwight. *A Buddhist Bible.* Boston: Beacon, 1994.

Goethe, Johann Wolfgang von. *Poetry and Truth From My Own Life, Volume 1.* Trans. Minna Steele Smith. London: George Bell & sons, 1908. <http://books.google.com/books?id=BYoNAAAAYAAJ>

Gorightly, Adam. *The Prankster and the Conspiracy.* New York: Paraview, 2003.

> A biography of Kerry Thornley - co-founder of the Discordian Society, Marine Corps buddy of Lee Harvey Oswald, political philosopher, possible pawn in CIA mind control experiments, and probable paranoid schizophrenic.

Grahame, Kenneth. *Pagan Papers* (5th ed.) London: John Lane, 1898.
<http://books.google.com/books?id=9ZAWAAAAYAAJ>

Grahame, Kenneth. *The Wind in the Willows*. New York: C. Scribner's Sons, 1908.
<http://books.google.com/books?id=-4UgAAAAMAAJ>

Greer, John Michael and Gordon Cooper. "The Red God: Woodcraft and the Origins of Wicca." *Gnosis* Summer 1998: 50-58.

Greer, Thomas. *A Brief History of the Western World*. Stamford: Thomson Learning, 1987.

> A standard college history text, Greer's Brief History is clear and concise, excellent for the autodidact.

Gribbin, John. *In Search of Schrödinger's Cat*. New York: Bantam, 1984.

Grigoriadis, Vanessa. "Daniel Pinchbeck and the New Psychedelic Elite." *Rolling Stone* 7 Sept. 2006: 88-90, 114, 116. <http://www.rollingstone.com/politics/story/11217201/daniel_pinchbeck_and_the_new_psychedelic_elite>

Hall, John, et. al. *The Cambridge History of Japan*. Cambridge: Cambridge University Press, 1997.
<http://books.google.com/books?id=A3_6lp8IOK8C>

Hamill, Sam. *The Essential Chuang Tzu*. Boulder: Shambhala, 1998.

Hanes, William Travis, and Sanello, Frank. *The Opium Wars: The Addiction of One Empire and the Corruption of Another*. Sourcebooks, Inc., 2004.
<http://books.google.com/books?id=8LOkbOxyNYwC>

Hanh, Thich Nhat. *The Heart of Understanding*. Berkeley: Parallax, 1988.

> A clear and understandable commentary on the Heart Sutra.

Hanh, Thich Nhat. *Old Path, White Clouds*. Berkeley: Parallax, 1991

> A novelization of the life of the Buddha. Very good.

Harada, K. and G. P. Glasby. "Human impact on the environment in Japan and New Zealand: a comparison." *The Science of The Total Environment* 263:1-3 (18 December 2000): 79-90. <http://dx.doi.org/10.1016/S0048-9697(00)00668-9>

Harris, Elizabeth J. *Ānanda Metteyya: The First British Emissary of Buddhism (Wheel No. 420/422).* Kandy: Buddhist Publication Society, 1998. <http://www.bps.lk/wheels_library/wheels_pdf/wh_420_422.pdf>

> From the Buddhist Publication Society site at http://www.bps.lk

Hazlitt, William. *Lectures Chiefly on the Dramatic Literature of the Age of Elizabeth: Delivered at the Surrey Institution (Second Edition).* London: Stoddart and Stewart, 1821. <http://books.google.com/books?id=DAYOAAAAQAAJ>

Heine, Steven and Dale Wright. *Zen Ritual.* Oxford, Oxfordshire: Oxford University Press, 2008. <http://books.google.com/books?id=Q_qAZWejjD4C>

Hesse, Herman. *Demian.* New York:Bantam, 1970.

Hieronimus, Robert R. *One People, One Planet, Hon! Hidden Meaning of Common Symbols.* Exhibit Guide 2009: One People, One Planet...Hon!. The Windup Space, Baltimore MD.

"Hoorin-ji The Daruma Temple in Kyoto" <http://www.amie.or.jp/daruma/Hoorin-ji.html> as of 28 Feb. 2009.

Horgan, John. *Rational Mysticism.* Boston: Mariner, 2004. <http://books.google.com/books?id=7dYV9UJszlUC>

Horner, Francis J. *Case History of Japan.* New York: Sheed & Ward, 1948.

Hutton, Ronald. *The Triumph of the Moon.* Oxford, Oxfordshire: Oxford University Press, 1999.

> Hutton is Professor of History at the University of Bristol, and this book is the premiere history of British Witchcraft (i.e., Wicca). Scholarly and dense, but if you are interested in the history of Neopaganism, Hutton's work is required reading.

Huxley, Aldous. *Island*. New York: Perennial, 2002.
<http://books.google.com/books?id=MB3VSMgJ5CkC>
> Island is Huxley's antidote to his Brave New World: an attempt to depict a sane society. Recommended.

Jalon, Allan M. "Meditating On War And Guilt, Zen Says It's Sorry." *New York Times* 11 January 2003, New York ed.: B9.
<http://www.nytimes.com/2003/01/11/books/meditating-on-war-and-guilt-zen-says-it-s-sorry.html>

Johnson, K. Paul. *The Masters Revealed*. Albany: State University of New York Press, 1994.
<http://books.google.com/books?id=bMVrr1XaADwC>

Johnson, Vera. "Letters of H.P. Blavatsky. Part XII." *The Path (New York)* Nov. 1895.
<http://blavatskyarchives.com/blavle12.htm>
> Part of an on-line reprint of a series of articles by Vera Johnston (Blavatsky's sister) in the monthly Path magazine of New York, December 1894 through December 1895. Published on line by the Blavatsky Study Center, http://blavatskyarchives.com/blavletc.htm

Kagan, Donald et.al. *The Western Heritage, Volume II: Since 1648*. Englewood Cliffs: Prentice Hall, 2001.

Kaplan, Justin. *Walt Whitman, a Life*. New York: Simon and Schuster, 1980.

Keats, John. "Endymion Book I." *Poetical Works*. London: Macmillan, 1884.
<http://www.bartleby.com/126/32.html>

Keats, John. "Endymion Book IV." *Poetical Works*. London: Macmillan, 1884.
<http://www.bartleby.com/126/35.html>

"Ken Wilber: Welcome". <http://wilber.shambhala.com> as of Jan 1 2010.

Kennedy, Gordon. *Children of the Sun*. Ojai, California: Nivaria, 1998.
> A fascinating account of how the values of 19th century German bohemianism, especially the Lebensreform and Naturmenschen ("life-reform" and "natural men") movements, came to influence later generations of Americans.

Keremidschieff, Vladimir. "Legends in Ch'an: the

Northern/Southern Schools Split, Hui-neng and the Platform Sutra." thezensite.com.
<http://www.thezensite.com/ZenEssays/HistoricalZen/Legends_in_Chan.pdf>
> This very nice essay is actually just attributed to "Vladimir K.", but outside links identify Keremidschieff as the founder of thezensite.com

Kerouac, Jack. *The Dharma Bums*. Harmondsworth Eng.: Penguin, 1986.
> The book that made Buddhism part of American popular culture.

Kipling, Rudyard. *Puck of Pook's Hill*. Project Gutenberg, June 1996 [Etext #557].
<http://www.gutenberg.org/dirs/etext96/pkpkh10.txt>

Knaul, Livia. "Chuang-Tzu And The Chinese Ancestry of Ch'an Buddhism." *Journal of Chinese Philosophy* 13 (1986): 411-428.
<http://ccbs.ntu.edu.tw/FULLTEXT/JR-JOCP/livia.htm>

Kornfield, Jack. *After the Ecstasy, the Laundry*. New York: Bantam, 2000.

Krassner, Paul. "Life Among the Neo-Pagans." *The Nation*. 24 Aug. 2005.
<http://www.thenation.com/doc/20050829/krassner>

Lacey, Marc. "New Age Guru Guilty in Sweat Lodge Deaths". *New York Times* 23 June 2001, New York ed.: A16.
<http://www.nytimes.com/2011/06/23/us/23sweat.html>

Lamond, Frederic. *Fifty Years of Wicca*. Sutton Mallet: Green Magic, 2004.

Lane, David Christopher. "Ken Wilber's Achilles' Heel: The Art of Spiritual Hyperbole, Part Two: EVOLUTION VERSUS MYSTERIONISM?"
<http://elearn.mtsac.edu/dlane/kendebates.htm>

Langford, Donald Stewart. *The Primacy of Place in Gary Snyder's Ecological Vision*. The Ohio State University, 1993.
<http://etd.ohiolink.edu/send-pdf.cgi/Langford%20Donald%20Stewart.pdf?acc_num=osu1234700675>

Lawrence, D.H. "Mystic." *The Complete Poems of D.H. Lawrence*. Wordsworth Poetry Library, 1994.
<http://books.google.com/books?id=cQYRp8EQrzUC>

Legge, James. *The Texts of Taoism*. Mineola: Dover, 1962.

<http://books.google.com/books?id=kXd_ZMpWvy8C>
Leighton, Taigen. *Faces of Compassion*. London: Wisdom Publications, 2003.
<http://books.google.com/books?id=XcvVUAhFwQIC>
Lowry, Dave. "Why Are There So Many Losers in the Martial Arts?" Excerpt of out-of-print article verified by the author.

> Originally published in Karate Illustrated circa 1994, this essay can be found on-line in several places, including <http://lklawson.isa-geek.org/sync/Martial_Arts/BB_Mag/kki/1986/feb86/traditions/traditions.html> and <http://sports.groups.yahoo.com/group/CyberDojo/message/51989>. The excerpt used appears by permission of Mr. Lowry.

Lutyens, Mary. *Krishnamurti*. Boulder: Shambhala, 1997.
<http://books.google.com/books?id=lhPFWXgxQCkC>
Malaclypse the Younger. *Principia Discordia*. Avondale Estates: Illuminet, 1991.

> Hail Eris! You can read the body of the Principia on-line at www.PrincipiaDiscordia.com; however, that version lacks the Kerry Thornley introduction in the Illuminet edition (though of course that too can be found on-line via the search engine of your choice.)

"Malaclypse the Younger." *Wikipedia, The Free Encyclopedia*. 11 Dec 2008 18:27 UTC.
<http://en.wikipedia.org/w/index.php?title=Malaclypse_the_Younger&oldid=257316602>.

> The mighty Wikipedia has been of great assistance for general background. And it was one of the few sources I could find for biographical information about Greg Hill (a.k.a. Malaclypse the Younger), though I'm breaking the hearts of all of my English teachers by citing an encyclopedia as a source. So be it.

Maltby, Samuel Edwin. *Manchester and the Movement for National Elementary Education, 1800-1870*. University Press, 1918.
<http://books.google.com/books?id=y5lDAAAAIAAJ>
Mann, Charles C. "The Birth of Religion." *National Geographic* 219.6 (Jun 2011): 35-59.
Martin, John and Phyllis Martin. *Kyoto: a Cultural Guide*. Boston:

Tuttle, 2002.
<http://books.google.com/books?id=YRCWtf_d5jgC>
Mathers, Samuel Liddell MacGregor. Introduction. *The Book of the Sacred Magic of Abramelin the Mage.* Trans. Mathers. Forgotten Books, 2008.
<http://books.google.com/books?id=mSLthPgiYq4C>
Mathers, S.L. MacGregor and Aleister Crowley. *The Lesser Key of Solomon: Geotia for Invocation and Convocation of Spirits, Necromancy, Witchcraft and Black Art.* Forgotten Books, 2008.
<http://books.google.com/?id=pXqeXi6T1D0C>

> It seems that this cheap reprint edition misspells "Goetia" on the cover, but it's still Mathers and Crowley's translation inside.

McClelland, Hardin T. "Religion and Philosophy in Ancient India." *The Open Court* Vol 35 No 8, Aug. Ed. Carus, Paul (1921): 463-474.
<http://books.google.com/books?id=zL8NAQAAIAAJ>
Metzger, Richard. "Interview with Grant Morrison." Disinfo Nation, 2 Feb. 2001. The Disinformation Company Ltd. Transcript.
<http://www.disinfo.com/archive/pages/dossier/id987/pg2/index.html>
Mullen, Eve. *The American Occupation of Tibetan Buddhism.* Münster: Waxmann, 2001.
<http://books.google.com/books?id=2F_9vXbQpzIC>
Murphy, Dan. "Norway spiral: A rocket scientist explains the mystery". Christian Science Monitor Global News Blog. 10 Dec. 2009. <http://www.csmonitor.com/World/Global-News/2009/1210/Norway-spiral-video-Mystery-solved>
Murray, Margaret. The God of the Witches. Oxford, Oxfordshire: Oxford University, 1970.
<http://books.google.com/books?id=hkayBkbOWfQC>
Nakamura, Tadashi. *One Day, One Lifetime: An Illustrated Guide to the Spirit, Practice and Philosophy of Seido Karate Meditation.* Mexico: World Seido Karate Organization, 1992.
Nanamoli (Bhikkhu), Bodhi (Bhikkhu). *The Middle Length Discourses of the Buddha.* Boston: Wisdom Publications in association with the Barre Center for Buddhist Studies, 1995.
<http://books.google.com/books?id=g5YfHBF10aoC>
Nara National Museum. *Shinto Gods and Buddhist Deities: Syncretic Faith in Japanese Art.* Trans. Michael Jamentz. Nara: Nara

National Museum, 2007.
O'Brien, Jack. "An Interview with Steven Wright". Cracked.com. <http://www.cracked.com/article_15330_interview-with-steven-wright.html>
O'Connor, Anahad. "2 Die and 16 Are Sickened at Spa in Arizona". *New York Times* 10 October 2009, New York ed.: A14. <http://www.nytimes.com/2009/10/10/us/10spa.html>
Oldmeadow, Harry. *Journeys East.* Bloomington: World Wisdom, 2004. <http://books.google.com/books?id=vC1qAj6RbRQC>
Paine, Jeffery. *Re-Enchantment.* New York: Norton, 2004. <http://books.google.com/books?id=fnOPOczzYrYC>
Pearson, Joanne. *A Popular Dictionary of Paganism.* Routledge, 2002. <http://books.google.com/books?id=3W02UMPejRwC>
Pearson, Jo. "Inappropriate Sexuality? Sex Magic, S/M and Wicca (or 'Whipping Harry Potter's Arse!')" *Theology & Sexuality.* 2005 11.2: 31-42 <http://tse.sagepub.com/cgi/content/abstract/11/2/31>
Perry, Bliss, Ed. *The Heart of Emerson's Journals.* Cambridge Massachusetts: Houghton Mifflin, 1926.
Philostratus. *The Life of of Apollonius of Tyana: the Epistles of Apollonius and the Treatise of Eusebius, Volume 1.* Trans. F.C. Conybeare. London: William Heinemann, 1912. <http://books.google.com/books?id=nzghyc2nJbMC>
Pinchbeck, Daniel. *2012: the Return of Quetzalcoatl.* Los Angeles: Tarcher, 2007.
Pinchbeck, Daniel. Foreward. *A Psychonaut's Guide to the Invisible Landscape: The Topography of the Psychedelic Experience.* By Dan Carpenter. Rochester: Park Street, 2006. vii-xi. <http://books.google.com/books?id=CcpjE-LIwvwC>
Pinchbeck, Daniel. "Thoughts on the Norway Spiral." Reality Sandwich. 10 Dec. 2009 <http://www.realitysandwich.com/thoughts_norway_spiral>
Pine, Red. *The Zen Teaching of Bodhidharma.* San Francisco: North Point, 1989.
Porter, Eleanor. *Pollyanna.* Boston: The Page Company, 1913. <http://books.google.com/books?id=bF81AAAAMAAJ>
"The Preaching of Buddha". *The Dial: A Magazine for Literature, Philosophy, and Religion* Vol IV. No. III, Jan. Ed. Fuller,

Margaret, et. al. Boston: J. Munroe (1844): 391-401.
<http://books.google.com/books?id=VnsAAAAAYAAJ>

Prothero, Stephen. Introduction. *Big Sky Mind*. Ed. Carol Tonkinson. New York: Riverhead Books, 1995.

"Ralph Borsodi: The Plowboy Interview" *Mother Earth News* No. 26 (March-April 1974) <http://www.motherearthnews.com/Sustainable-Farming/1974-03-01/The-Plowboy-Interview-Dr-Ralph-Borsodi.aspx>

Regardie, Israel. *Eye in the Triangle*. Tempe: New Falcon Publications, 1993.

Rice, David Gerard and John E. Stambaugh. *Sources For the Study of Greek religion*. The Society of Biblical Literature, 1979. <http://books.google.com/books?id=fkwkgUEZjrkC>

Robbins, John. *The Food Revolution: How Your Diet Can Help Save Your Life and Our World*. Berkeley: Conari, 2001.

> The whole story about the pig farmer is available on-line: <http://www.foodrevolution.org/pig_farmer.htm>. Read it, it will make you weep.

Robinson, Howard, and James Thomson Shotwell. *The Development of the British Empire*. Houghton Mifflin, 1922. <http://books.google.com/books?id=woRdQlGbL_oC>

Sadler, Roger. *Electronic Media Law*. Thousand Oaks: Sage, 2005. <http://books.google.com/books?id=i4egPXh4OoEC>

Sagan, Carl and Ann Druyan. *The Varieties of Scientific Experience*. New York: Penguin Group, 2006. <http://books.google.com/books?id=a2iouZybD8sC>

Sahn, Seung. *Teaching Letters of Zen Master Seung Sahn: Letters 101 through 200*. Kwan Um School of Zen, 2008. <http://www.kwanumzen.com/teaching_letters/0101_0200.pdf>

Sahn, Seung. *The Compass of Zen*. Boulder: Shambhala, 1997. <http://books.google.com/books?id=xUrZsugB4r4C>

Sahn, Seung. *Dropping Ashes on the Buddha*. New York: Grove, 1976. <http://books.google.com/books?id=U-7KFCPt3P0C>

> Seung Sahn's "Kwan Um" school of Korean Zen is wonderfully earthy.

Satterthwaite, David. "Streets ahead". The Guardian, Wednesday 17 Jan. 2007.

<http://www.guardian.co.uk/environment/2007/jan/17/society.pollution>

Schiller, Friedrich. *The Poems and Ballads of Schiller*. Trans. Sir Edward Bulwer Lytton. New York: Clark & Maynard, 1864. <http://books.google.com/books?id=3BxKAAAAIAAJ>

Seton, Anya. Preface. *Green Darkness*. By Seton. Chicago: Chicago Review Press, 2005.

Seton, Ernest and Julia Seton. *The Gospel of the Redman*. Bloomington: World Wisdom, 2005.

Seton, Ernest Thompson. *The Woodcraft Manual for Boys: The Fifteenth Birch Bark Roll*. New York: Doubleday, Page & Company, 1917. <http://books.google.com/books?id=I7g2AAAAMAAJ>

Seton, Ernest Thompson. *The Red Lodge*. 1912. <http://www.etsetoninstitute.org/digitized-works-by-seton/The%20Red%20Lodge.pdf>

Seton, Ernest Thompson. *Trail of an Artist-Naturalist*. New York: Charles Scribner's Sons, 1940.

> Seton's autobiography. Unfortunately it is rare, out of print, and not available on-line.

Shaku, Soyen. "An Address Delivered at a Service Held in Memory of Those Who Died in The Russo-Japanese War." *Zen for Americans*. Trans. Daisetz Teitaro Suzuki. Chicago: Open Court, 1906. <http://www.sacred-texts.com/bud/zfa/zfa24.htm>

Shaw, Miranda. *Buddhist Goddesses of India*. Princeton: Princeton University Press, 2006. <http://books.google.com/books?id=MvDKOK1h3zMC>

Shea, Robert and Robert Wilson. *The Illuminatus! Trilogy*. New York: Dell, 1988. <http://books.google.com/books?id=gnO76vZELmQC>

Shelley, Percy Bysshe, and Harry Buxton Forman. *The Works of Percy Bysshe Shelley in Verse and Prose, Now First Brought Together with Many Pieces Not Before Published (Volume 5)*. Reeves and Turner, 1880. <http://books.google.com/books?id=JIwMAAAAYAAJ>

Shelley, Percy Bysshe. "A Defence of Poetry". *English Essays: Sidney to Macaulay. Vol. XXVII. The Harvard Classics*. New York: P.F. Collier & Son, 1909-14; Bartleby.com, 2001. <http://www.bartleby.com/27/>

Shelley, Percy Bysshe. "Song Of Proserpine While Gathering

Flowers on the Plain Of Enna". *The Complete Poetical Works of Percy Bysshe Shelley Volume I*. Project Gutenberg, December, 2003 [Etext #4800].
<http://www.gutenberg.org/dirs/etext03/shlyc10.txt>

Shelley, Percy Bysshe. "Hymn Of Pan". *The Complete Poetical Works of Percy Bysshe Shelley Volume I*. Project Gutenberg, December, 2003 [Etext #4800].
<http://www.gutenberg.org/dirs/etext03/shlyc10.txt>

Shih, Hu. "Ch'an (Zen) Buddhism in China: Its History and Method" *Philosophy East and West* 3.1 (January, 1953): 3-24
<http://ccbs.ntu.edu.tw/FULLTEXT/JR-PHIL/ew87728.htm>

Shimazono, Susumu. *From Salvation to Spirituality: Popular Religious Movements in Modern Japan*. Trans Pacific Press, 2004.
<http://books.google.com/books?id=W5bveVtxGV0C>

Smith, Huston. *The World's Religions*. San Francisco: HarperSanFrancisco, 1991.
> If you live on Earth, and encounter people of religions different from your own, you ought to read this book. The original version, *The Religions of Man*, will do if you find a cheap copy in a used bookstore.

Smullyan, Raymond. *The Tao Is Silent*. San Francisco: Harper & Row, 1977.

Snyder, Gary. *A Place in Space: Ethics, Aesthetics, and Watersheds*. Washington: Counterpoint, 1995.
> Prose by Gary Snyder. Great stuff.

Sŏsan, Taesa, Pŏpchŏng, and Hyŏn'gak. *The Mirror of Zen: the Classic Guide to Buddhist Practice by Zen Master So Sahn*. Boston: Shambhala, 2006.
<http://books.google.com/books?id=MP_9WyyFptYC>

Starhawk. *The Spiral Dance (20th Anniversary Edition)*. San Francisco: HarperCollins, 1999.

Steinbeck, John and Robert Demott. *The Grapes of Wrath*. New York: Penguin, 1992.

Stevens, Jay. *Storming Heaven*. San Francisco: Harper & Row, 1988.
<http://books.google.com/books?id=rKlGAdNUDAkC>
> An outstanding history of the psychedelic movement.

Stevenson, David. *The Origins of Freemasonry: Scotland's Century, 1590-1710.* Cambridge University Press, 1990. <http://books.google.com/books?id=6WzkgXaSSeIC>

Stöver, Dietrich Johann Heinrich. *The life of Sir Charles Linnæus.* Trans. Joseph Trapp. London: B. and J. White, 1794. <http://books.google.com/books?id=AoidX8bJK-oC>

Suiter, John. *Poets on the Peaks.* Cambridge: Perseus Books, 2003.

Sunfellow, David. "Ken Wilber Describes His Savant-Like Abilities - Integral NHNE." <http://integralnhne.ning.com/forum/topics/1870157:Topic:563>, also at <http://kenwilber.meetup.com/boards/view/viewthread?thread=2824036>. See also the audio file of the interview with Wilber at <http://integralnhne.ning.com/forum/attachment/download?id=1870157%3AUploadedFi58%3A562> or <http://www.nhne.com/files/integral/audio/wilber_savant.mp3>; these appear to be extracted from the interview "Idiot Savant, or Just an Idiot?" behind a paywall at <http://in.integralinstitute.org/live/listen_to_Ken_Wilber.aspx>. All as of 26 Jul. 2010.

Surrey County Council. "Parliamentary enclosure." <http://www.surreycc.gov.uk/sccwebsite/sccwspages.nsf/LookupWebPagesByTITLE_RTF/Parliamentary+enclosure> as of 2 Feb. 2010.

> Some valuable facts and figures about the process of land enclosure in the U.K.

Suzuki, Daisetz Teitaro. Foreward. *Zen in the Art of Archery.* By Eugen Herrigel. London: Routledge & Kegan Paul, 1953. <http://books.google.com/books?id=Wo4VAAAAIAAJ>

Suzuki, Daisetz T. *Zen and Japanese Culture.* Trans. Momo'o Kitagawa. Tokyo: Kodansha International, 2005

Suzuki, Teitaro and Carus, Paul, trans. *Yin Chih Wen: The Tract of the Quiet Way.* Chicago: Open Court, 1906. <http://books.google.com/books?id=UEgOAAAAYAAJ>

Suzuki, Shunryu. *Zen Mind, Beginner's Mind.* New York: Weatherhill, 1988.

Swinburne, Algernon. *The Yale Edition of the Swinburne Letters.* New Haven: Yale University Press, 1959. <http://books.google.com/books?id=8XoTs_xQmNkC>

Swinburne, Algernon. "Hertha". *Songs before Sunrise.* Project

Gutenberg, May 2003 [Etext #4072]
<http://www.gutenberg.org/dirs/etext03/sbsun10.txt>
Tarlo, Luna. *The Mother of God*. New York: Plover, 1997.
Tolkein, Christopher. Introduction. *The Silmarillion*. By J.R.R. Tolkien. Boston: Houghton Mifflin, 1977.
Tonkinson, Carole ed. *Big Sky Mind*. New York: Riverhead, 1995.
Thoreau, Henry David, and Will H. Dircks. *A Week on the Concord and Merrimack Rivers*. Walter Scott, 1895.
<http://books.google.com/books?id=rMwgAAAAMAAJ>
Thorpe, William J. "Fire Circle Rap."
<http://www.bardobrothers.com/rap.php> as of 2 Aug 2010.
Turner, Frank. *The Greek Heritage in Victorian Britain*. New Haven: Yale University Press, 1981.
<http://books.google.com/books?id=KfbEsQ5WkdUC>
Turner, Steve. *The Gospel According to the Beatles*. Louisville: Westminster John Knox, 2006.
Varley, H. Paul. *Japanese Culture*. Honolulu: University of Hawaii, 2000.
<http://books.google.com/books?id=BvUEzBin61AC>
Versluis, Arthur. *American Transcendentalism and Asian Religions*. Oxford University Press US, 1993.
<http://books.google.com/books?id=mNPMzoVEv3sC>
Victoria, Daizen. *Zen War Stories*. London: RoutledgeCurzon, 2003.
<http://books.google.com/books?id=_tDuLWU3kUcC>
Victoria, Daizen. "Japanese Corporate Zen". *Bulletin of Concerned Asian Scholars*, 12.1, 1980: 61.
<http://criticalasianstudies.org/assets/files/bcas/v12n01.pdf>
von Eckartshausen, Karl. *The Cloud Upon the Sanctuary*. Book Tree, 2006. <http://books.google.com/books?id=y-PFe4rScYQC>
Wadland, John Henry. *Ernest Thompson Seton: Man in Nature and the Progressive Era*. New York: Arno, 1978.
Waller, P. *Town, City, and Nation*. Oxford Oxfordshire: Oxford University Press, 1983.
<http://books.google.com/books?id=1GOWTUYFPRQC>
Wagstaff, William R. *A History of the Society of Friends: Compiled From Its Standard Records, and Other Authentic Sources*. Wiley and Putnam, 1845.

<http://books.google.com/books?id=JuYpAAAAYAAJ>
Warner, Brad. "Better Way, Dengue Fever, Vegetarianism, Interviews." hardcorezen.blogspot.com. 13 Feb. 2008. <http://hardcorezen.blogspot.com/2008/02/better-way-dengue-fever-vegetarianism.html>
Warner, Bard. Rev. of *Enlightenment Blues*, by André van der Braak <http://www.monkfishpublishing.com/pages/Enlightenment-Reviews2.htm> as of 2 Feb. 2010
Warren, Henry Clarke. *Buddhism in Translations: Passages Selected from the Buddhist Sacred Books*. Harvard University Press, 1896. <http://www.sacred-texts.com/bud/bits/index.htm>
Watson, Richard. *The Life of Rev. John Wesley: Founder of the Methodist Societies.* L. Swormstedt & A. Poe, for the Methodist Episcopal Church, 1853. <http://books.google.com/books?id=f3WH1BtbH1cC>
Watterson, Bill. *The Calvin and Hobbes Tenth Anniversary Book*. Kansas City, Missouri: Andrews and McMeel, 1995.
Watts, Alan. "Beat Zen, Square Zen." *Chicago Review* 12.2, Summer 1958. <http://humanities.uchicago.edu/orgs/review/60th/pdfs/15watts.pdf>
Watts, Alan. *Does It Matter? Essays on Man's Relation to Materiality.* New York: Vintage, 1971.
Watts, Alan. *The Way of Zen.* New York: Mentor (New American Library), 1961.
> If Alan Watts wrote it, read it. An extended version of "Beat Zen, Square Zen" was published as a chapbook by City Lights Books in 1959.

Wells, H.G., revised by Raymond Postgate. *The Outline of History.* New York: Garden City, 1961.
> This is "Book Club Edition" printed in two volumes. A bit outdated in spots, and not exactly free of Well's own biases, but still an ambitious and worthwhile overview of human history.

Wilber, Ken. *A Brief History of Everything.* Boston: Shambhala, 2007. <http://books.google.com/books?id=c9shMX7HLY0C>

Wilber, Ken. "Integral Transformative Practice: In this world or out of it?" *What Is Enlightenment?* Issue 18 (Fall/Winter 2000): 34-39, 126-131

Wilber, Ken. *One Taste.* Boston: Shambhala, 1999.

Willson, A. Leslie. *A Mythical Image: The Ideal of India in German Romanticism.* Durham: Duke University Press, 1964.

Wilson, Robert. *Cosmic Trigger Volume I.* Tempe: New Falcon, 1991.

Wilson, Robert Anton. Introduction. *Eye in the Triangle.* By Israel Regardie. Tempe: New Falcon Publications, 1993.

Winckelmann, Johann Joachim. Excerpt from "Reflections on the Imitation of Greek Works in Painting and Scultpture." *Architectural Theory.* Ed. Harry Mallgrave. Blackwell, 2005. <http://books.google.com/books?id=Fxo8t5cZf6MC>

Whalen, Philip et.al. *The Collected Poems of Philip Whalen.* Middletown: Weseleyan University Press, 2007. <http://books.google.com/books?id=SxEI33KubpQC>

"Where No Man Has Gone Before." *Star Trek (Season 1).* Created and produced by Gene Roddenberry. CBS. <http://www.cbs.com/classics/star_trek/video/?pid=YXxaF37VKwyE0ZnWmhGKYbidQQyj0Uje&vs=Default&play=true>

Whitman, Walt. *Complete Poetry and Collected Prose.* New York: Literary Classics of the United States, 1982.

Whitman, Walt. "Preface to Leaves of Grass (1855)." *Prefaces and Prologues. Vol. XXXIX. The Harvard Classics.* New York: P.F. Collier & Son,1909-14; Bartleby.com, 2001. <http://www.bartleby.com/39/>

White, T.H. *The Sword in the Stone.* London: Collins, 1998.

Yamakage, Motohisa et.al. *The Essence of Shinto.* Tokyo: Kodansha International, 2006.

About the Author

Photo by Alison Chicosky

Tom Swiss has been both a practicing Pagan and a student of Asian culture through the lens of traditional martial and healing arts for over two decades. A well-known lecturer at events such as the Starwood Festival and the Free Spirit Gathering, he has taught classes on subjects spanning the gamut from acupressure to Zen and from self-defense to sexuality to a wide variety of audiences. He has served as President of the Free Spirit Alliance, a pantheist/pagan networking organization based in Maryland.

Tom holds a *yondan* (fourth degree black belt) in a traditional Japanese school of karate, and is an NCCAOM Diplomate in Asian Bodywork Therapy with a small private practice in shiatsu acupressure. He also has a Master's degree in Computer Science from the University of Maryland.

As one of the coordinators of the weekly "Zelda's Inferno" poetry workshop, he is a fixture in the Baltimore poetry scene. He has performed his poetry at venues too numerous to count, and on film in the documentary *The Poets from Planet X*. His work has appeared in the anthology *Octopus Dreams*, in *Zelda's Zine*, and in *the indie*.